drawnandquarterly.com

First edition: June 2018 | Printed in China | 10 9 8 7 6 5 4 3 2 1

Library and Archives Canada Cataloguing in Publication
Ruillier, Jérôme
[*Étrange*. English]
The Strange / Jérôme Ruillier ; Helge Dascher, translator.
Translation of: *L'étrange*.
ISBN 978-1-77046-317-2 (softcover)
1. Graphic novels. I. Dascher, Helge, 1965–, translator
II. Title. III. Title: Étrange. English.
PN6747.R855E8713 2018 741.5'944 C2017-905442-2

Published in the USA by Drawn & Quarterly, a client publisher of Farrar, Straus and Giroux. Orders: 888.330.8477. Published in Canada by Drawn & Quarterly, a client publisher of Raincoast Books. Orders: 800.663.5714. Published in the United Kingdom by Drawn & Quarterly, a client publisher of Publishers Group UK. Orders: info@pguk.co.uk

Drawn & Quarterly acknowledges the support of the Government of Canada and the Canada Council for the Arts for our publishing program, and the National Translation Program for Book Publishing, an initiative of the Roadmap for Canada's Official Languages 2013–2018: Education, Immigration, Communities, for our translation activities.

Drawn & Quarterly reconnaît l'aide financière du gouvernement du Québec par l'entremise de la Société de développement des entreprises culturelles (SODEC) pour nos activités d'édition. Gouvernement du Québec—Programme de crédit d'impôt pour l'édition de livres—Gestion SODEC

Cet ouvrage a bénéficié du soutien des Programmes d'aide à la publication de l'Institut Français.

Canada CNL CENTRE NATIONAL DU LIVRE

The Strange

JÉRÔME RUILLIER

TRANSLATED BY
HELGE DASCHER

DRAWN & QUARTERLY

ᒪᔑᖁᖕᖃᓐᔑᕆᖓ*

* WE HAD DECIDED TO LEAVE.

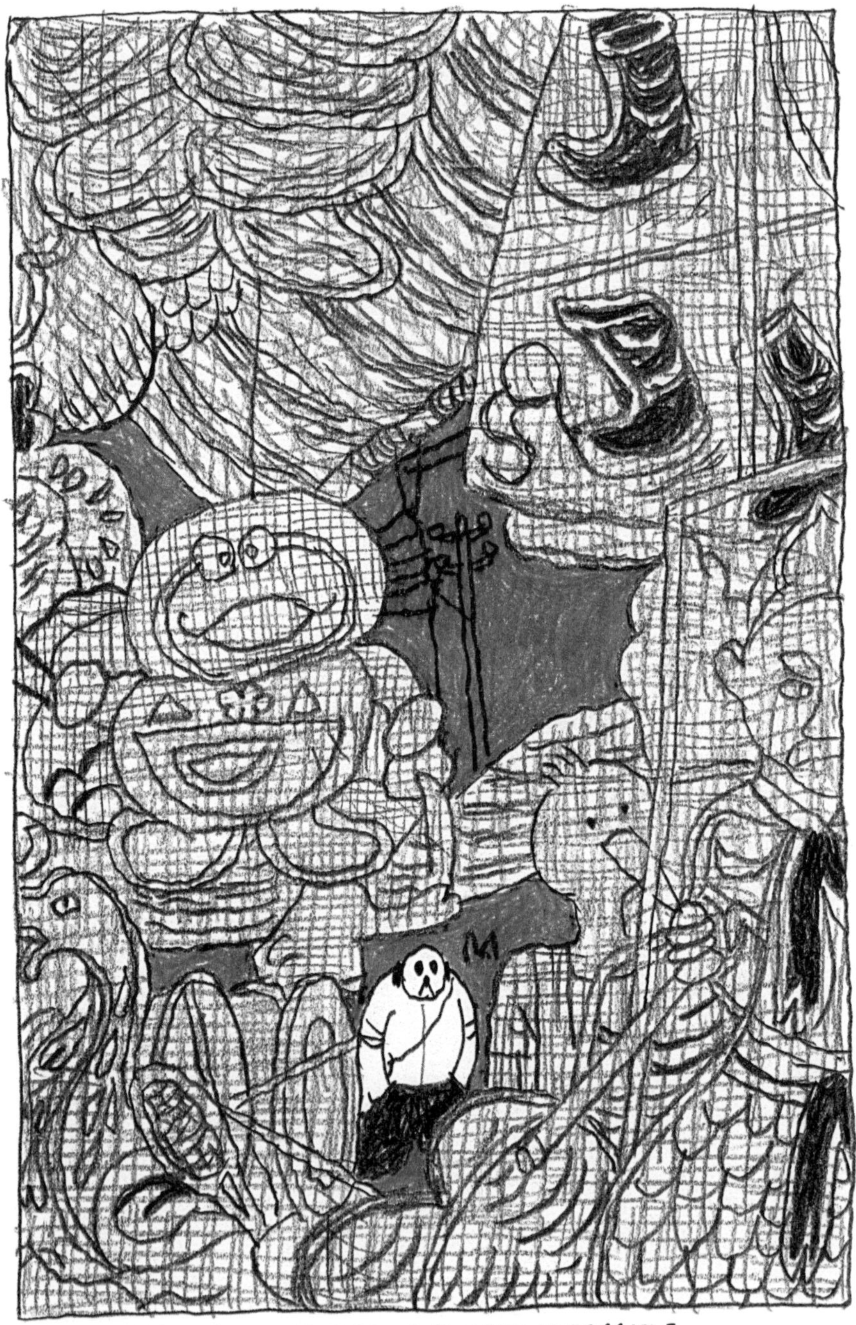

* UNFORTUNATELY, IT HAD BECOME ALMOST IMPOSSIBLE.

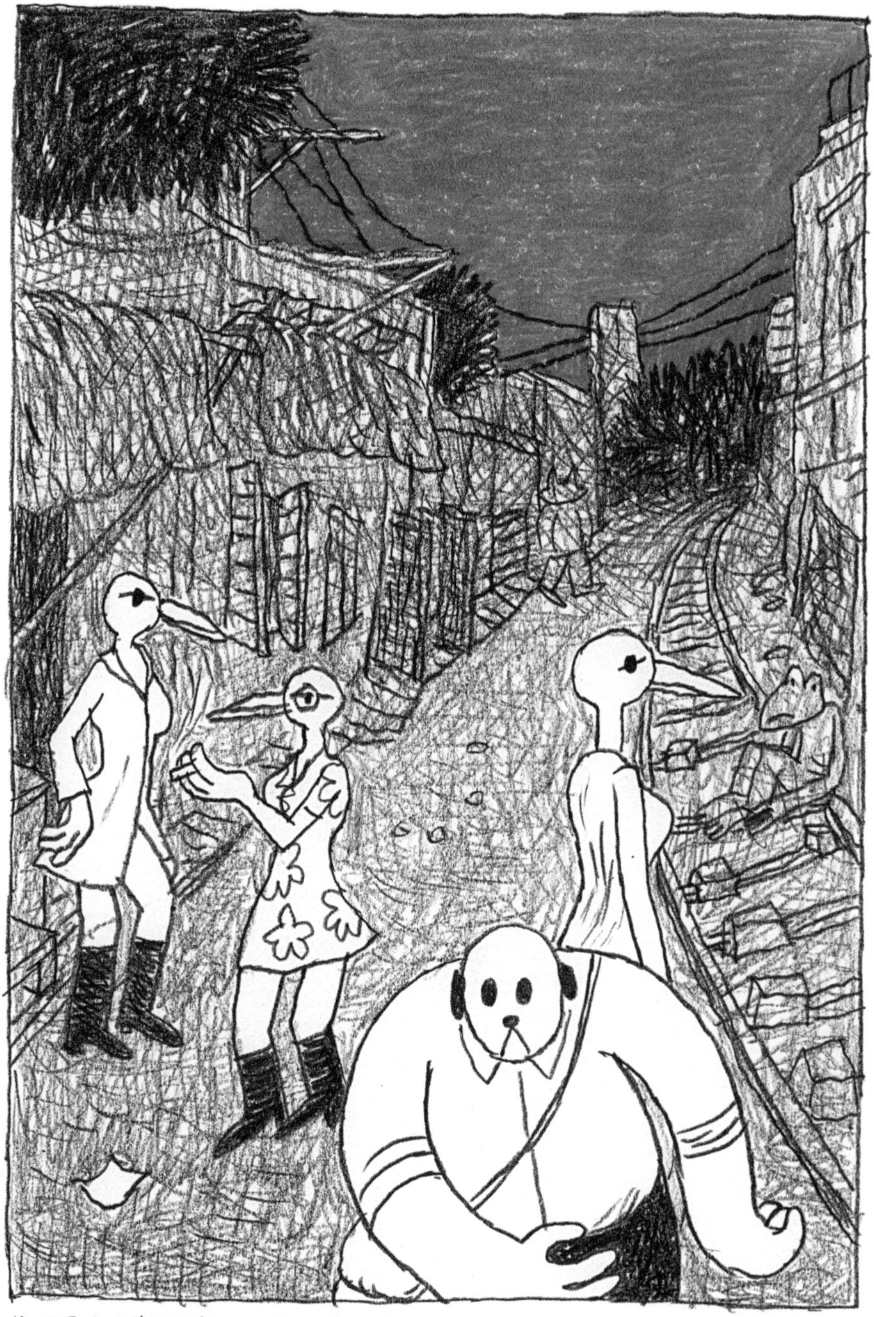

* THE ONLY PERSON WE COULD FIND TO HELP US WAS THAT WOMAN WHO WAS WELL KNOWN IN OUR SMALL TOWN.

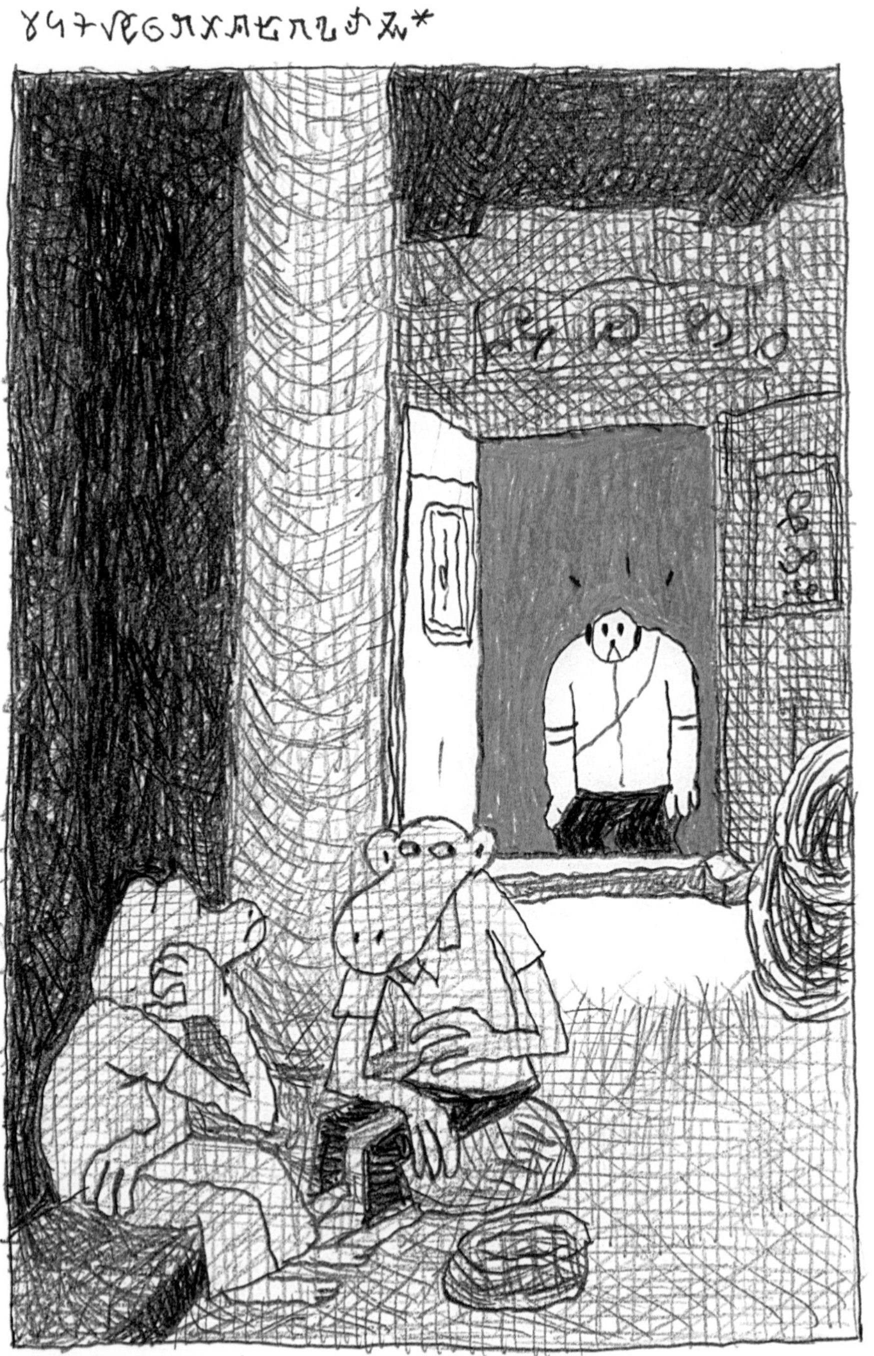

* SHE HAD CONTACTS.

ᴧ℠ℳℳ℟ℤ⅂ℰ℥ℶᴪ*

* SHE WAS A "FIXER," AS SHE SAID.

ℤℳℤℝℨℵℳℳ℟ℤ℟ℳℤℝℽℭℕℱℳℋℰℕℝℳℾ℟
℥℥℠ℳ℟℥℥℟ℤ℟*

* WE KNEW ABOUT HER BECAUSE SHE HAD ALREADY HELPED MANY
OTHER PEOPLE GET PAPERS.

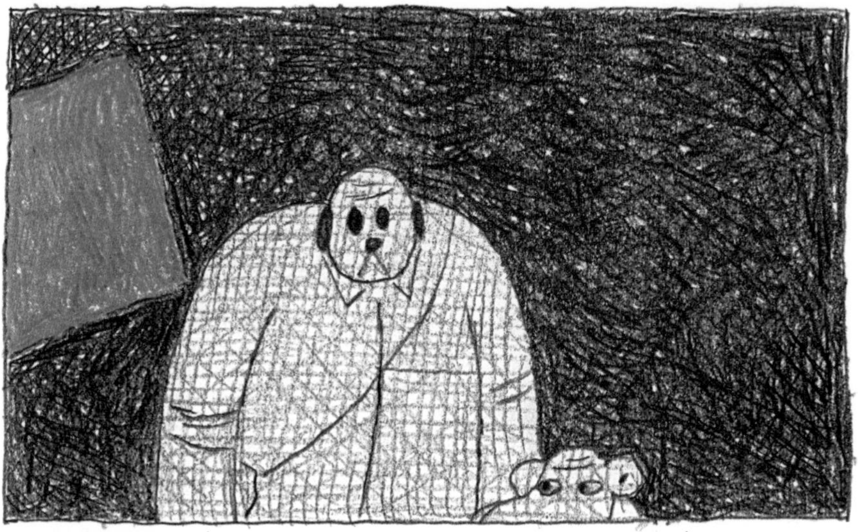

* WE SOLD EVERYTHING WE OWNED, WE BORROWED MONEY FROM FRIENDS AND FAMILY...

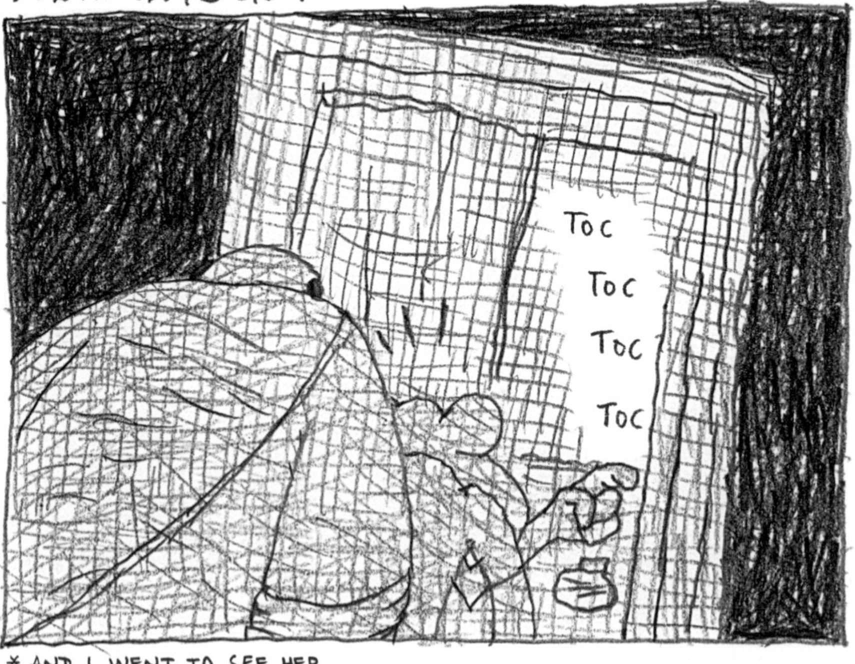
TOC
TOC
TOC
TOC

* AND I WENT TO SEE HER.

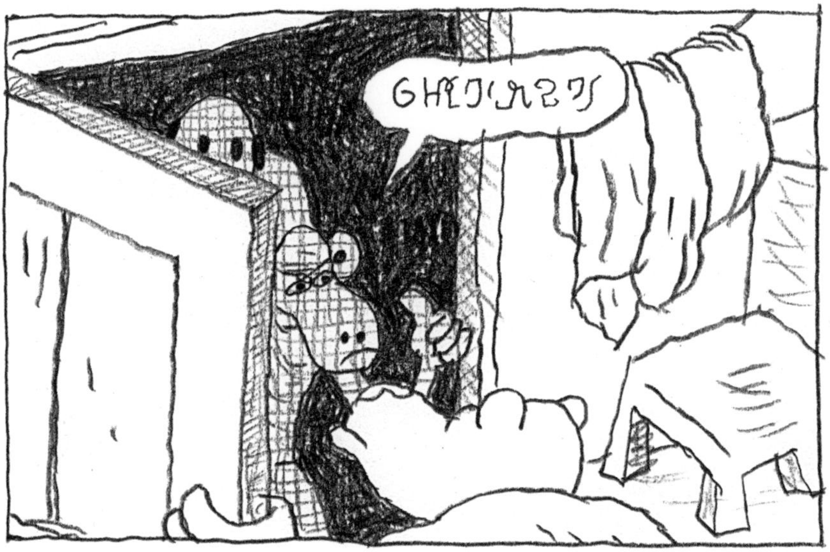

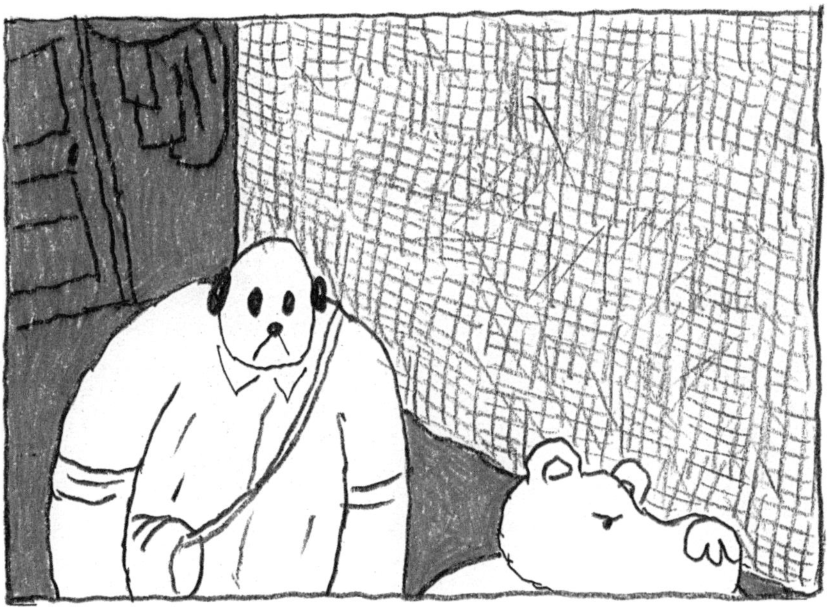

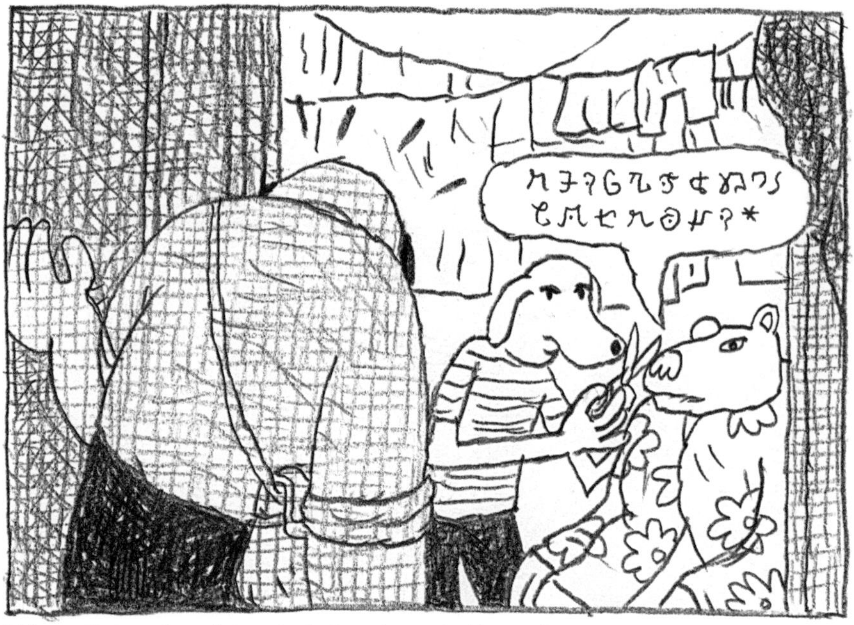

* YOU WANT TO LEAVE. YOU'RE RIGHT, YOU DON'T BELONG HERE.

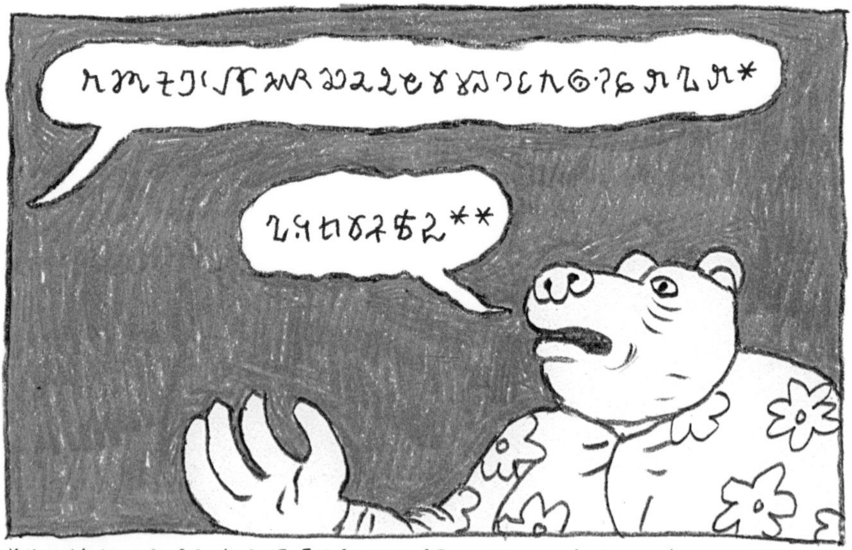

* I WANT TO GO ALONE FIRST TO SEE HOW IT IS, AND I'LL BRING MY FAMILY LATER.
** DON'T WORRY, I HAVE CONTACTS.

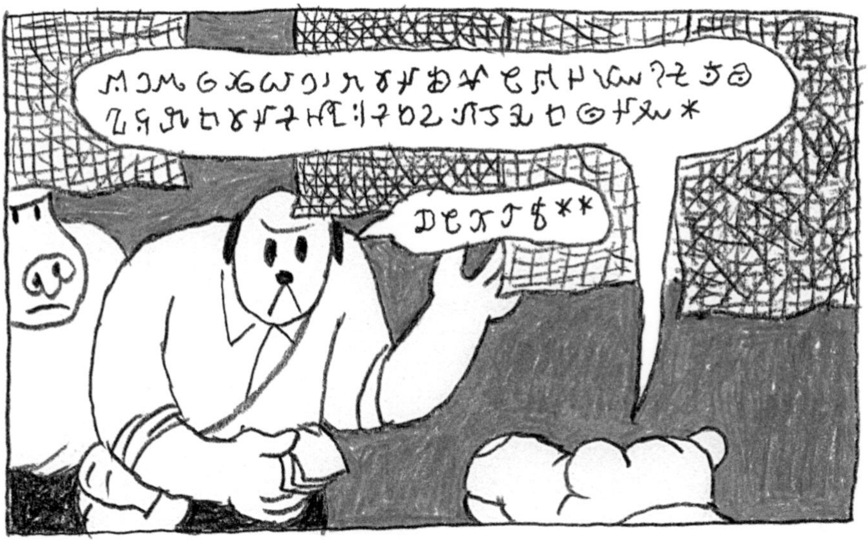

* IT WON'T BE EASY, OF COURSE, BUT WE'LL WORK IT OUT. IT'LL BE 12,000 CASH PER PERSON. THESE ARE HIGH-LEVEL CONTACTS...
** THAT'S TOO MUCH!

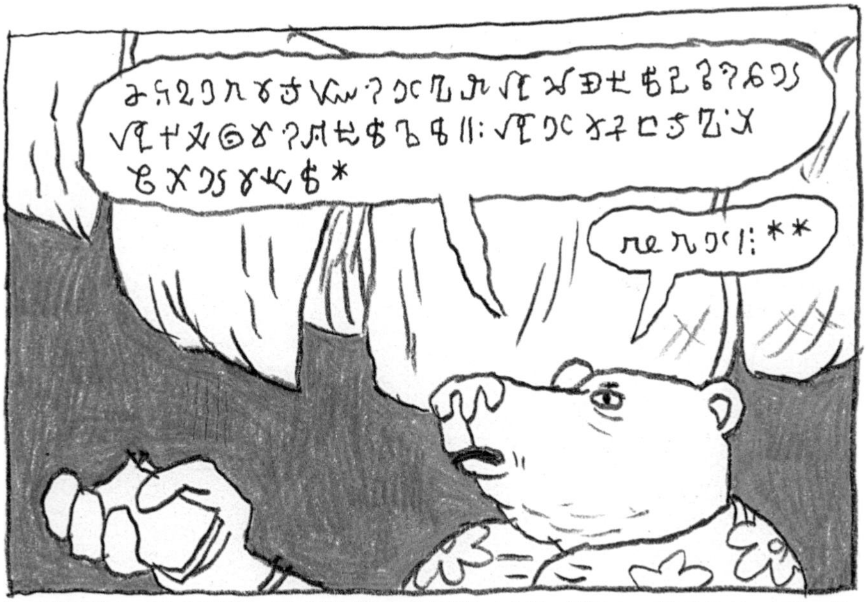

* THERE'LL BE BRIBES TO PAY FOR EVERYTHING, EVEN THE BIRTH CERTIFICATES. SOMEONE WILL PICK YOU UP AT THE AIRPORT. HE'LL RECOGNIZE YOU BY THE CLOTHES WE'LL GIVE YOU.
** AND 2000 MORE...

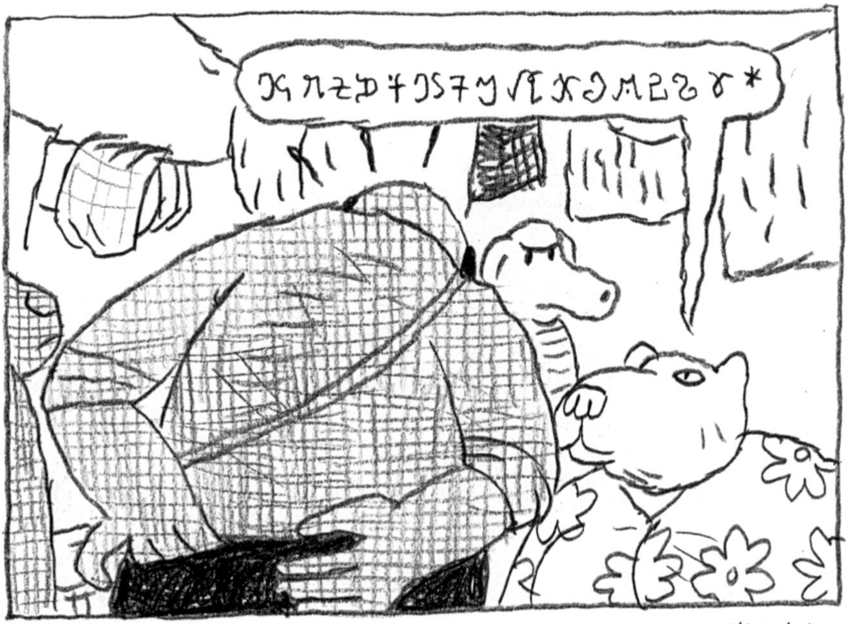

* YOU'LL GIVE HIM YOUR PAPERS, AND IN RETURN HE'LL GIVE YOU AN ADDRESS WHERE YOU CAN STAY UNTIL YOU SORT THINGS OUT.

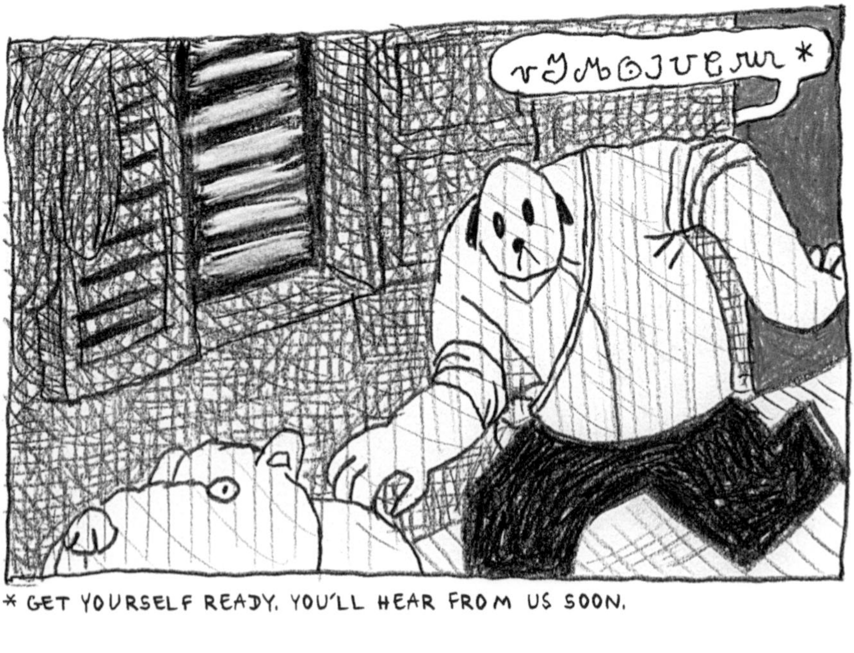

* GET YOURSELF READY. YOU'LL HEAR FROM US SOON.

* A MONTH LATER, I WAS ON A PLANE WITH A FAKE PASSPORT AND A TOURIST VISA, HEADED FOR A BETTER LIFE.

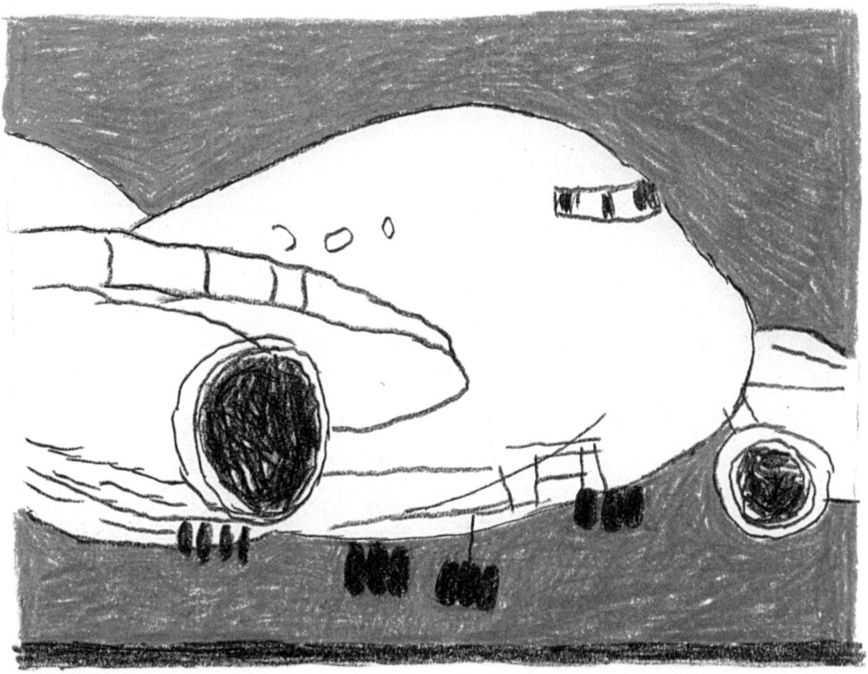

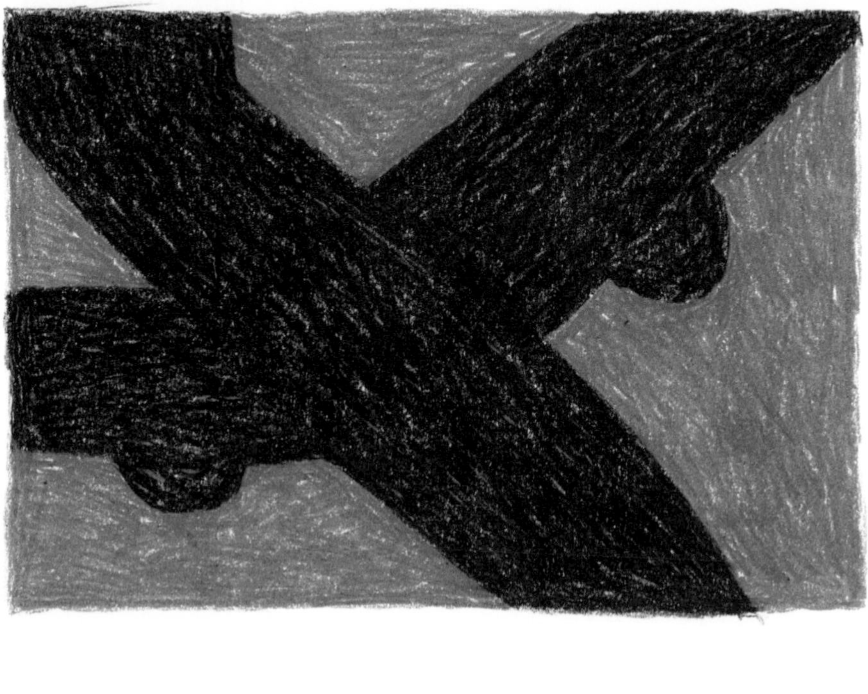

WHERE IS OZ? "SOMEWHERE, OVER THE RAINBOW."

The Strange

"I AM A LIBERAL, IN THE SENSE THAT I BELIEVE IN FREEDOM. BUT I AM ALSO A HUMANIST, IN THE SENSE THAT I BELIEVE THAT THE PRODUCTION OF WEALTH SHOULD BE MEANINGFUL, THAT MORALITY MATTERS, THAT SPIRITUALITY DOES EXIST, THAT WE HAVE A DESTINY, AND THAT YOU CAN'T TREAT PEOPLE ANY WAY YOU WANT, BECAUSE A HUMAN BEING IS MORE THAN JUST A COMMODITY."

The crow

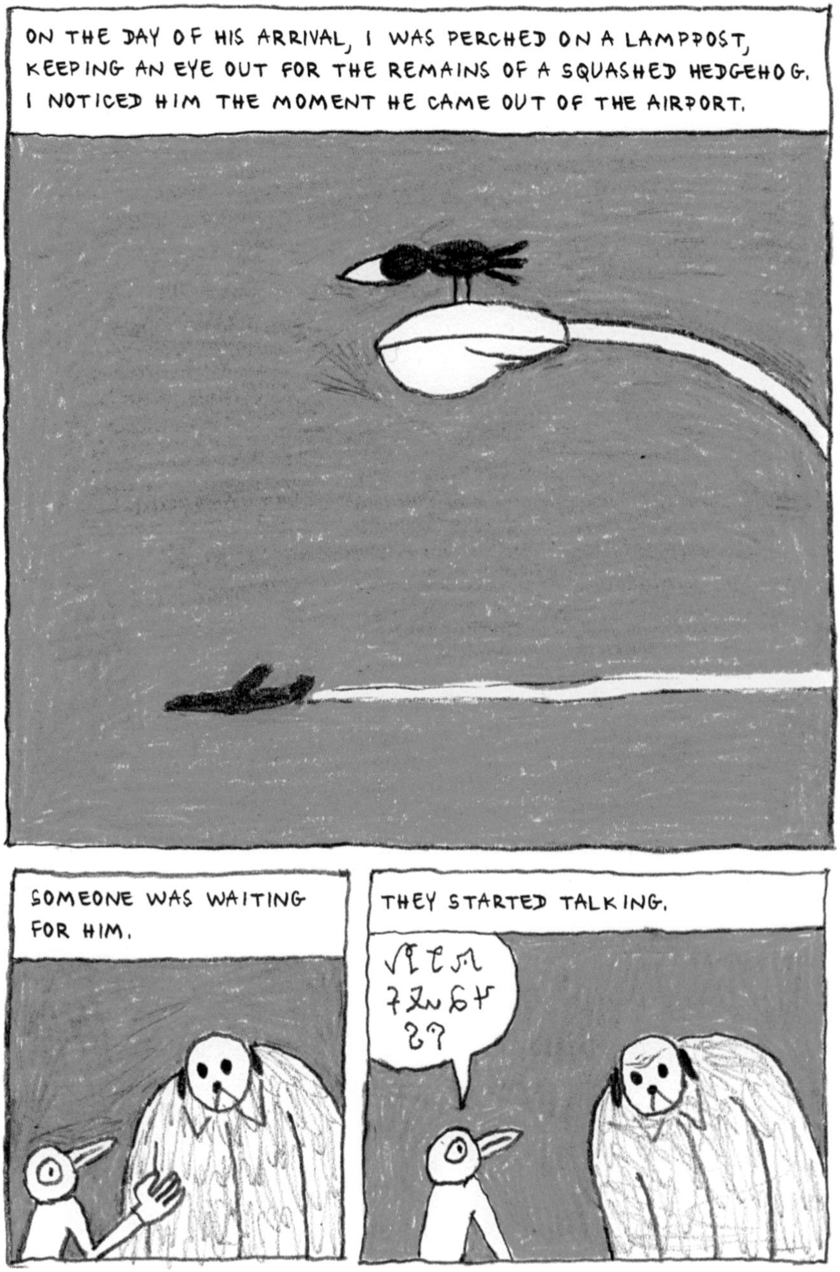
ON THE DAY OF HIS ARRIVAL, I WAS PERCHED ON A LAMPPOST, KEEPING AN EYE OUT FOR THE REMAINS OF A SQUASHED HEDGEHOG. I NOTICED HIM THE MOMENT HE CAME OUT OF THE AIRPORT.
SOMEONE WAS WAITING FOR HIM.
THEY STARTED TALKING.

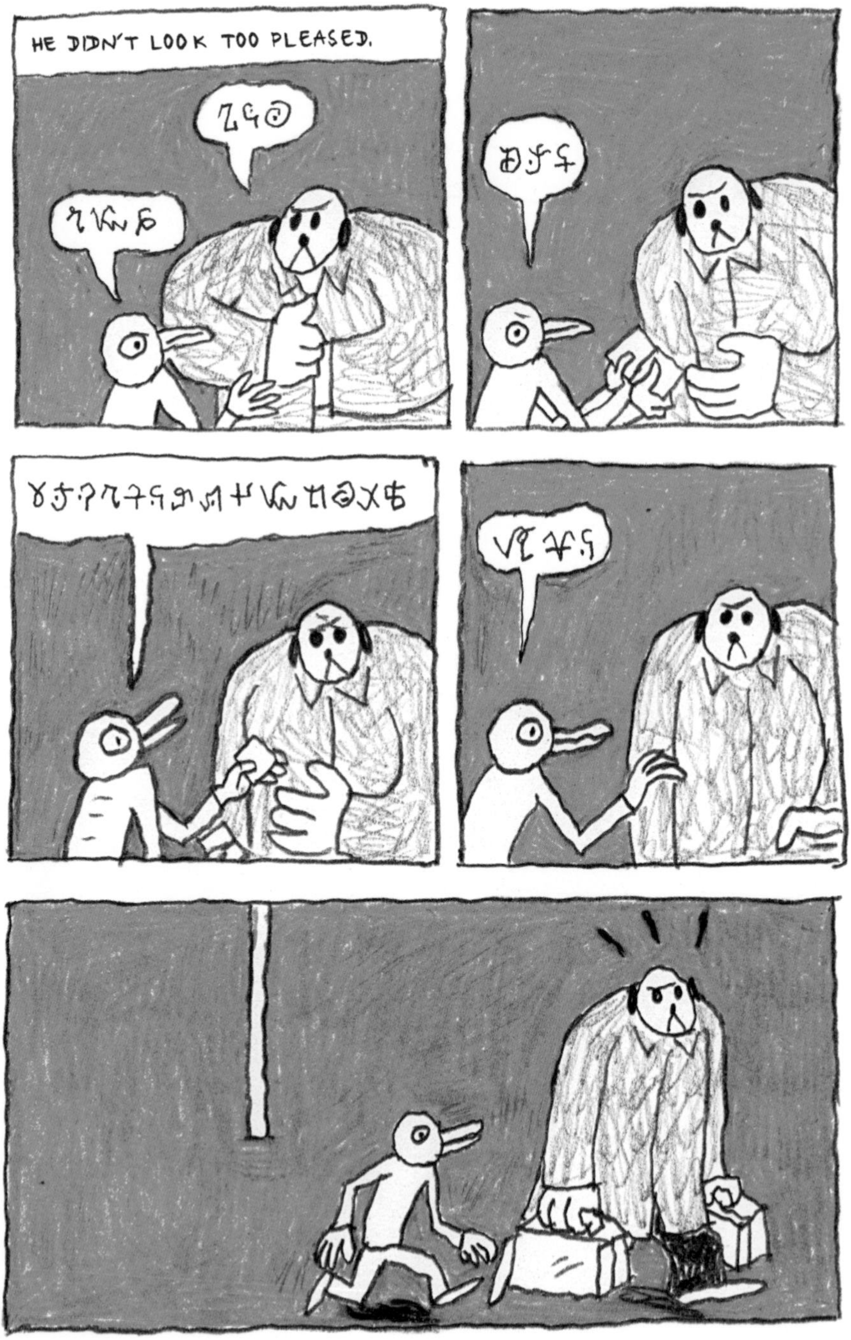
HE DIDN'T LOOK TOO PLEASED.

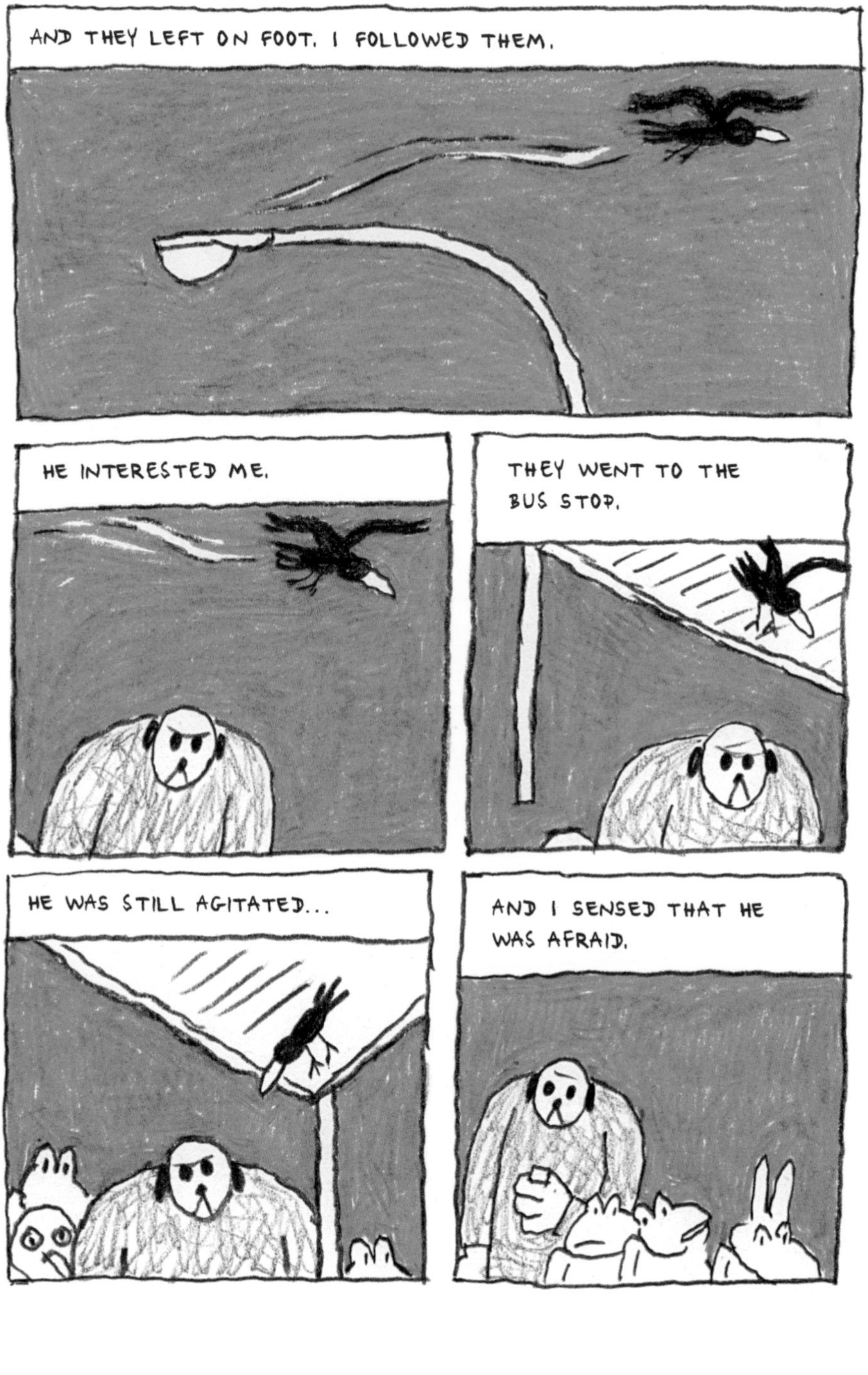
AND THEY LEFT ON FOOT. I FOLLOWED THEM.
HE INTERESTED ME.
THEY WENT TO THE BUS STOP.
HE WAS STILL AGITATED...
AND I SENSED THAT HE WAS AFRAID.

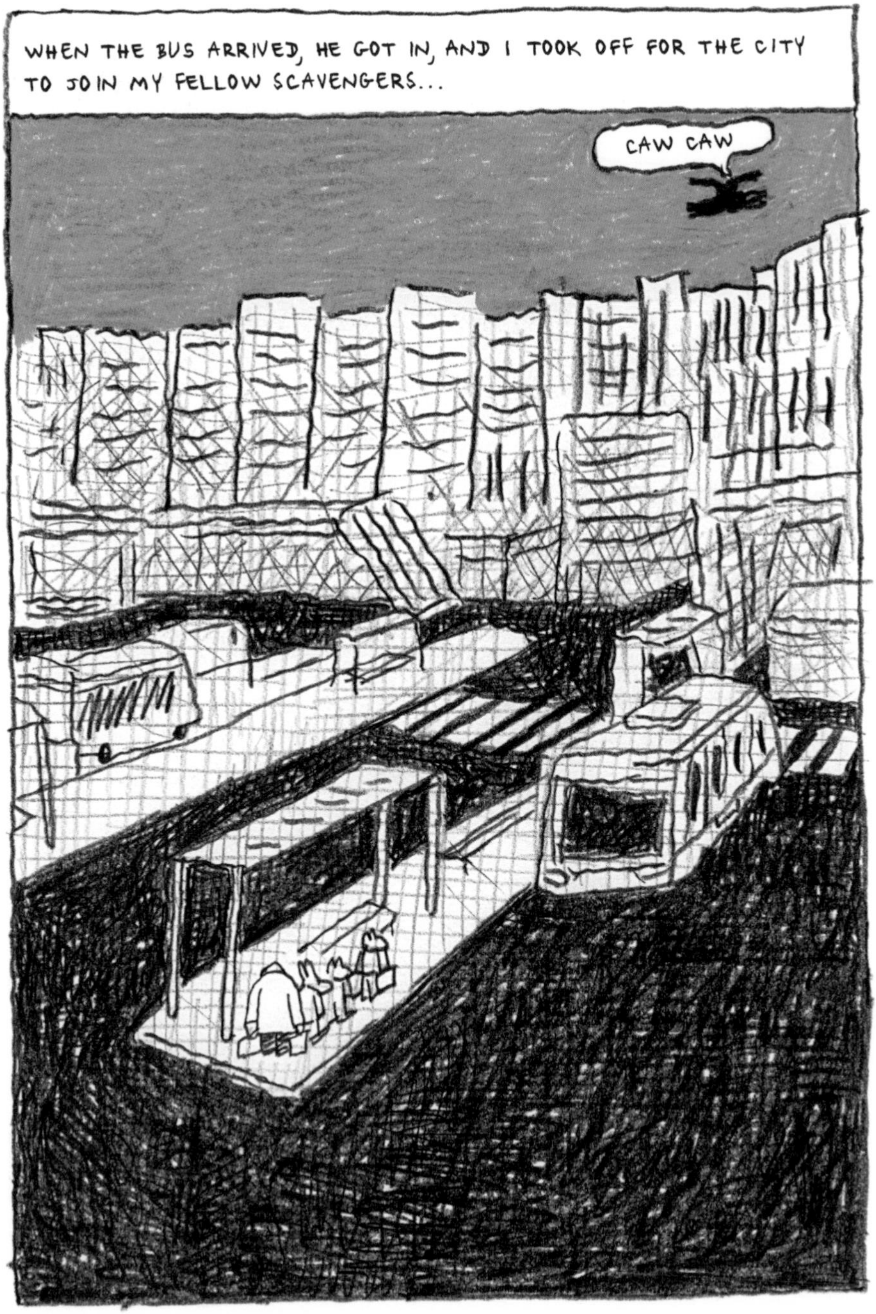
WHEN THE BUS ARRIVED, HE GOT IN, AND I TOOK OFF FOR THE CITY TO JOIN MY FELLOW SCAVENGERS...
CAW CAW

The passenger

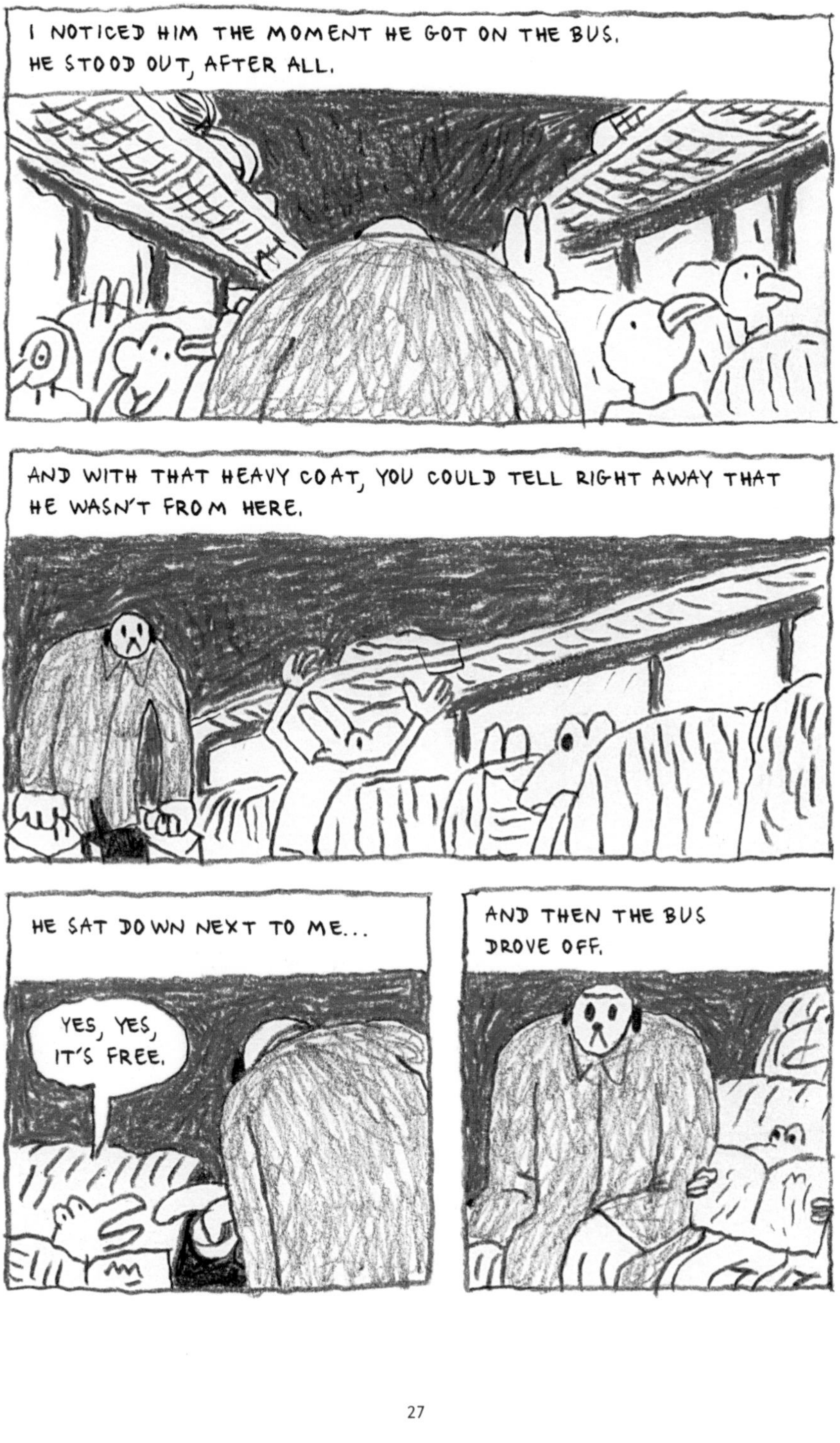
I NOTICED HIM THE MOMENT HE GOT ON THE BUS.
HE STOOD OUT, AFTER ALL.
AND WITH THAT HEAVY COAT, YOU COULD TELL RIGHT AWAY THAT HE WASN'T FROM HERE.
HE SAT DOWN NEXT TO ME...
YES, YES, IT'S FREE.
AND THEN THE BUS DROVE OFF.

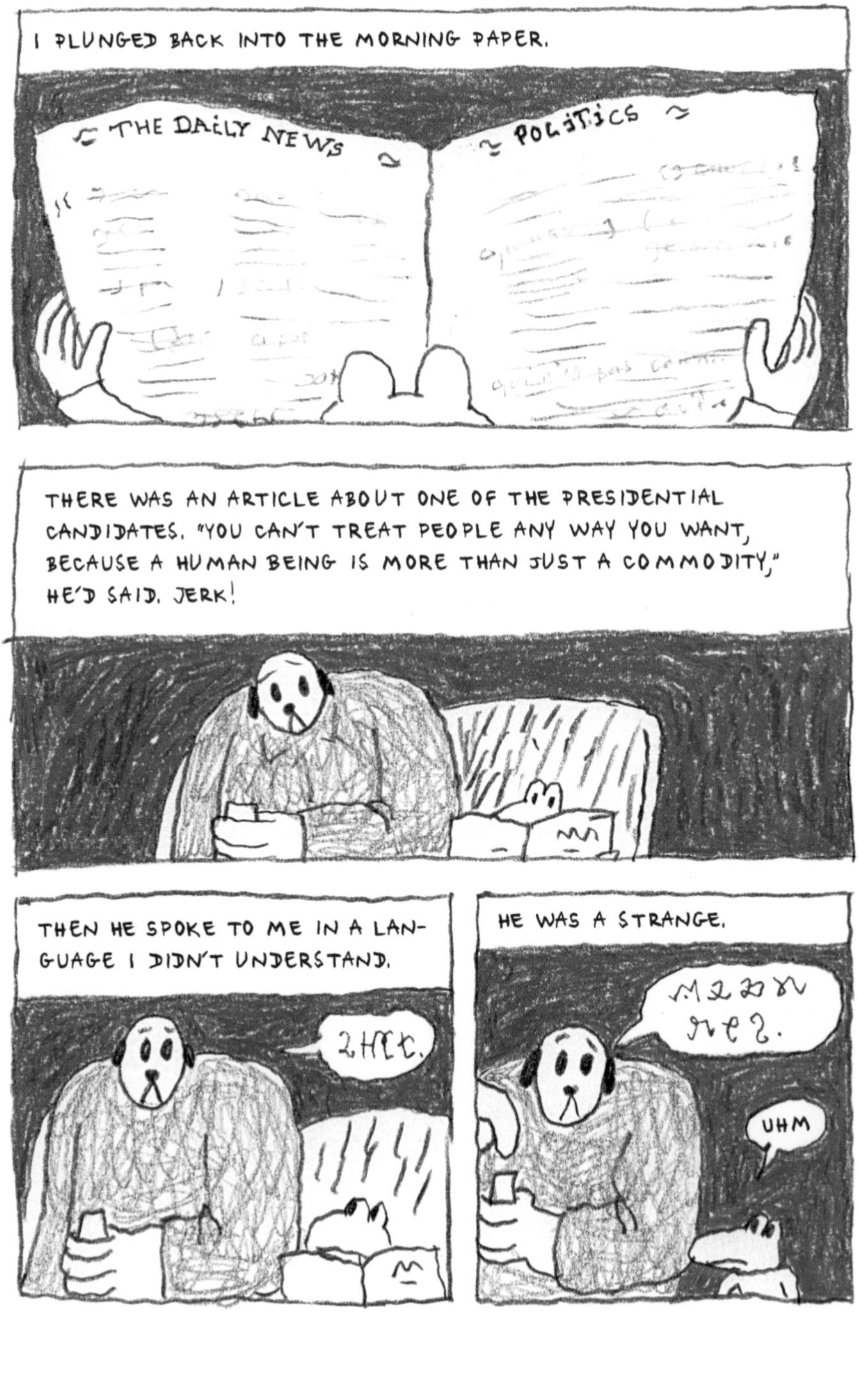
I PLUNGED BACK INTO THE MORNING PAPER.
THE DAILY NEWS
POLITICS
THERE WAS AN ARTICLE ABOUT ONE OF THE PRESIDENTIAL CANDIDATES. "YOU CAN'T TREAT PEOPLE ANY WAY YOU WANT, BECAUSE A HUMAN BEING IS MORE THAN JUST A COMMODITY," HE'D SAID. JERK!
THEN HE SPOKE TO ME IN A LANGUAGE I DIDN'T UNDERSTAND.
HE WAS A STRANGE.
UHM

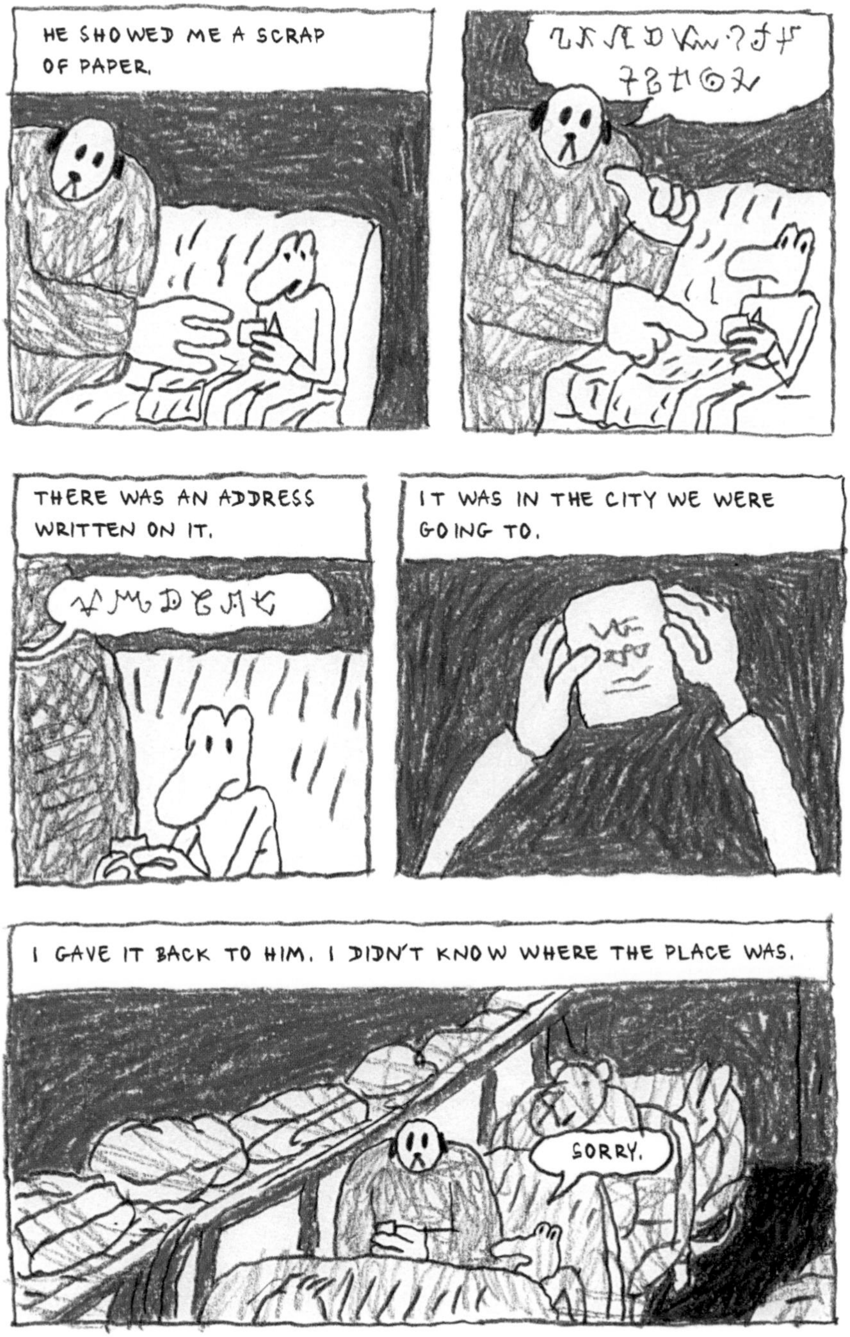
HE SHOWED ME A SCRAP OF PAPER.
THERE WAS AN ADDRESS WRITTEN ON IT.
IT WAS IN THE CITY WE WERE GOING TO.
I GAVE IT BACK TO HIM. I DIDN'T KNOW WHERE THE PLACE WAS.
SORRY.

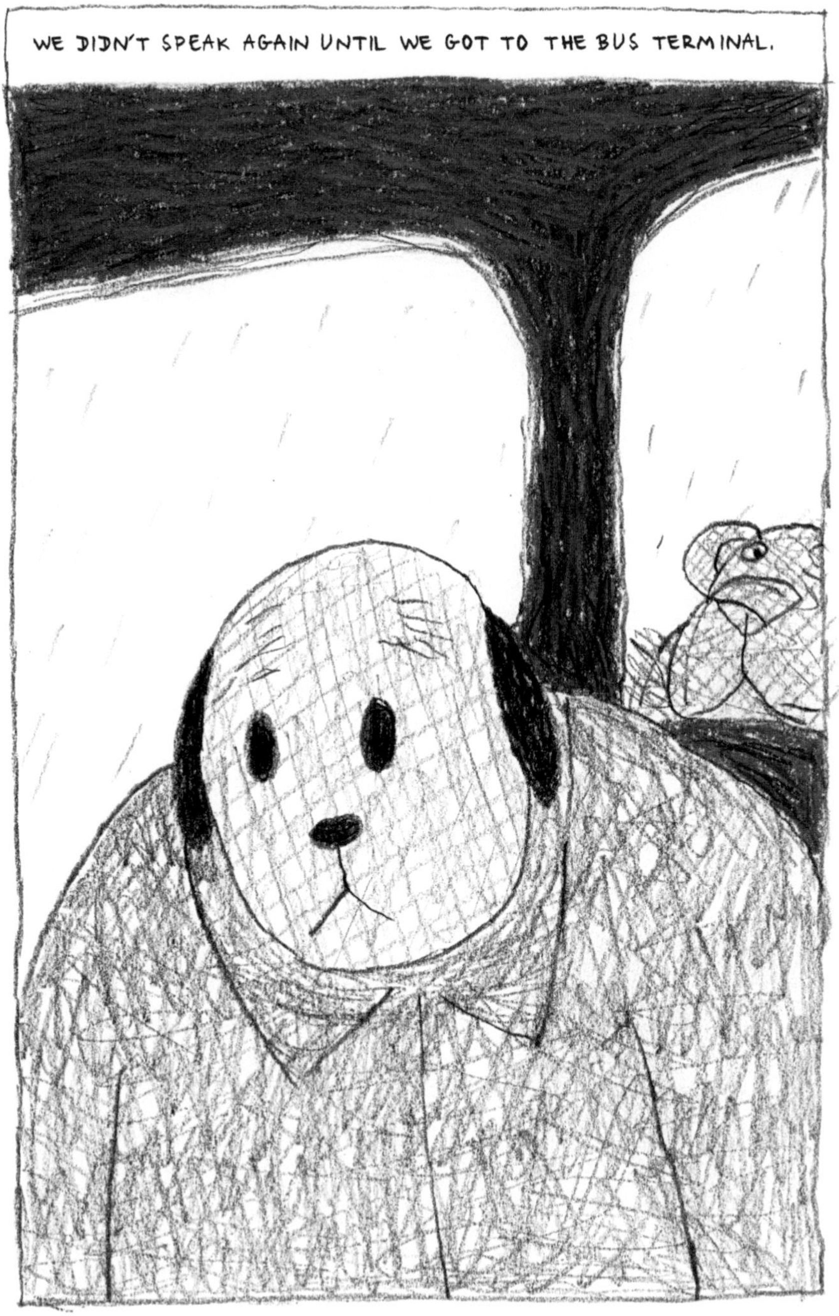
WE DIDN'T SPEAK AGAIN UNTIL WE GOT TO THE BUS TERMINAL.

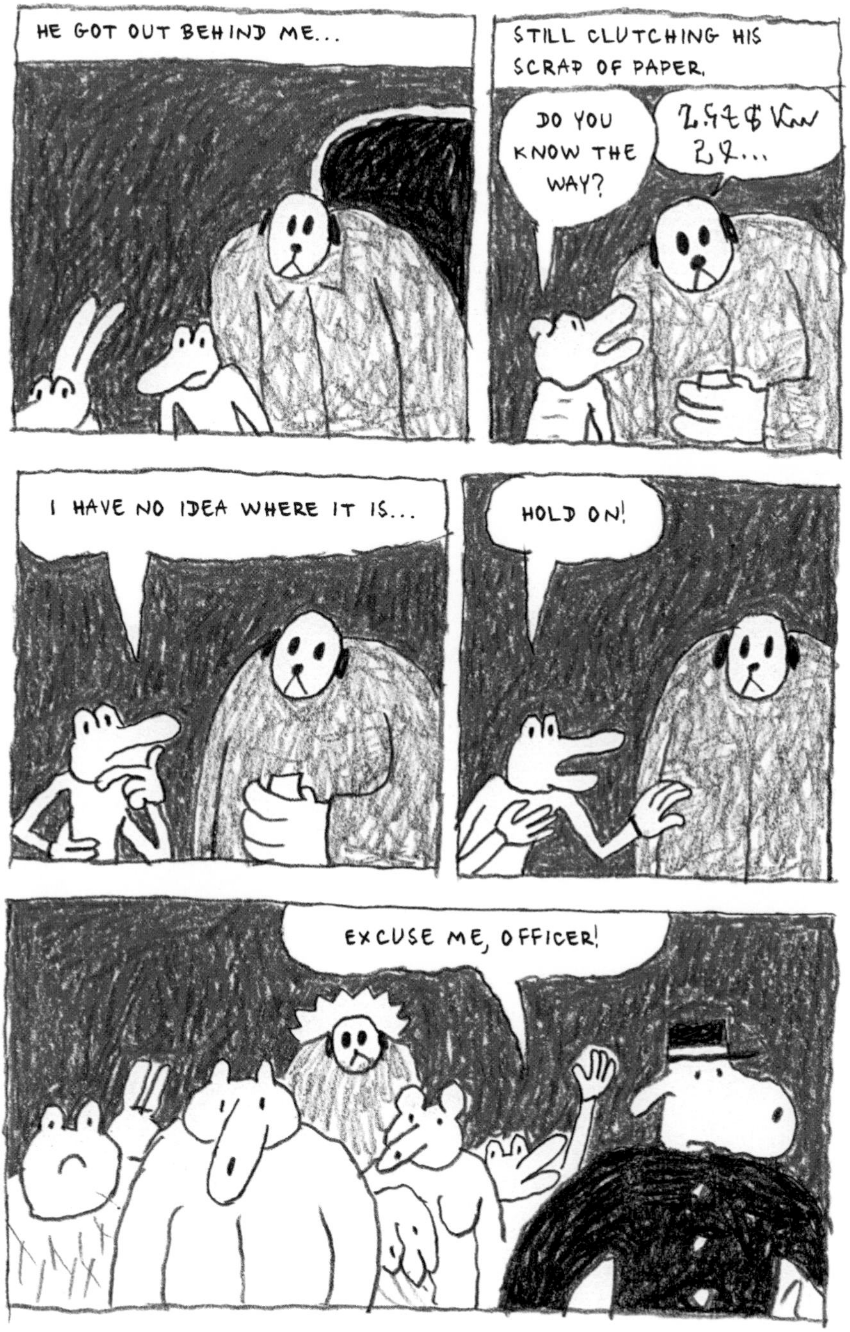
HE GOT OUT BEHIND ME...
STILL CLUTCHING HIS SCRAP OF PAPER.
DO YOU KNOW THE WAY?
I HAVE NO IDEA WHERE IT IS...
HOLD ON!
EXCUSE ME, OFFICER!

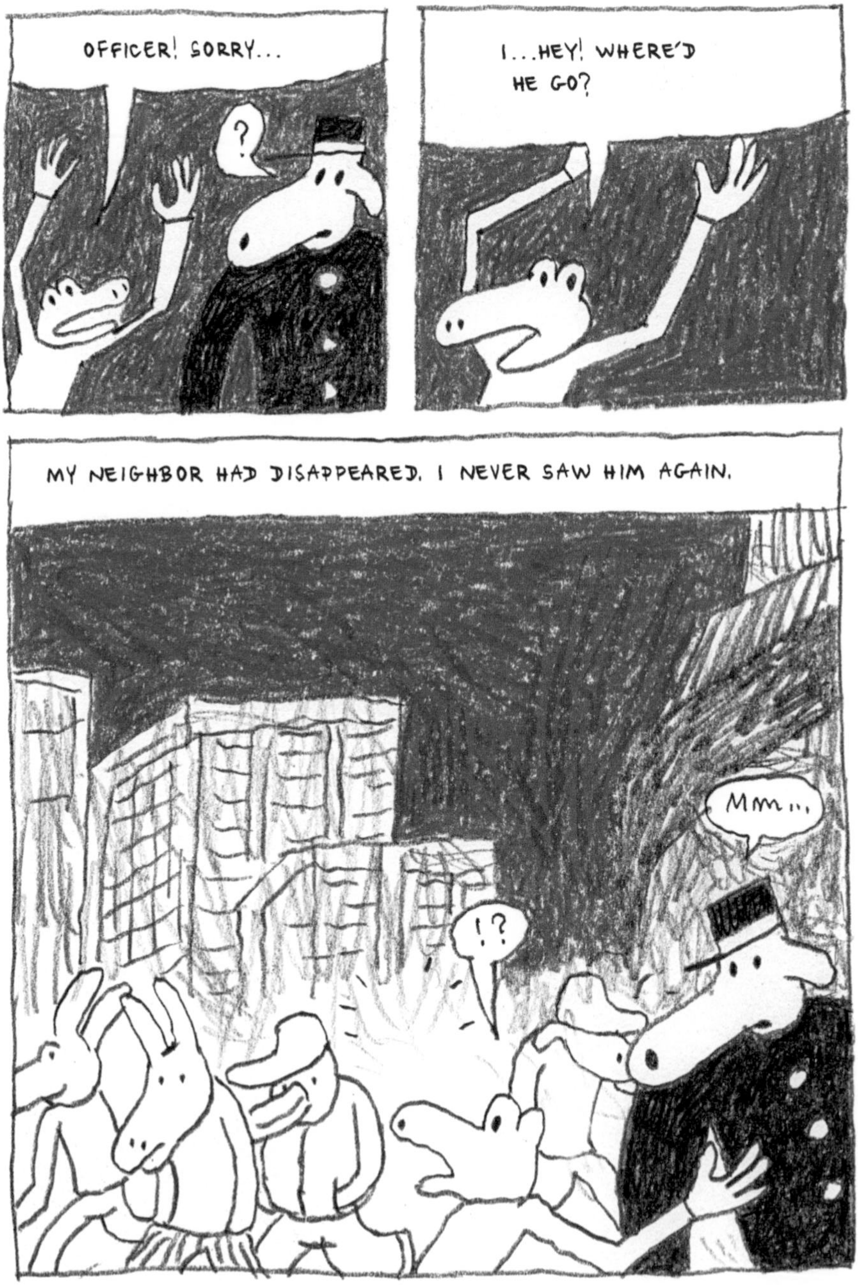
OFFICER! SORRY...
?
I...HEY! WHERE'D HE GO?
MY NEIGHBOR HAD DISAPPEARED. I NEVER SAW HIM AGAIN.
Mm...
!?

The taxi driver

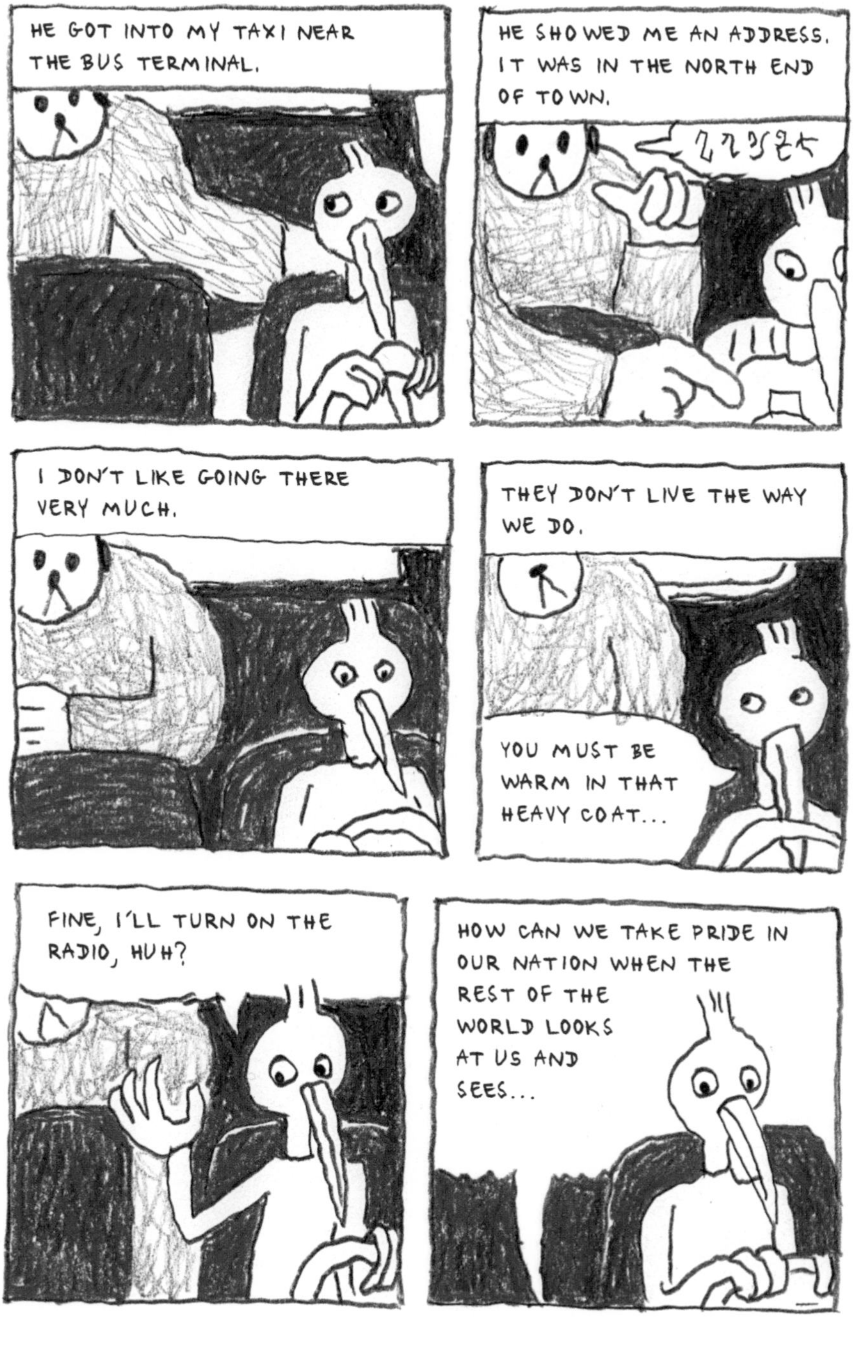
HE GOT INTO MY TAXI NEAR THE BUS TERMINAL.
HE SHOWED ME AN ADDRESS. IT WAS IN THE NORTH END OF TOWN.
I DON'T LIKE GOING THERE VERY MUCH.
THEY DON'T LIVE THE WAY WE DO.
YOU MUST BE WARM IN THAT HEAVY COAT...
FINE, I'LL TURN ON THE RADIO, HUH?
HOW CAN WE TAKE PRIDE IN OUR NATION WHEN THE REST OF THE WORLD LOOKS AT US AND SEES...

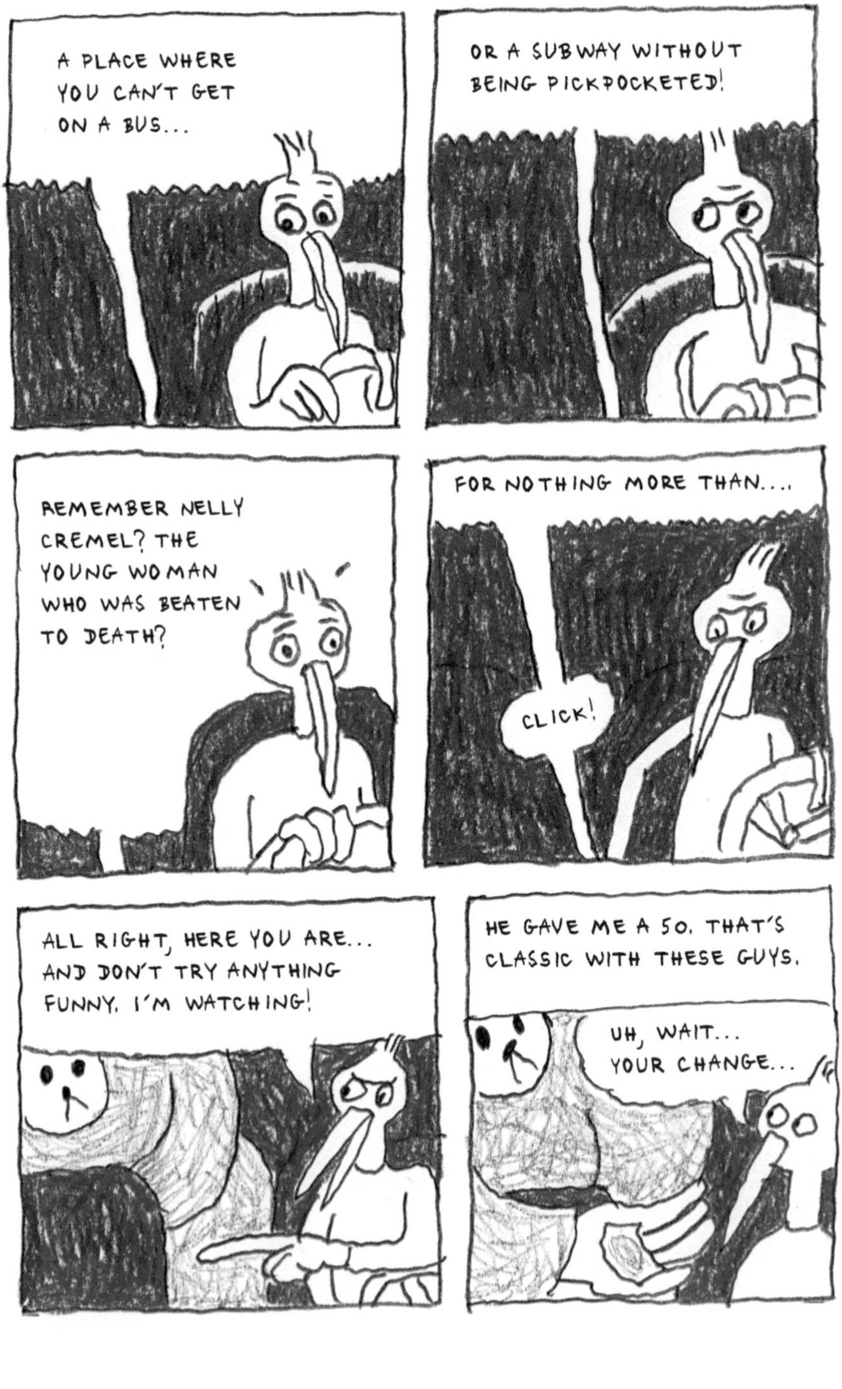
A PLACE WHERE YOU CAN'T GET ON A BUS...
OR A SUBWAY WITHOUT BEING PICKPOCKETED!
REMEMBER NELLY CREMEL? THE YOUNG WOMAN WHO WAS BEATEN TO DEATH?
FOR NOTHING MORE THAN....
CLICK!
ALL RIGHT, HERE YOU ARE... AND DON'T TRY ANYTHING FUNNY. I'M WATCHING!
HE GAVE ME A 50. THAT'S CLASSIC WITH THESE GUYS.
UH, WAIT... YOUR CHANGE...

The crow

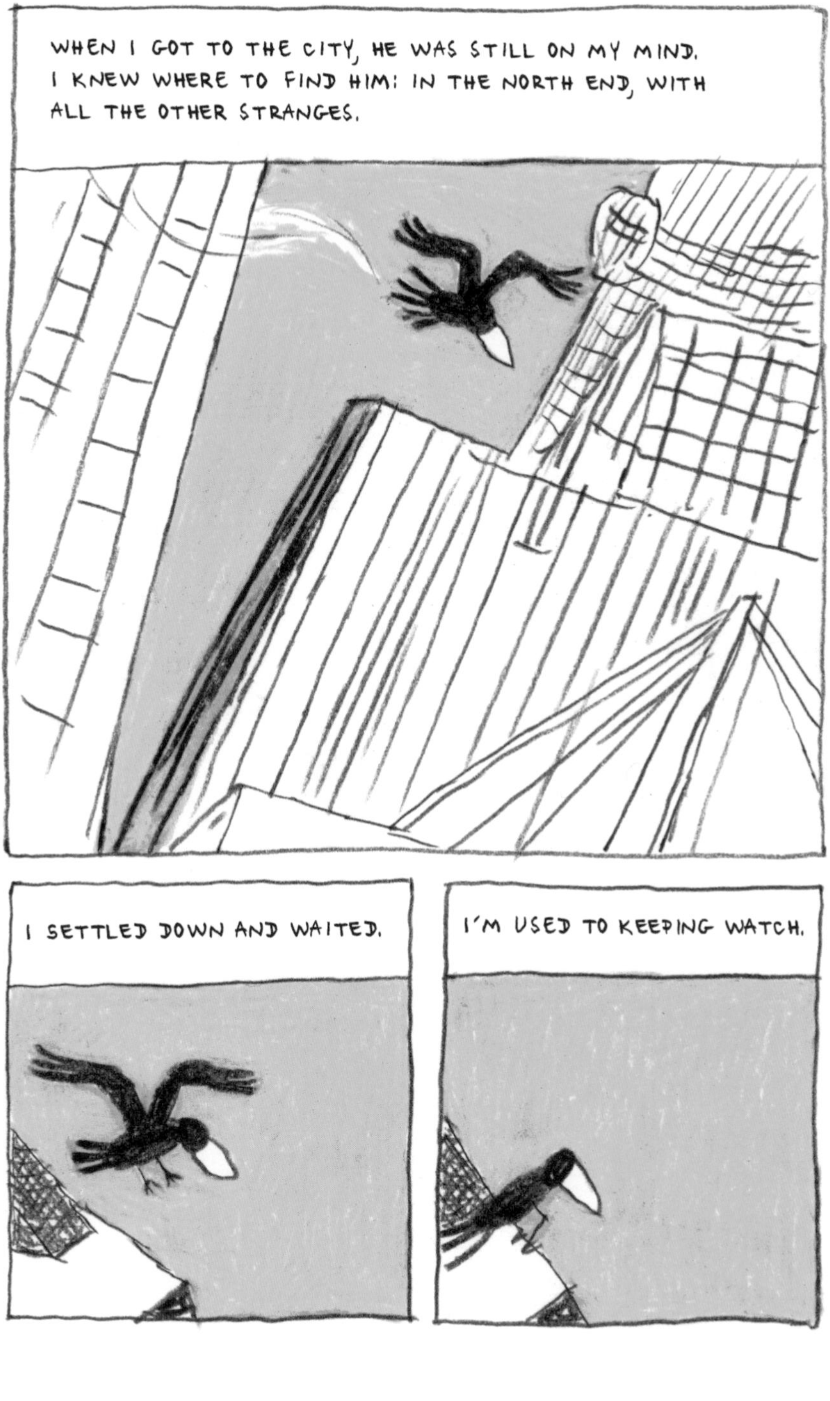
WHEN I GOT TO THE CITY, HE WAS STILL ON MY MIND. I KNEW WHERE TO FIND HIM: IN THE NORTH END, WITH ALL THE OTHER STRANGES.
I SETTLED DOWN AND WAITED.
I'M USED TO KEEPING WATCH.

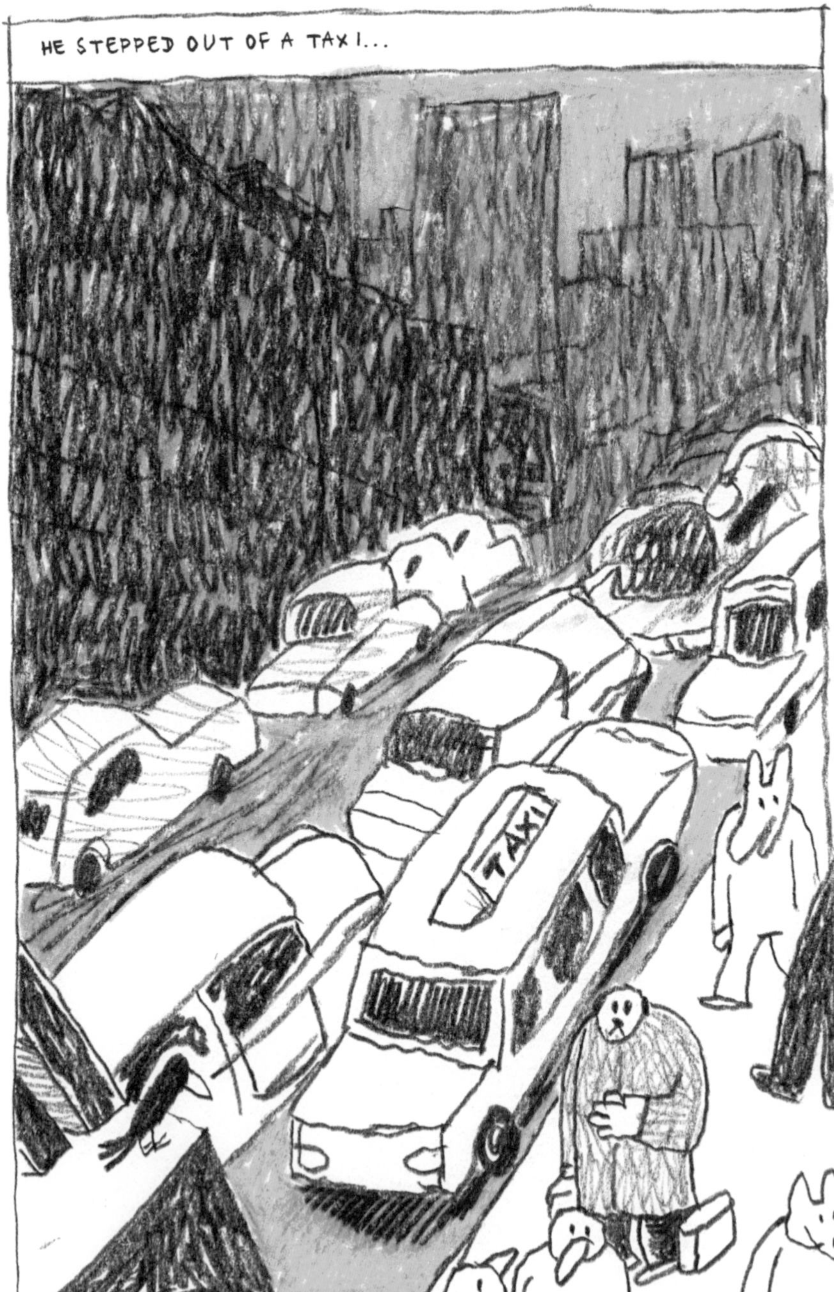
HE STEPPED OUT OF A TAXI...
TAXI

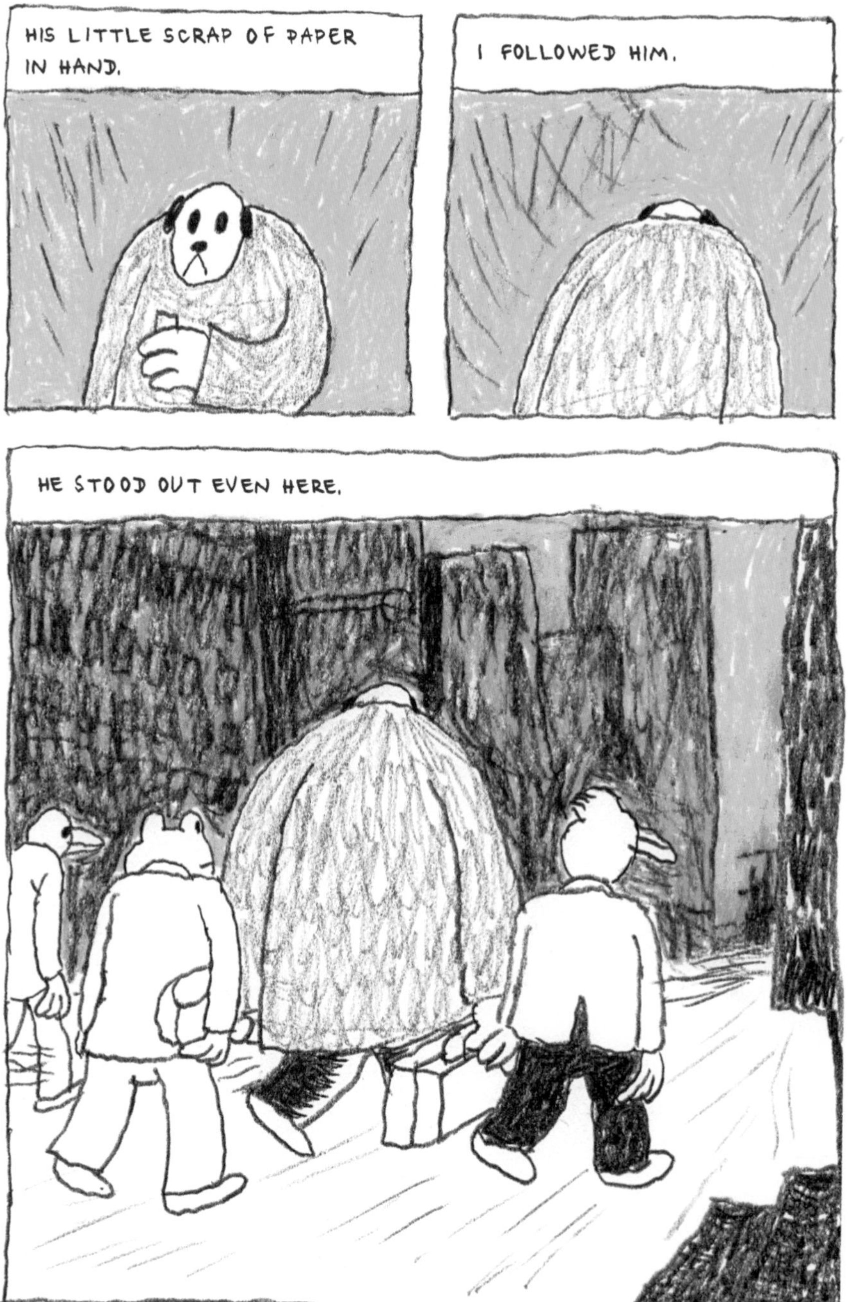
HIS LITTLE SCRAP OF PAPER IN HAND.
I FOLLOWED HIM.
HE STOOD OUT EVEN HERE.

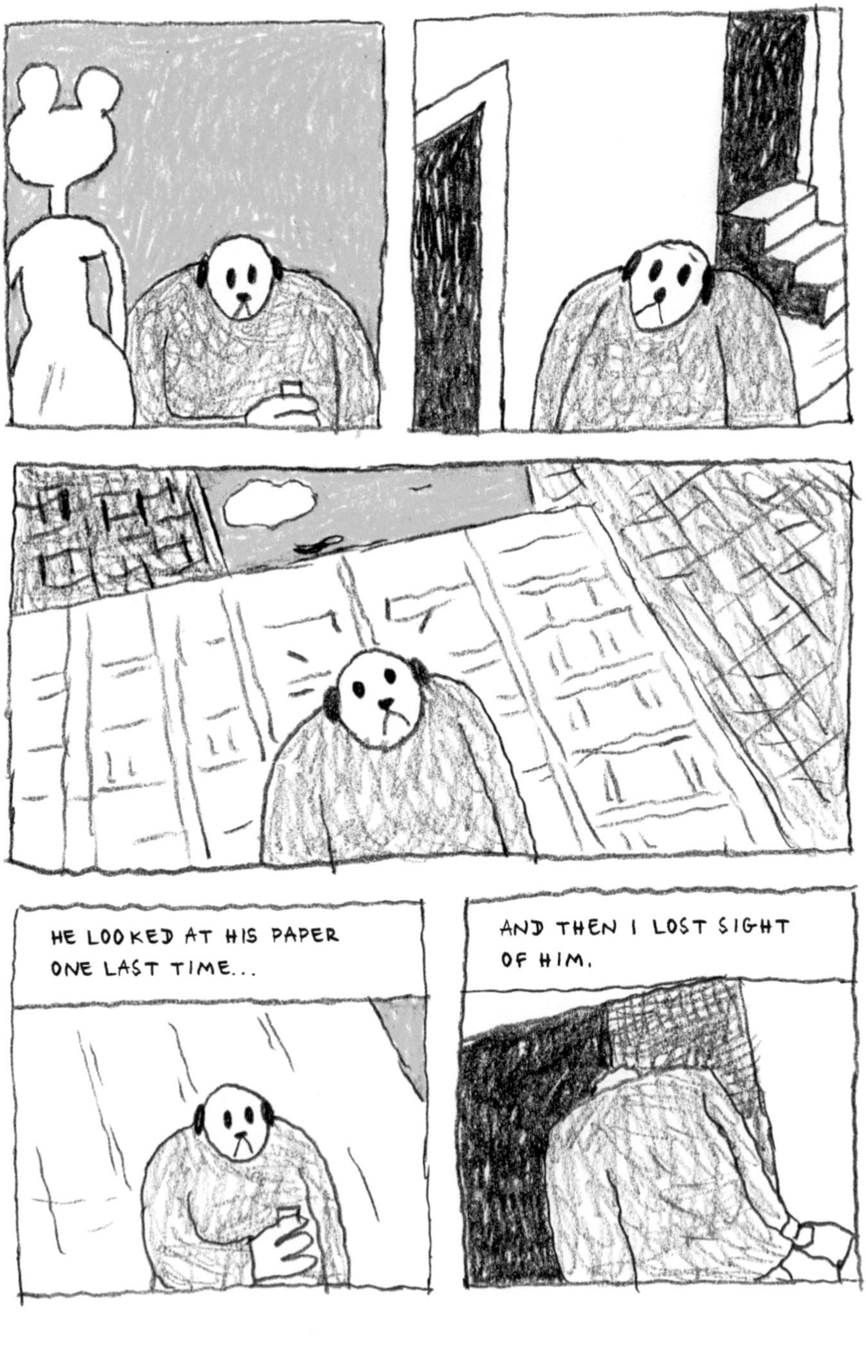
HE LOOKED AT HIS PAPER ONE LAST TIME...
AND THEN I LOST SIGHT OF HIM.

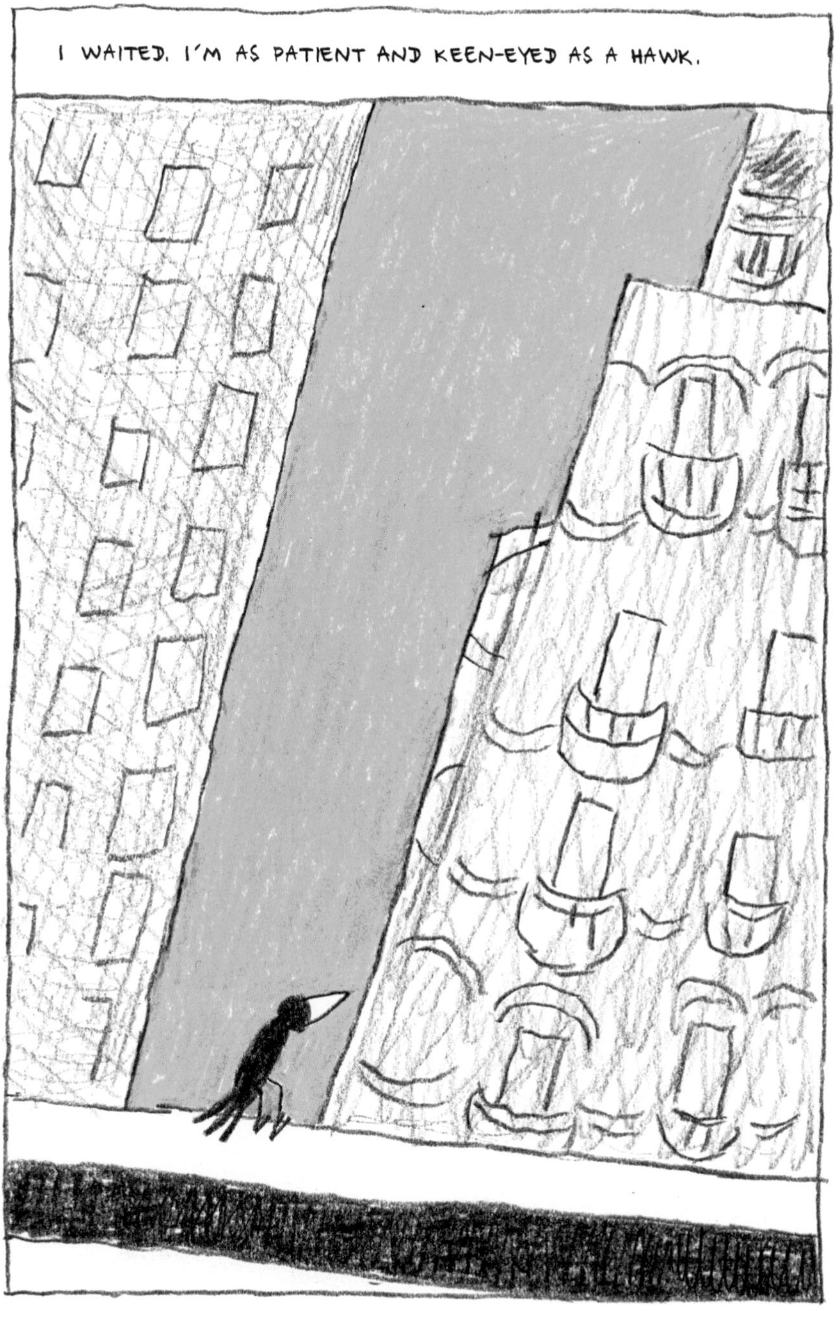
I WAITED. I'M AS PATIENT AND KEEN-EYED AS A HAWK.

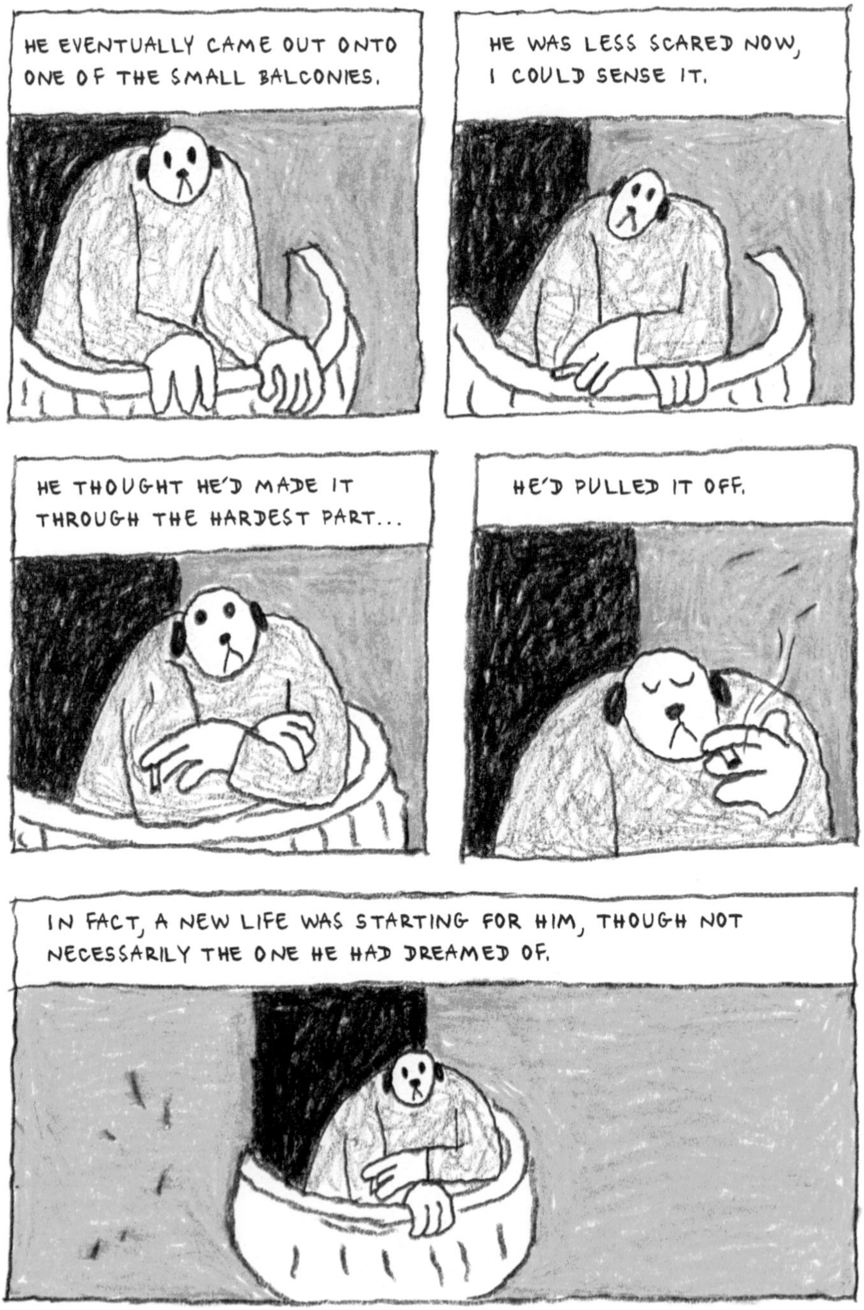
HE EVENTUALLY CAME OUT ONTO ONE OF THE SMALL BALCONIES.
HE WAS LESS SCARED NOW, I COULD SENSE IT.
HE THOUGHT HE'D MADE IT THROUGH THE HARDEST PART...
HE'D PULLED IT OFF.
IN FACT, A NEW LIFE WAS STARTING FOR HIM, THOUGH NOT NECESSARILY THE ONE HE HAD DREAMED OF.

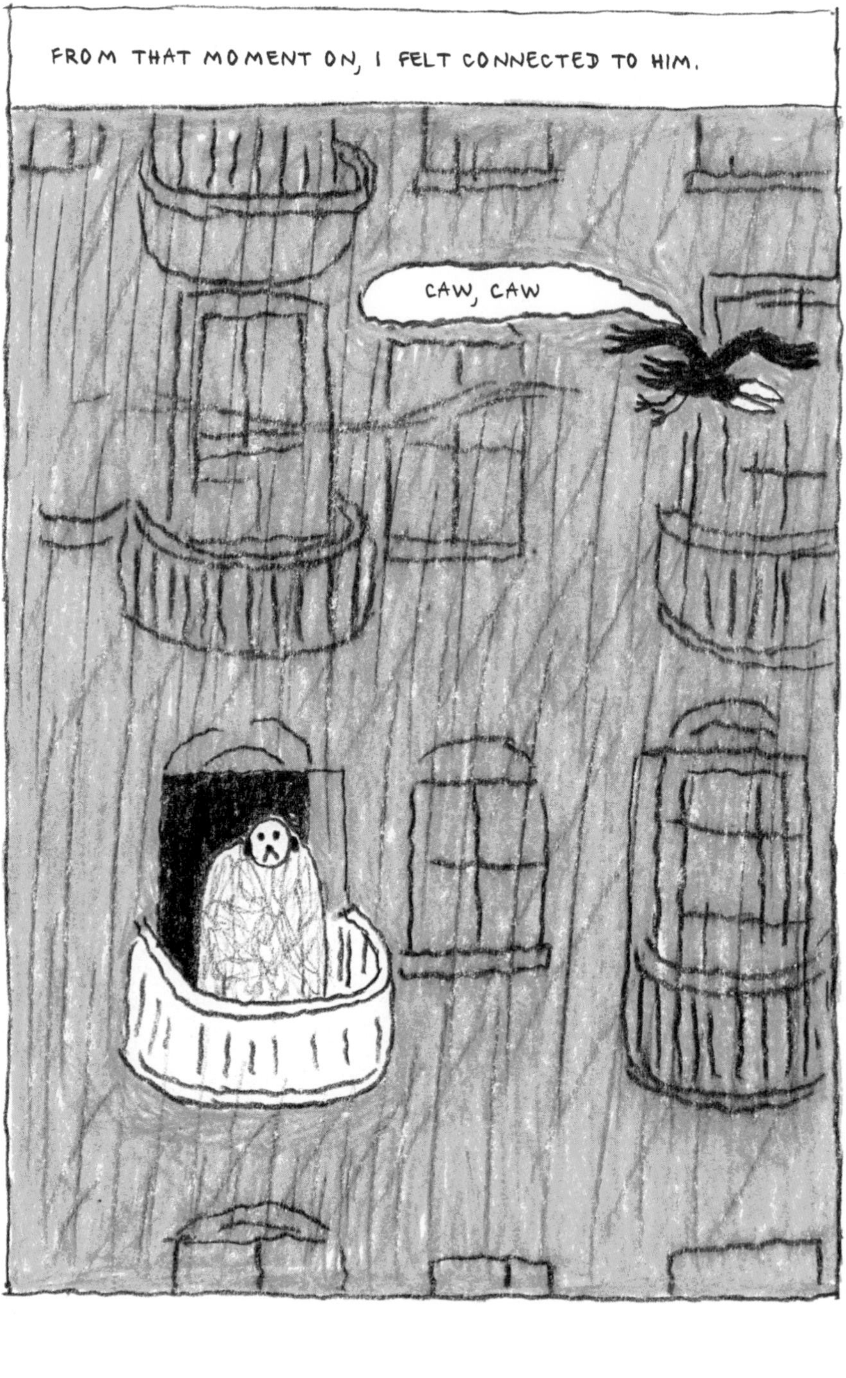
FROM THAT MOMENT ON, I FELT CONNECTED TO HIM.
CAW, CAW

"WE'LL FLUSH THEM OUT ONE BY ONE."

The middleman

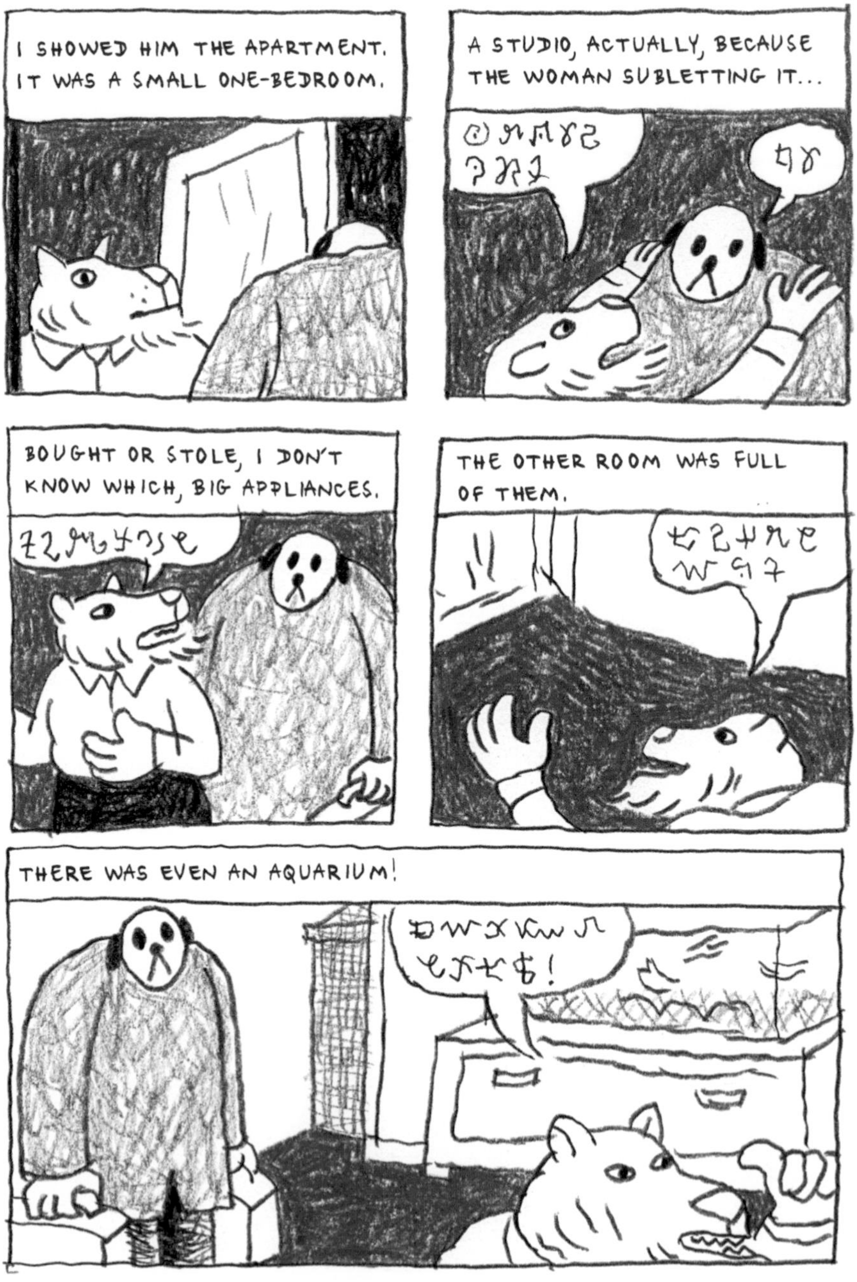
I SHOWED HIM THE APARTMENT. IT WAS A SMALL ONE-BEDROOM.
A STUDIO, ACTUALLY, BECAUSE THE WOMAN SUBLETTING IT...
BOUGHT OR STOLE, I DON'T KNOW WHICH, BIG APPLIANCES.
THE OTHER ROOM WAS FULL OF THEM.
THERE WAS EVEN AN AQUARIUM!

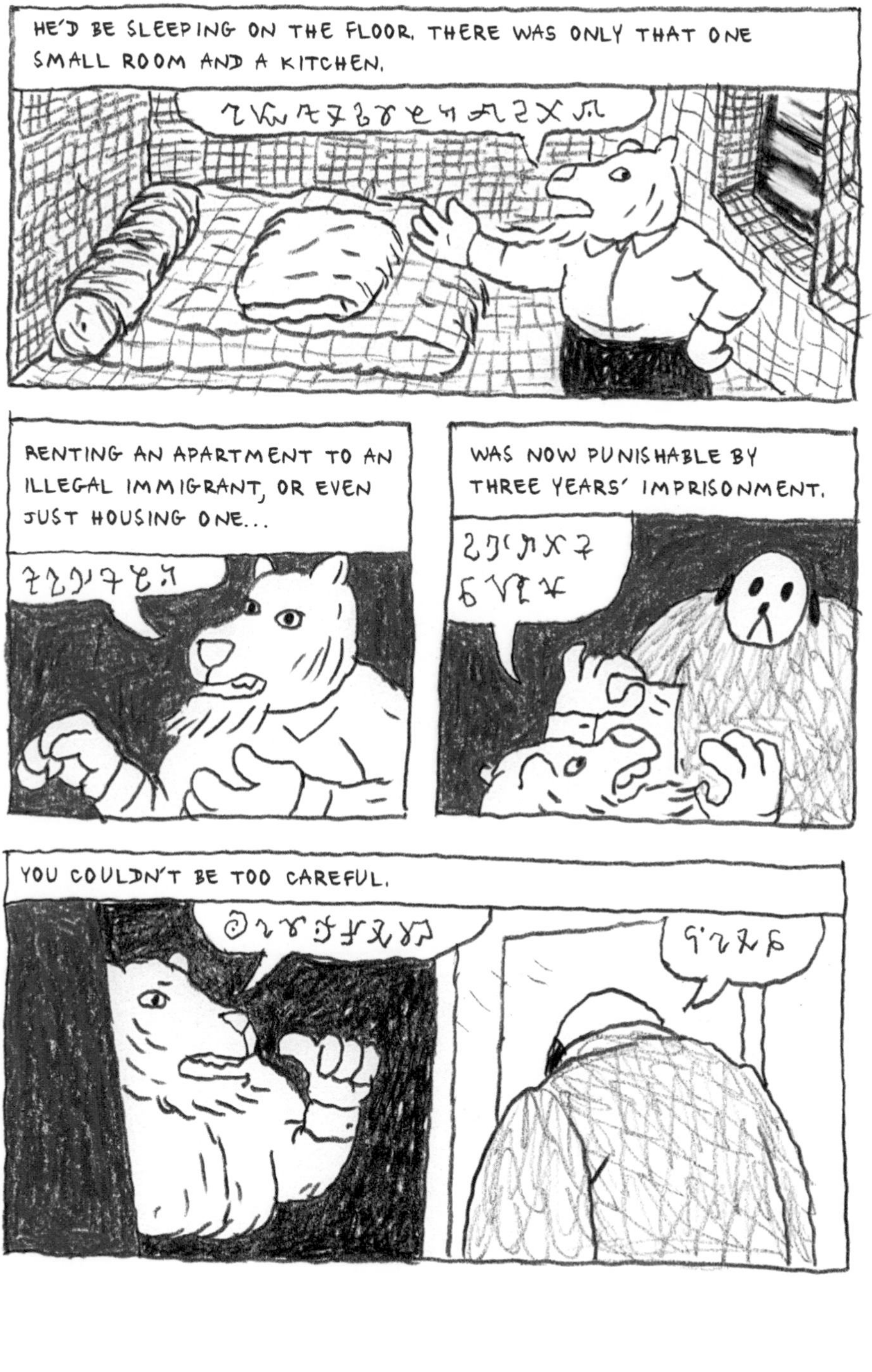
HE'D BE SLEEPING ON THE FLOOR. THERE WAS ONLY THAT ONE SMALL ROOM AND A KITCHEN.
RENTING AN APARTMENT TO AN ILLEGAL IMMIGRANT, OR EVEN JUST HOUSING ONE...
WAS NOW PUNISHABLE BY THREE YEARS' IMPRISONMENT.
YOU COULDN'T BE TOO CAREFUL.

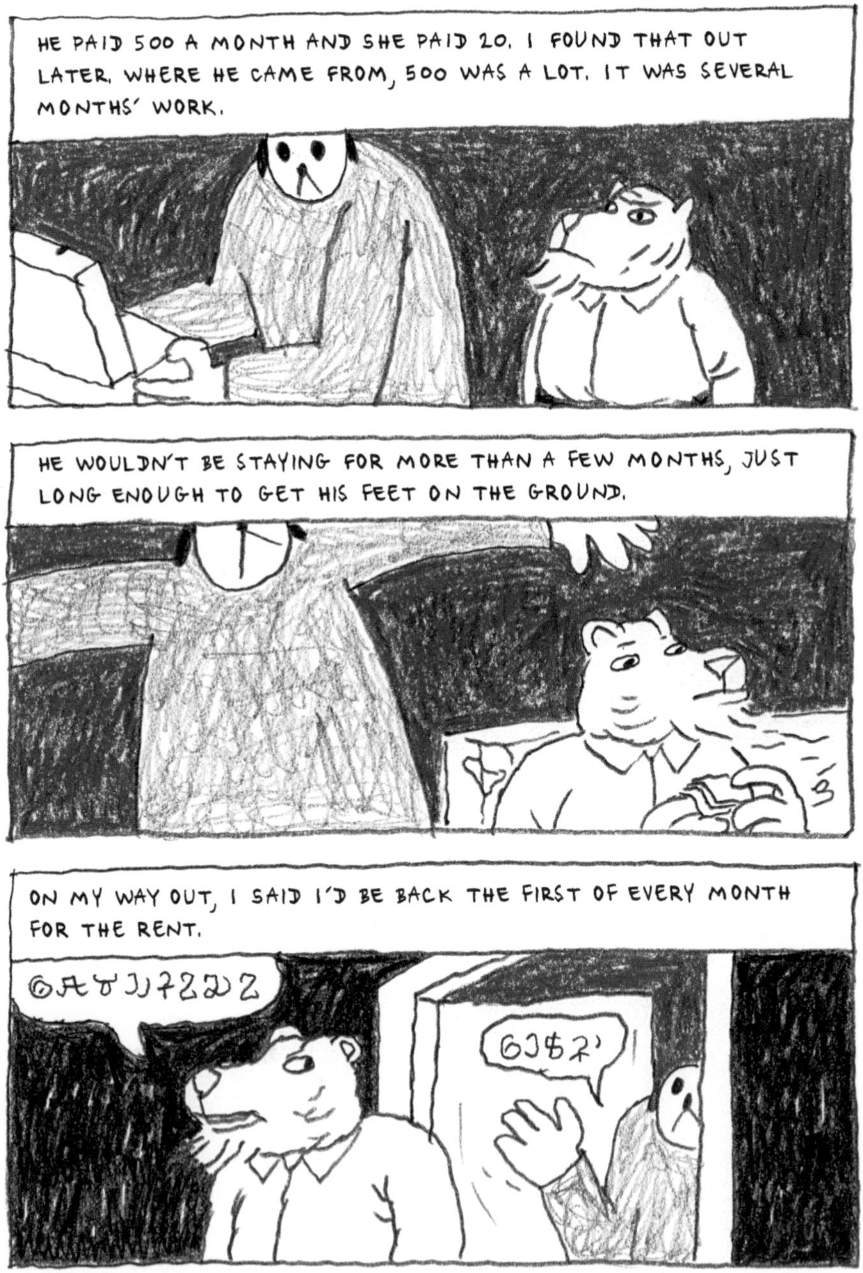
HE PAID 500 A MONTH AND SHE PAID 20. I FOUND THAT OUT LATER. WHERE HE CAME FROM, 500 WAS A LOT. IT WAS SEVERAL MONTHS' WORK.
HE WOULDN'T BE STAYING FOR MORE THAN A FEW MONTHS, JUST LONG ENOUGH TO GET HIS FEET ON THE GROUND.
ON MY WAY OUT, I SAID I'D BE BACK THE FIRST OF EVERY MONTH FOR THE RENT.

The fish

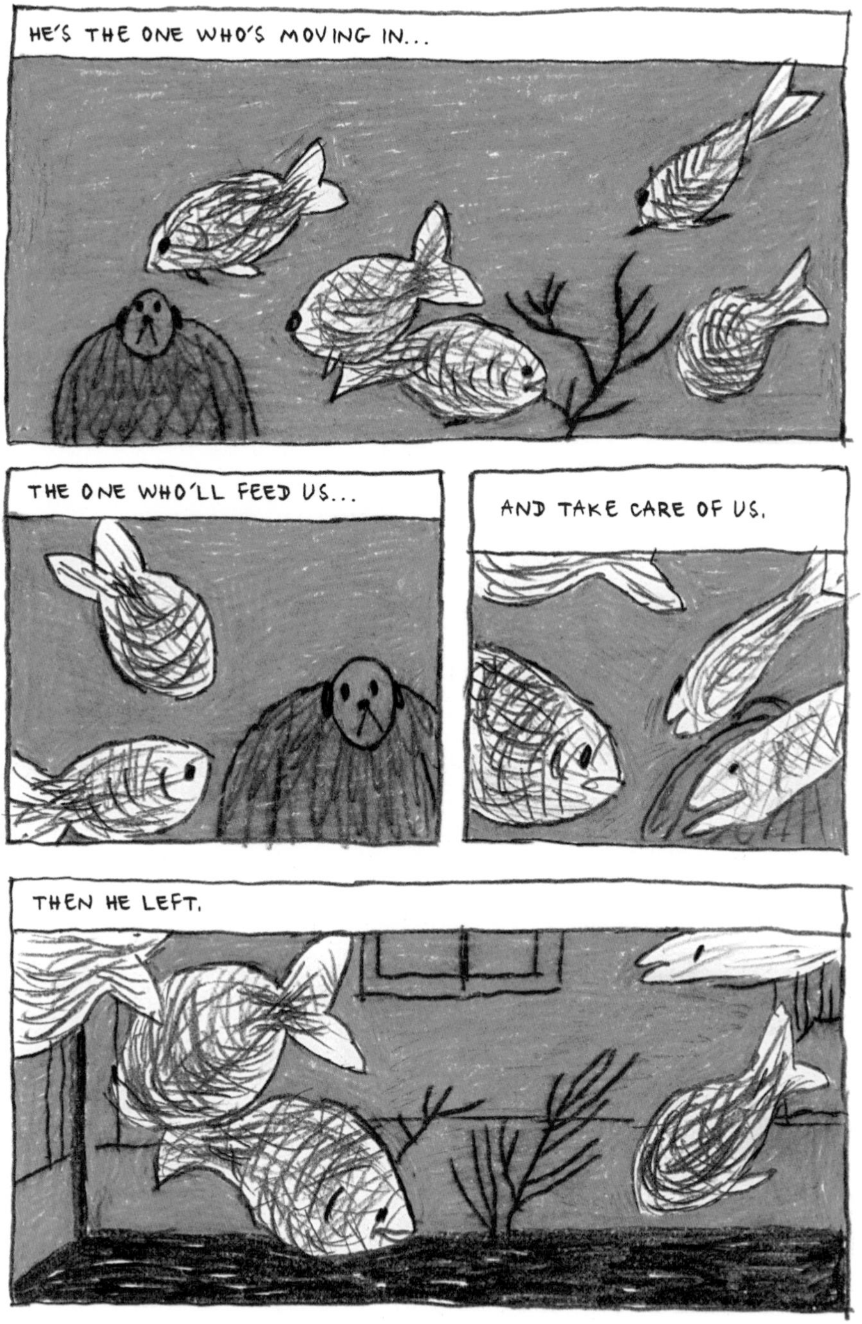
HE'S THE ONE WHO'S MOVING IN...
THE ONE WHO'LL FEED US...
AND TAKE CARE OF US.
THEN HE LEFT.

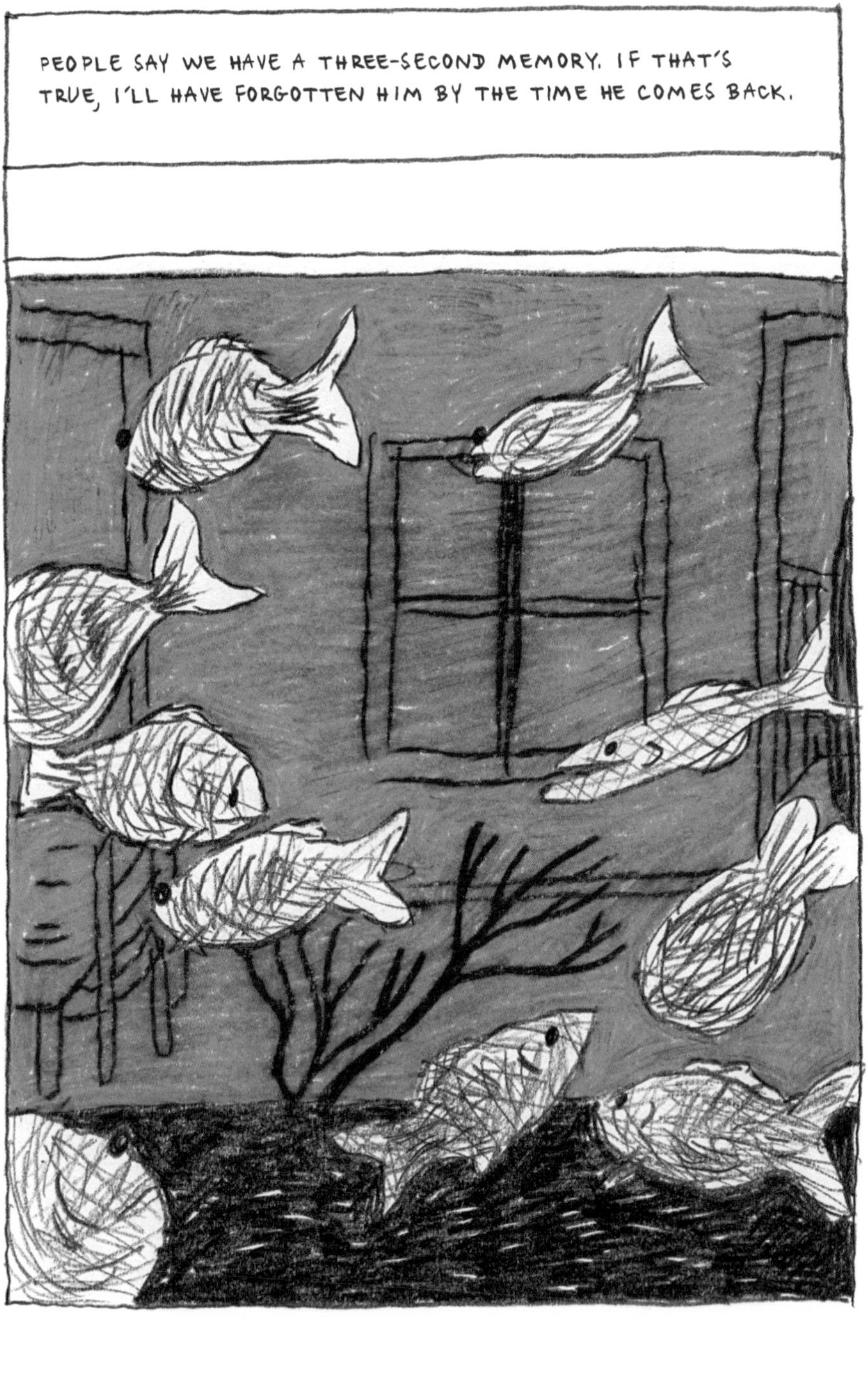
PEOPLE SAY WE HAVE A THREE-SECOND MEMORY. IF THAT'S TRUE, I'LL HAVE FORGOTTEN HIM BY THE TIME HE COMES BACK.

Bernard

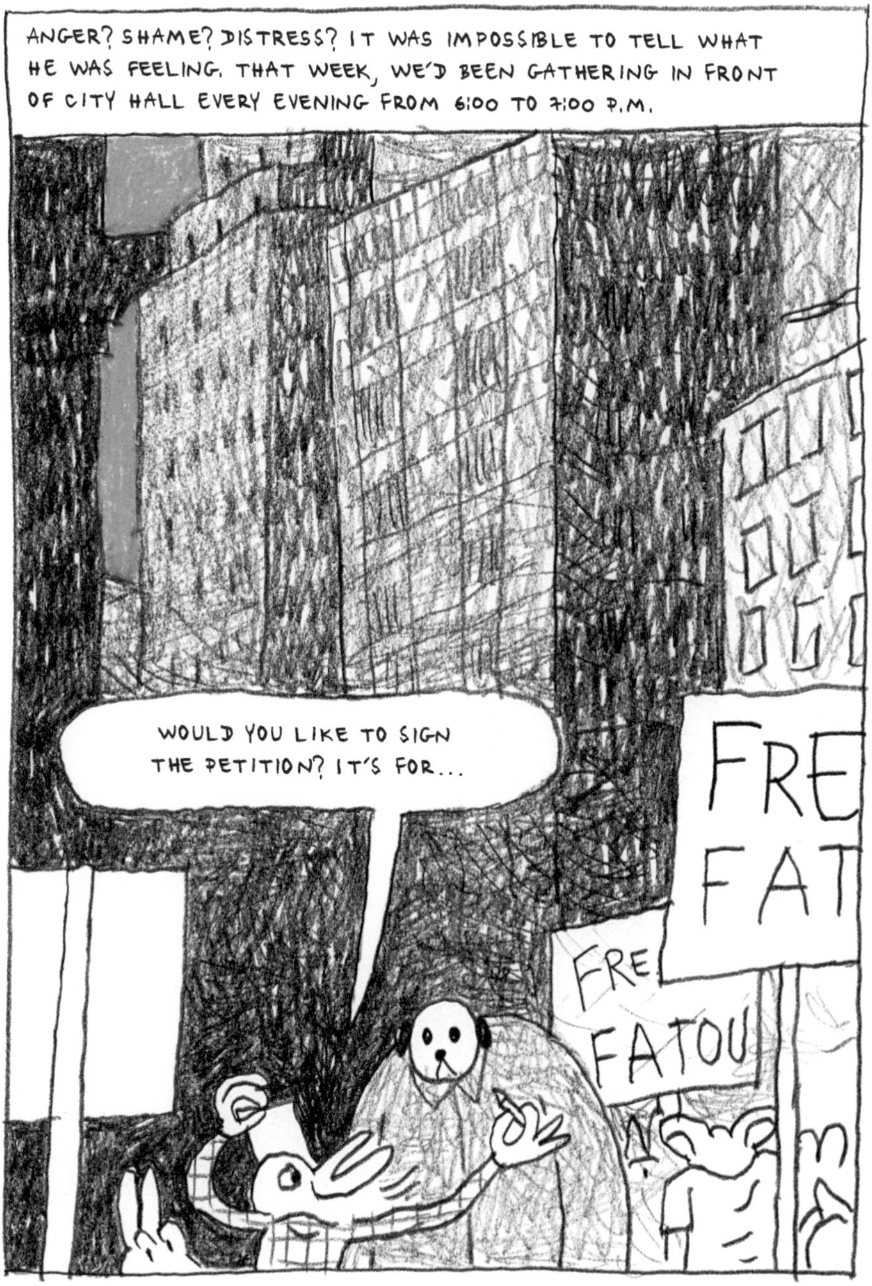
ANGER? SHAME? DISTRESS? IT WAS IMPOSSIBLE TO TELL WHAT HE WAS FEELING. THAT WEEK, WE'D BEEN GATHERING IN FRONT OF CITY HALL EVERY EVENING FROM 6:00 TO 7:00 P.M.
WOULD YOU LIKE TO SIGN THE PETITION? IT'S FOR...
FRE
FAT
FRE
FATOU

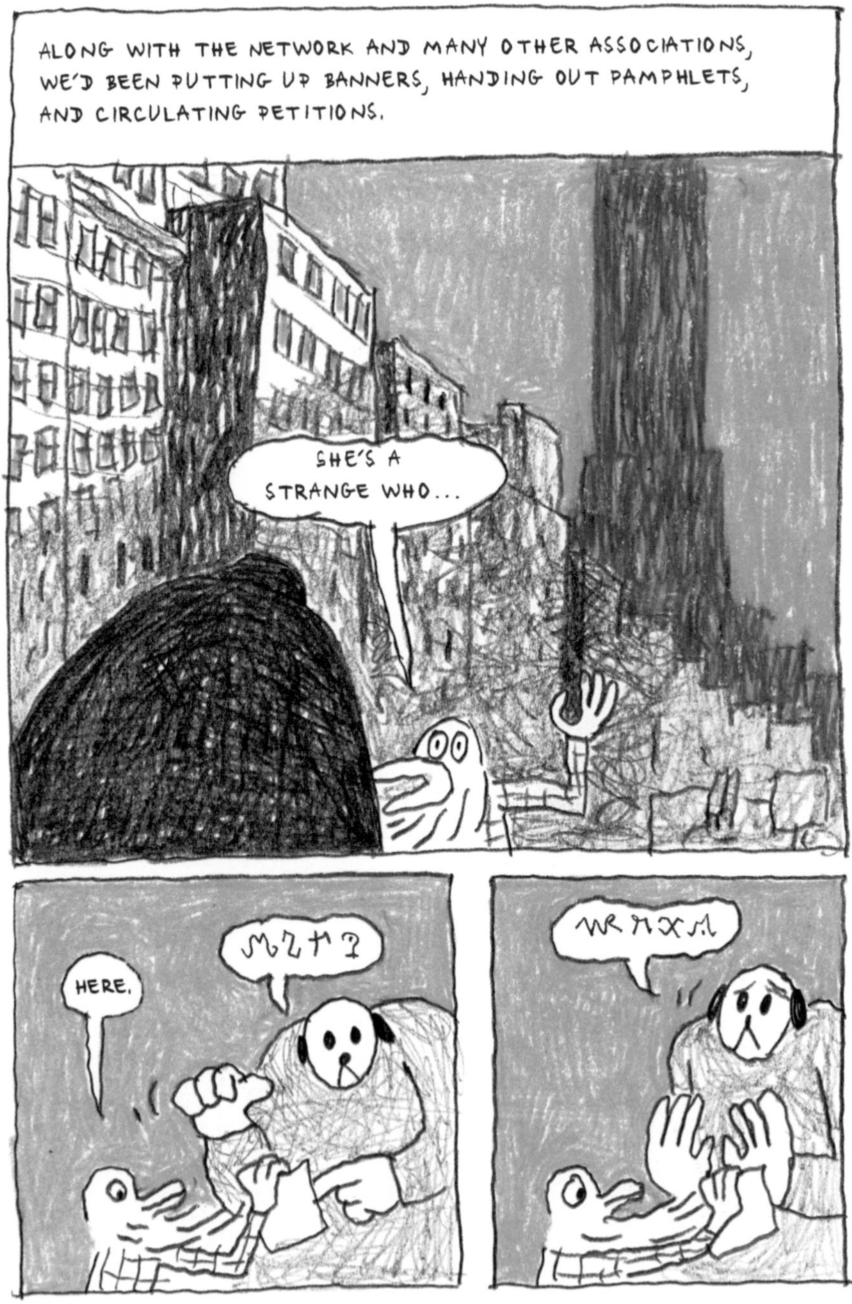
ALONG WITH THE NETWORK AND MANY OTHER ASSOCIATIONS, WE'D BEEN PUTTING UP BANNERS, HANDING OUT PAMPHLETS, AND CIRCULATING PETITIONS.
SHE'S A STRANGE WHO...
HERE.

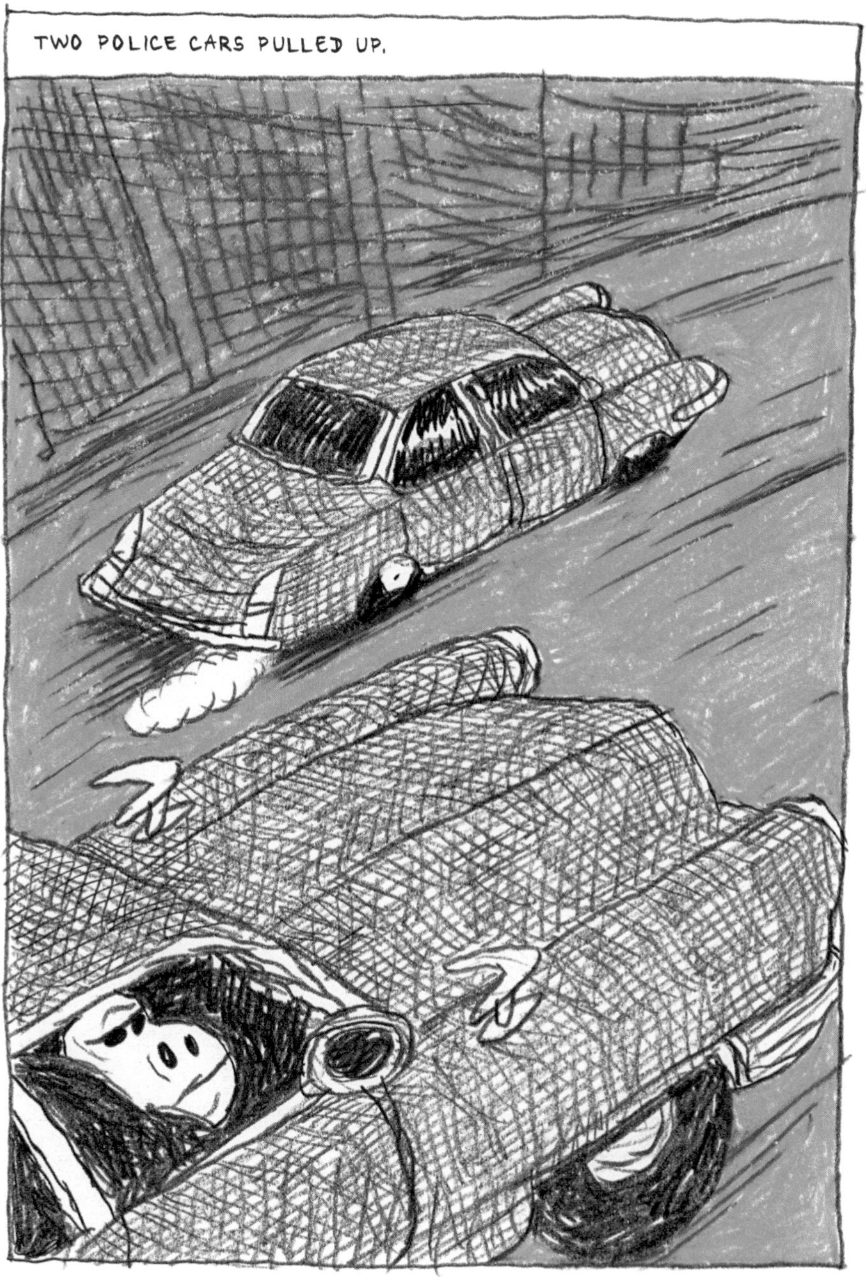
TWO POLICE CARS PULLED UP.

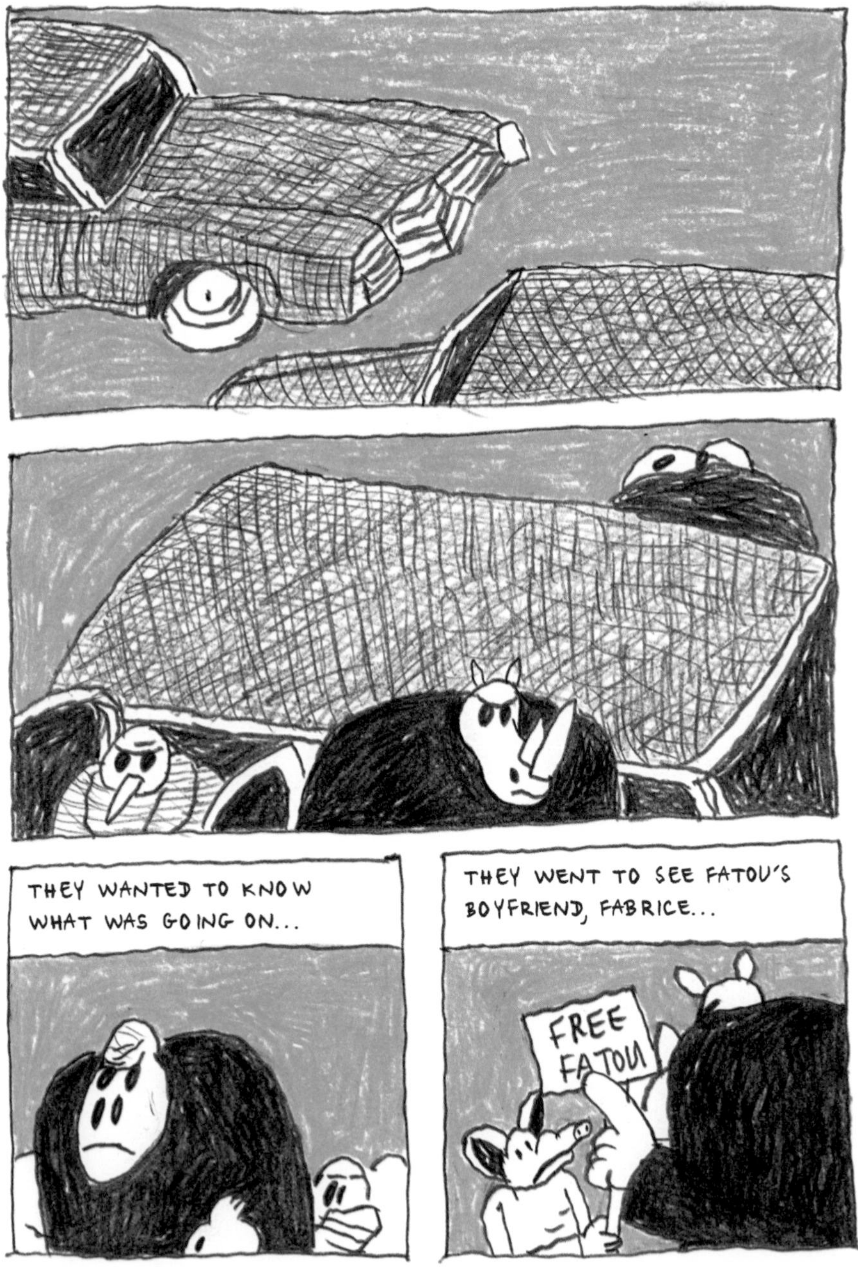
THEY WANTED TO KNOW WHAT WAS GOING ON...
THEY WENT TO SEE FATOU'S BOYFRIEND, FABRICE...
FREE FATOU

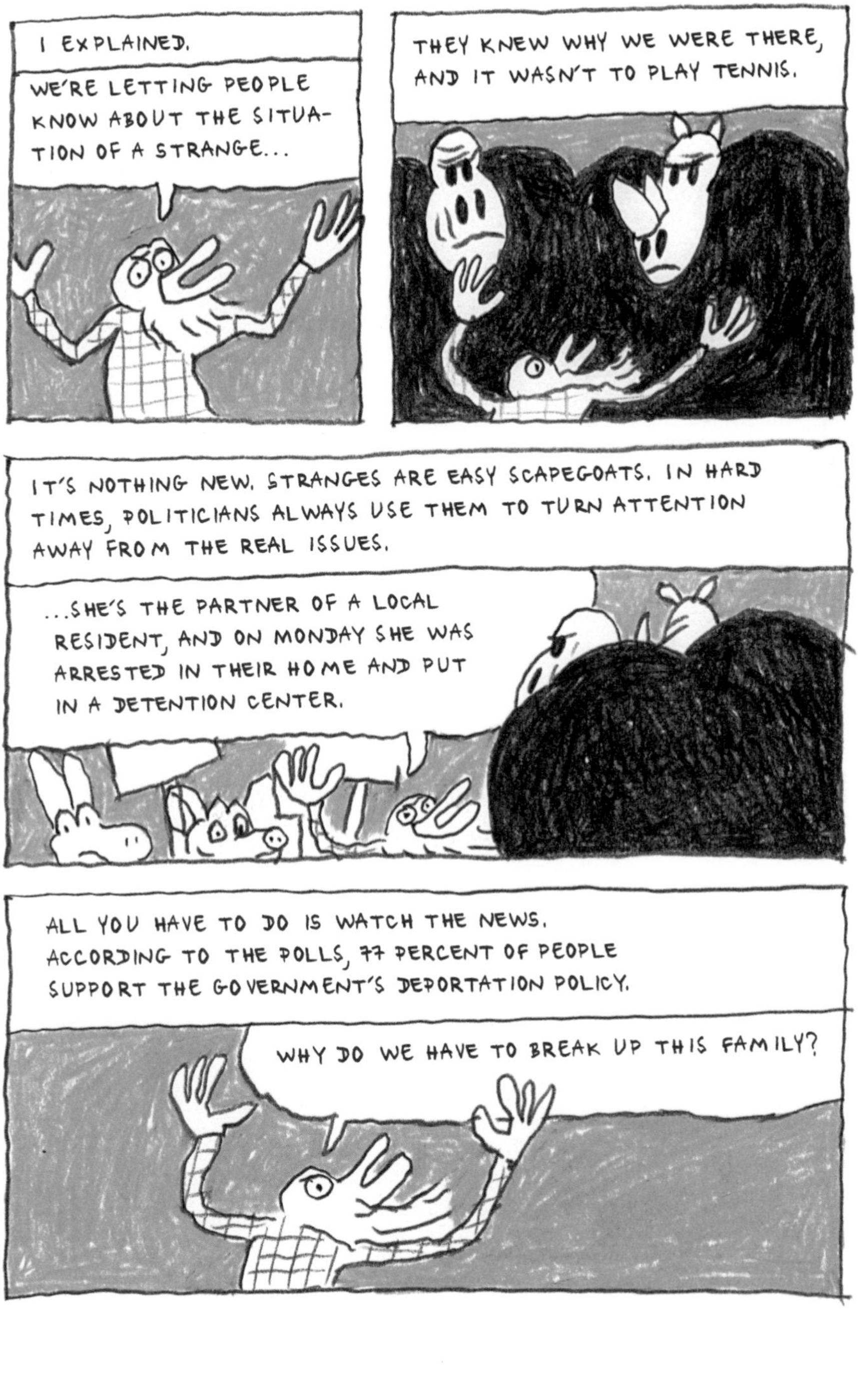
I EXPLAINED.
WE'RE LETTING PEOPLE KNOW ABOUT THE SITUATION OF A STRANGE...
THEY KNEW WHY WE WERE THERE, AND IT WASN'T TO PLAY TENNIS.
IT'S NOTHING NEW. STRANGES ARE EASY SCAPEGOATS. IN HARD TIMES, POLITICIANS ALWAYS USE THEM TO TURN ATTENTION AWAY FROM THE REAL ISSUES.
...SHE'S THE PARTNER OF A LOCAL RESIDENT, AND ON MONDAY SHE WAS ARRESTED IN THEIR HOME AND PUT IN A DETENTION CENTER.
ALL YOU HAVE TO DO IS WATCH THE NEWS. ACCORDING TO THE POLLS, 77 PERCENT OF PEOPLE SUPPORT THE GOVERNMENT'S DEPORTATION POLICY.
WHY DO WE HAVE TO BREAK UP THIS FAMILY?

MORE AND MORE STRANGES ARE BEING EXPELLED HERE,
LIKE EVERYWHERE ELSE. IT GOT WORSE LAST YEAR AFTER
THE NEW POLICE PREFECT WAS APPOINTED, WITH ORDERS
TO KEEP UP THE QUOTAS.

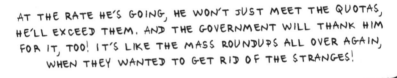

THE PREFECT HAS NO RESPECT FOR BASIC HUMAN
RIGHTS. HIS LACK OF HUMANITY IS A DISGRACE!

AT THE RATE HE'S GOING, HE WON'T JUST MEET THE QUOTAS,
HE'LL EXCEED THEM. AND THE GOVERNMENT WILL THANK HIM
FOR IT, TOO! IT'S LIKE THE MASS ROUNDUPS ALL OVER AGAIN,
WHEN THEY WANTED TO GET RID OF THE STRANGES!

THE COMMISSIONER GOT BACK INTO HER CAR. SHE MUST HAVE
CALLED THE PREFECT TO TELL HIM THERE WAS TROUBLE.

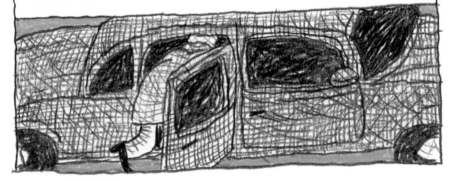

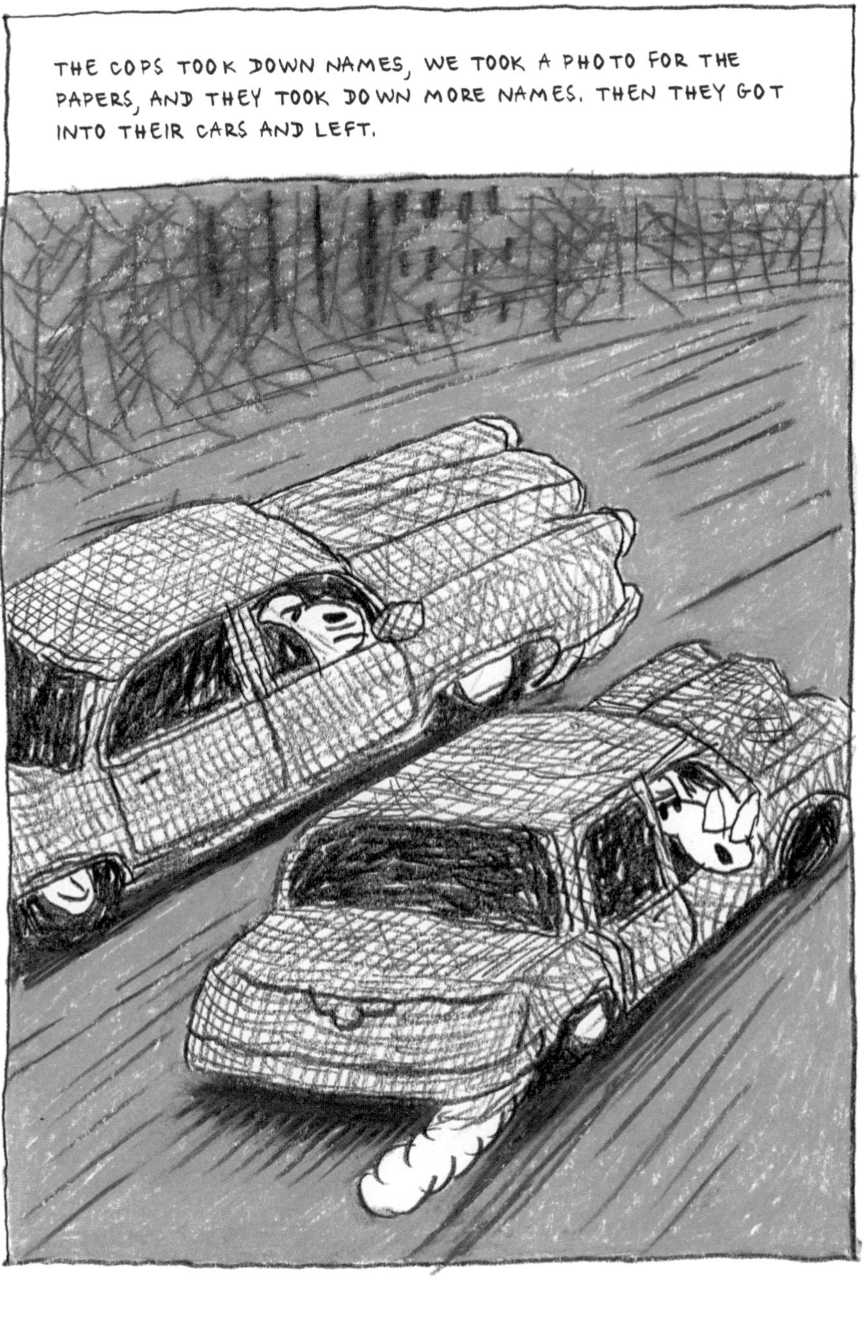
THE COPS TOOK DOWN NAMES, WE TOOK A PHOTO FOR THE PAPERS, AND THEY TOOK DOWN MORE NAMES. THEN THEY GOT INTO THEIR CARS AND LEFT.

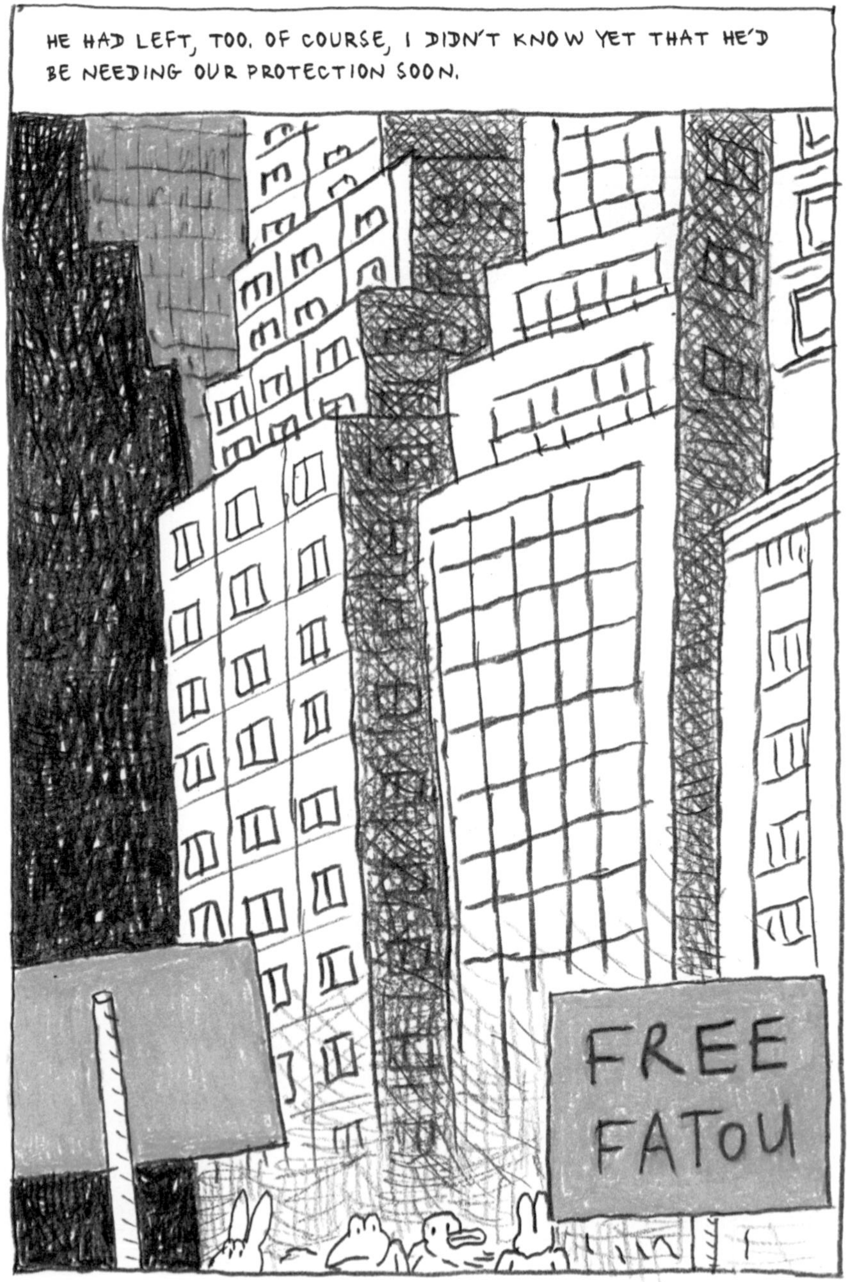
HE HAD LEFT, TOO. OF COURSE, I DIDN'T KNOW YET THAT HE'D BE NEEDING OUR PROTECTION SOON.
FREE FATOU

A passerby

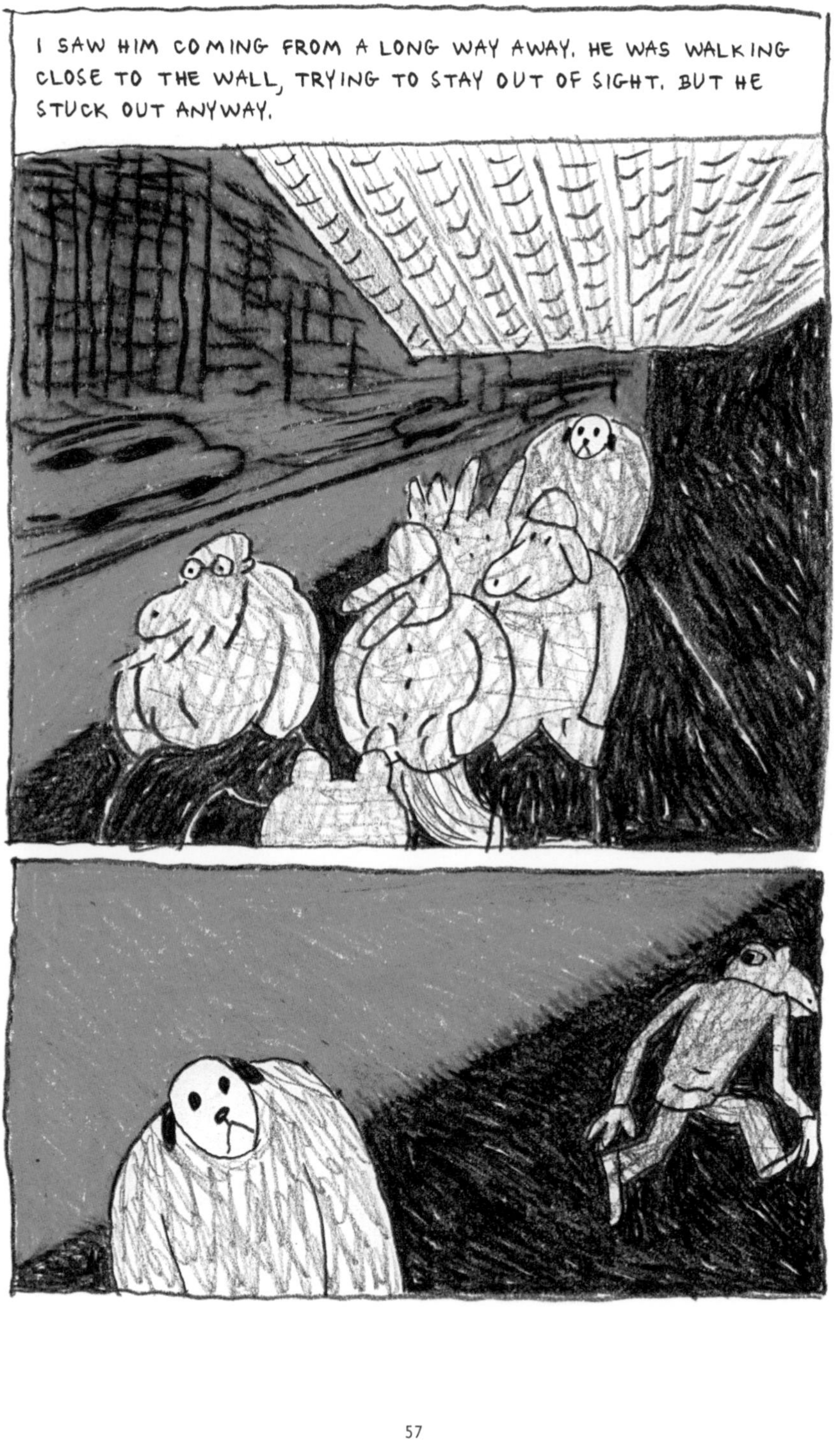
I SAW HIM COMING FROM A LONG WAY AWAY. HE WAS WALKING CLOSE TO THE WALL, TRYING TO STAY OUT OF SIGHT. BUT HE STUCK OUT ANYWAY.

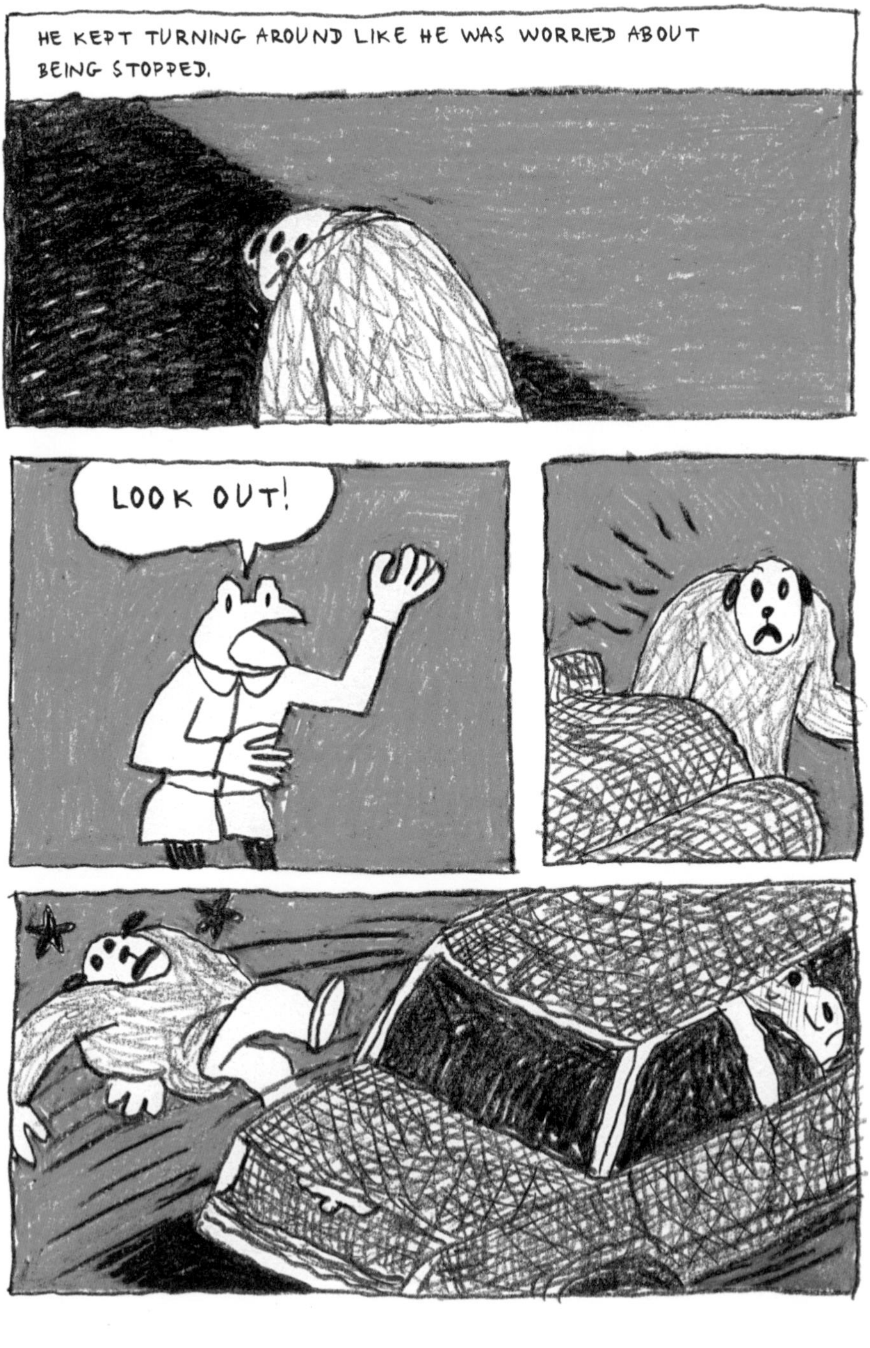
HE KEPT TURNING AROUND LIKE HE WAS WORRIED ABOUT BEING STOPPED.
LOOK OUT!

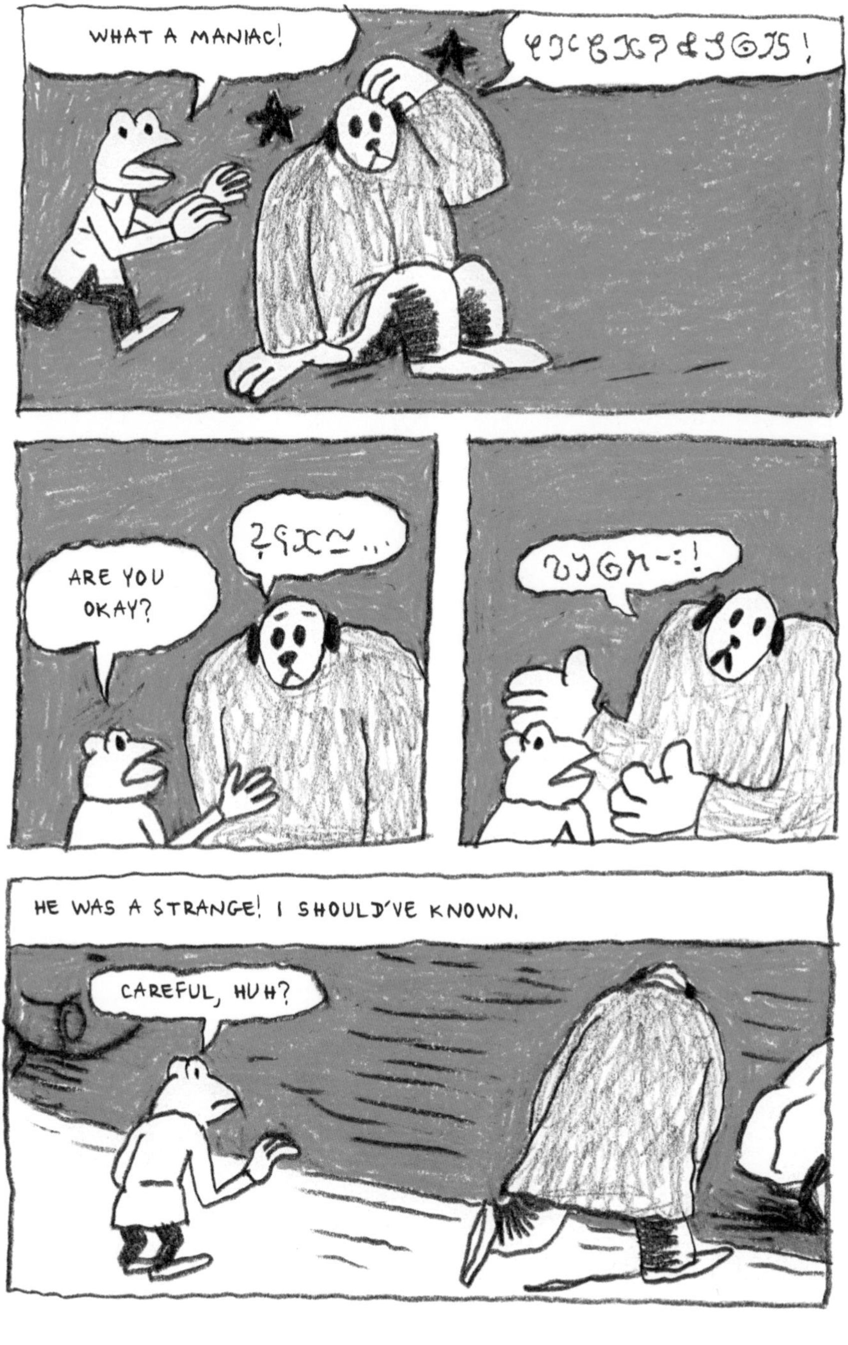
WHAT A MANIAC!
ARE YOU OKAY?
HE WAS A STRANGE! I SHOULD'VE KNOWN.
CAREFUL, HUH?

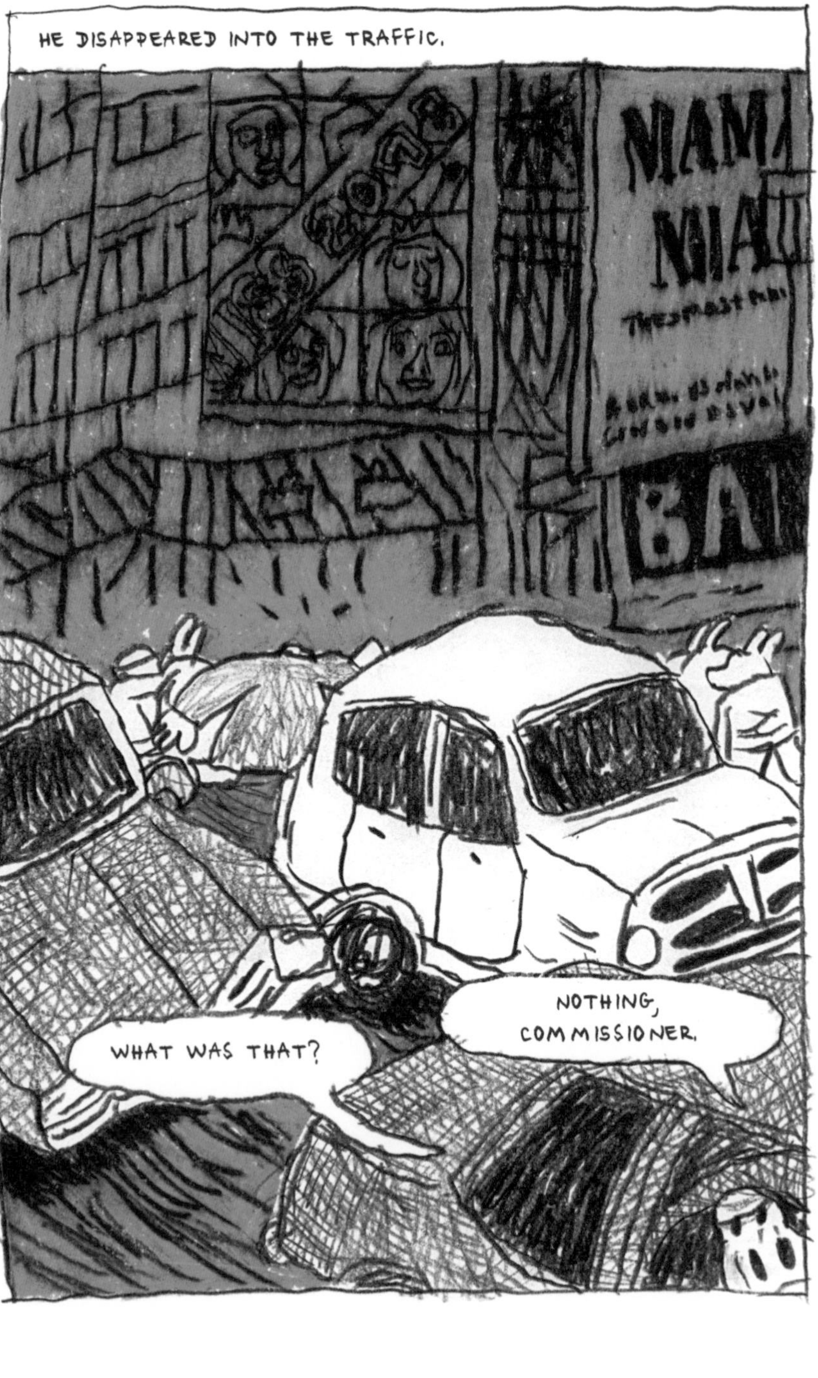
HE DISAPPEARED INTO THE TRAFFIC.
WHAT WAS THAT?
NOTHING, COMMISSIONER.

The officer

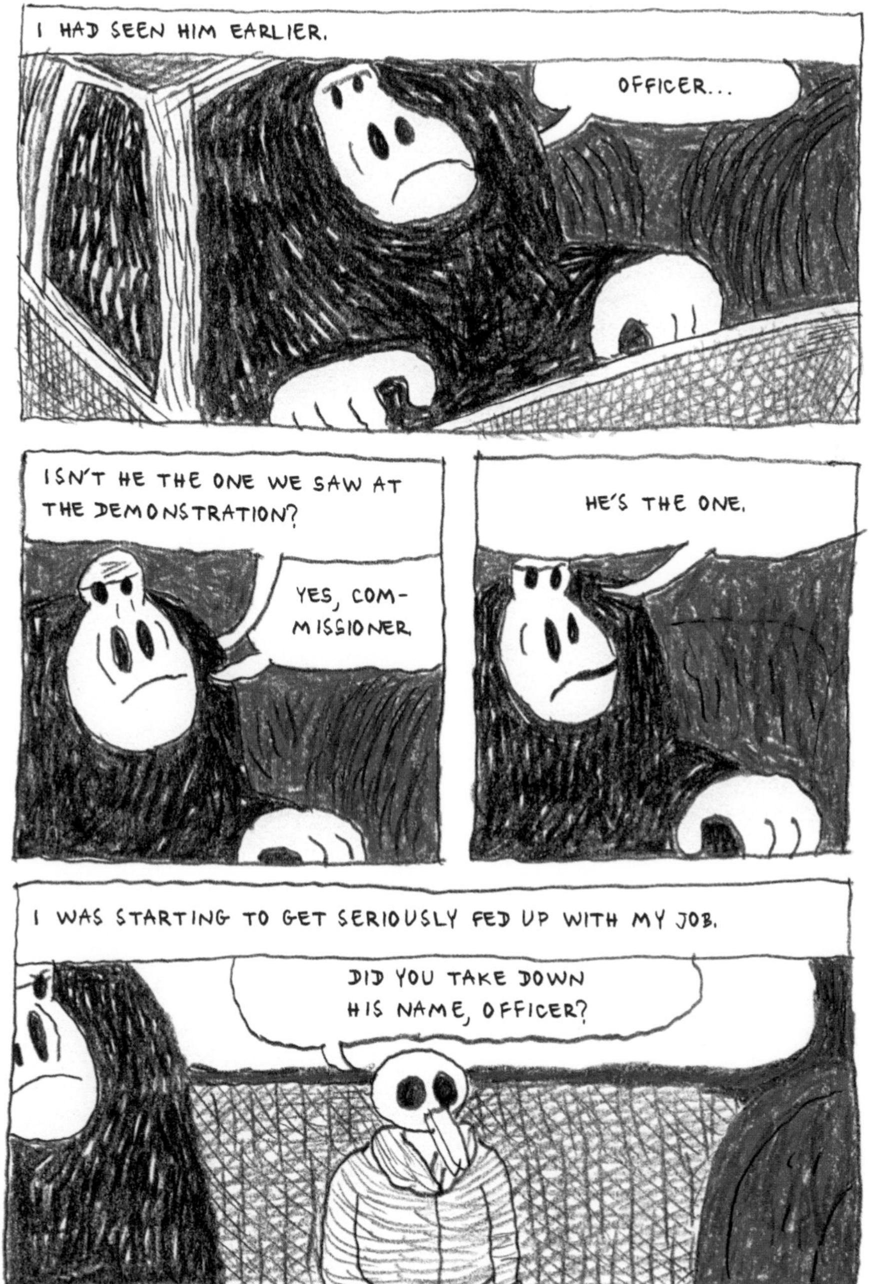
I HAD SEEN HIM EARLIER.
OFFICER...
ISN'T HE THE ONE WE SAW AT THE DEMONSTRATION?
YES, COM-MISSIONER.
HE'S THE ONE.
I WAS STARTING TO GET SERIOUSLY FED UP WITH MY JOB.
DID YOU TAKE DOWN HIS NAME, OFFICER?

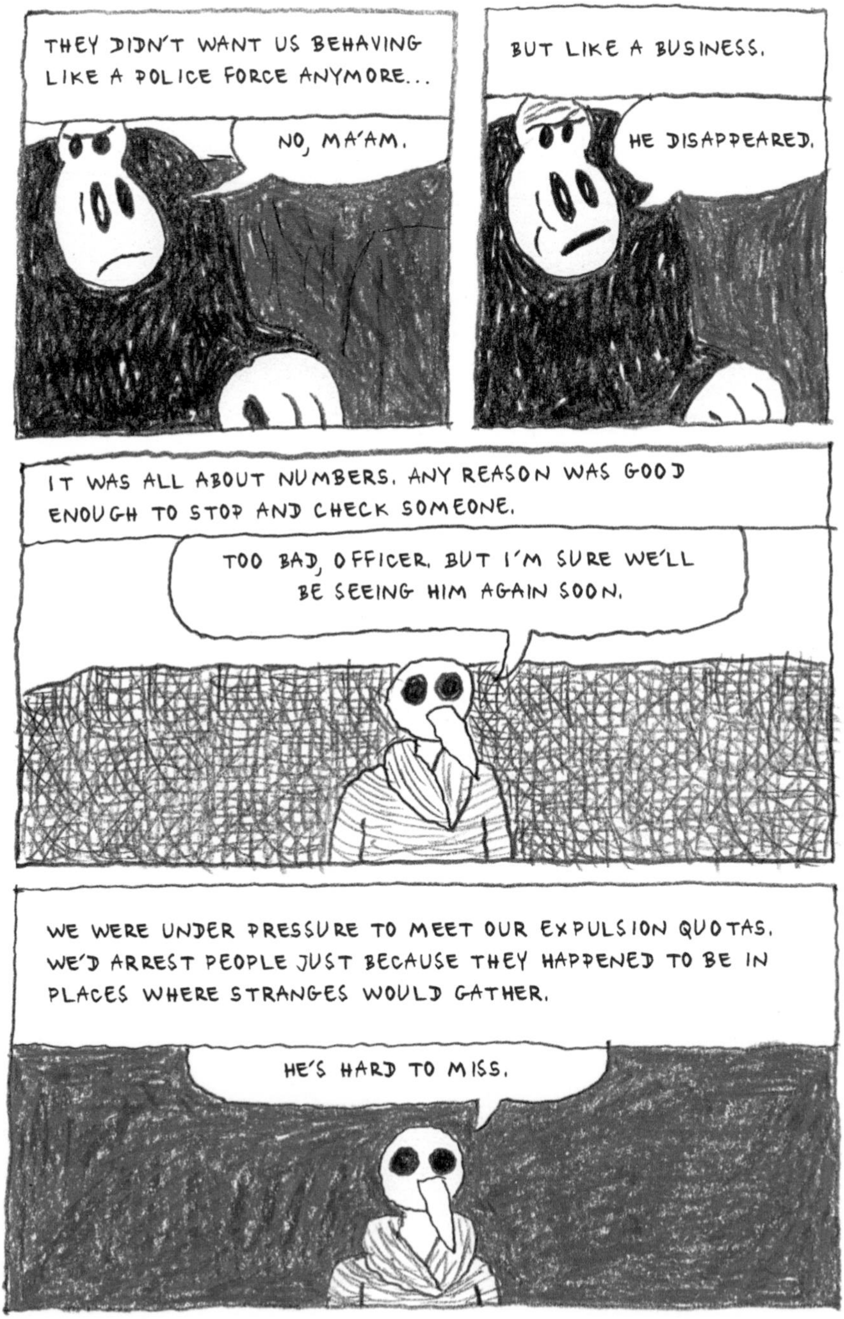
THEY DIDN'T WANT US BEHAVING LIKE A POLICE FORCE ANYMORE...
NO, MA'AM.
BUT LIKE A BUSINESS.
HE DISAPPEARED.
IT WAS ALL ABOUT NUMBERS. ANY REASON WAS GOOD ENOUGH TO STOP AND CHECK SOMEONE.
TOO BAD, OFFICER. BUT I'M SURE WE'LL BE SEEING HIM AGAIN SOON.
WE WERE UNDER PRESSURE TO MEET OUR EXPULSION QUOTAS. WE'D ARREST PEOPLE JUST BECAUSE THEY HAPPENED TO BE IN PLACES WHERE STRANGES WOULD GATHER.
HE'S HARD TO MISS.

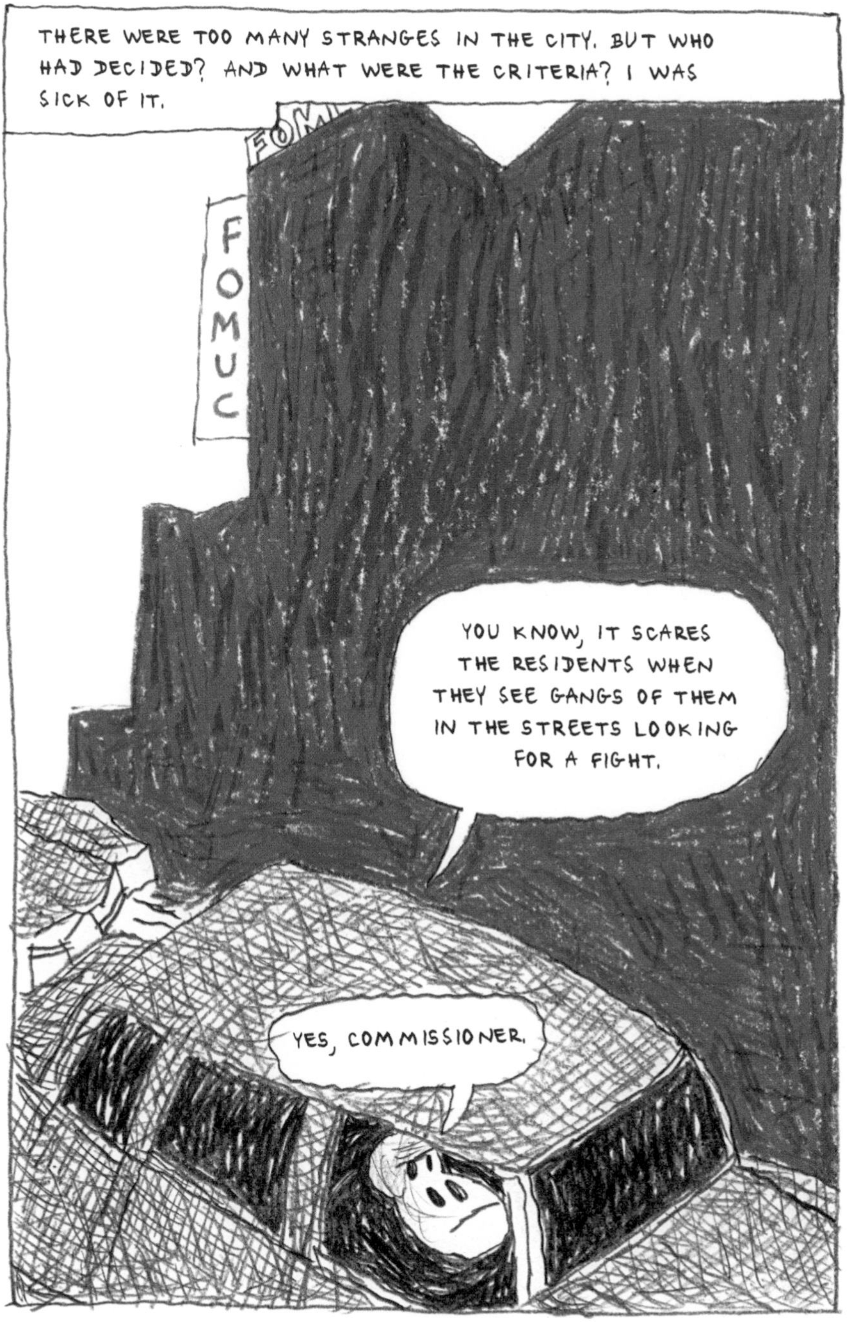
THERE WERE TOO MANY STRANGES IN THE CITY. BUT WHO HAD DECIDED? AND WHAT WERE THE CRITERIA? I WAS SICK OF IT.
FOMUC
YOU KNOW, IT SCARES THE RESIDENTS WHEN THEY SEE GANGS OF THEM IN THE STREETS LOOKING FOR A FIGHT.
YES, COMMISSIONER.

"THIS IS ALSO FOR THE SILENT MAJORITY, FOR ALL THOSE
PEOPLE WHO CAN'T AFFORD TO STRIKE OR DEMONSTRATE,
OR WHO CHOOSE TO PUT THEIR WORK FIRST. I HAVE TO
THINK OF THEM, TOO, AND ACT ON THEIR BEHALF."

The neighbor

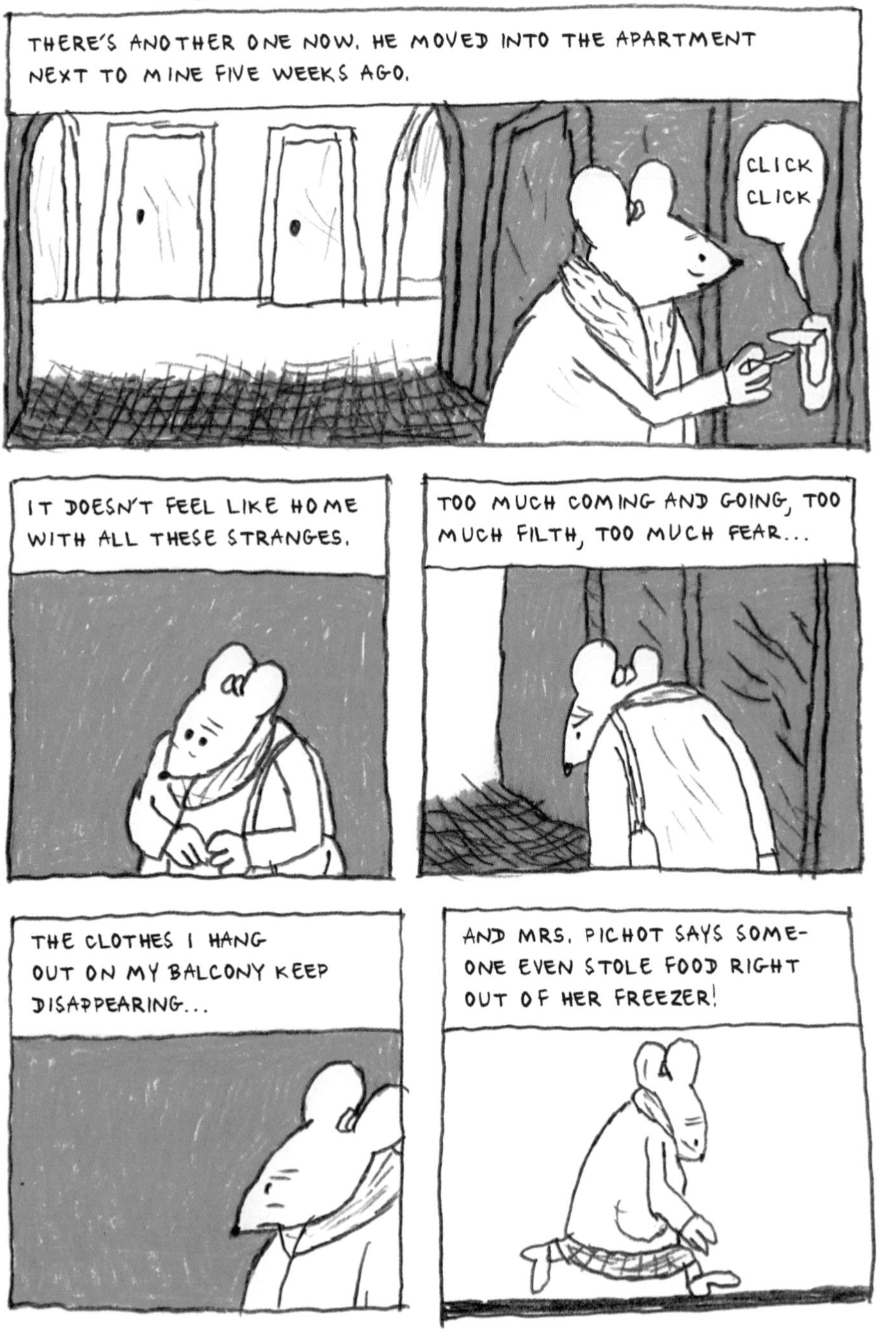

THERE'S ANOTHER ONE NOW. HE MOVED INTO THE APARTMENT NEXT TO MINE FIVE WEEKS AGO.
CLICK CLICK
IT DOESN'T FEEL LIKE HOME WITH ALL THESE STRANGES.
TOO MUCH COMING AND GOING, TOO MUCH FILTH, TOO MUCH FEAR...
THE CLOTHES I HANG OUT ON MY BALCONY KEEP DISAPPEARING...
AND MRS. PICHOT SAYS SOMEONE EVEN STOLE FOOD RIGHT OUT OF HER FREEZER!

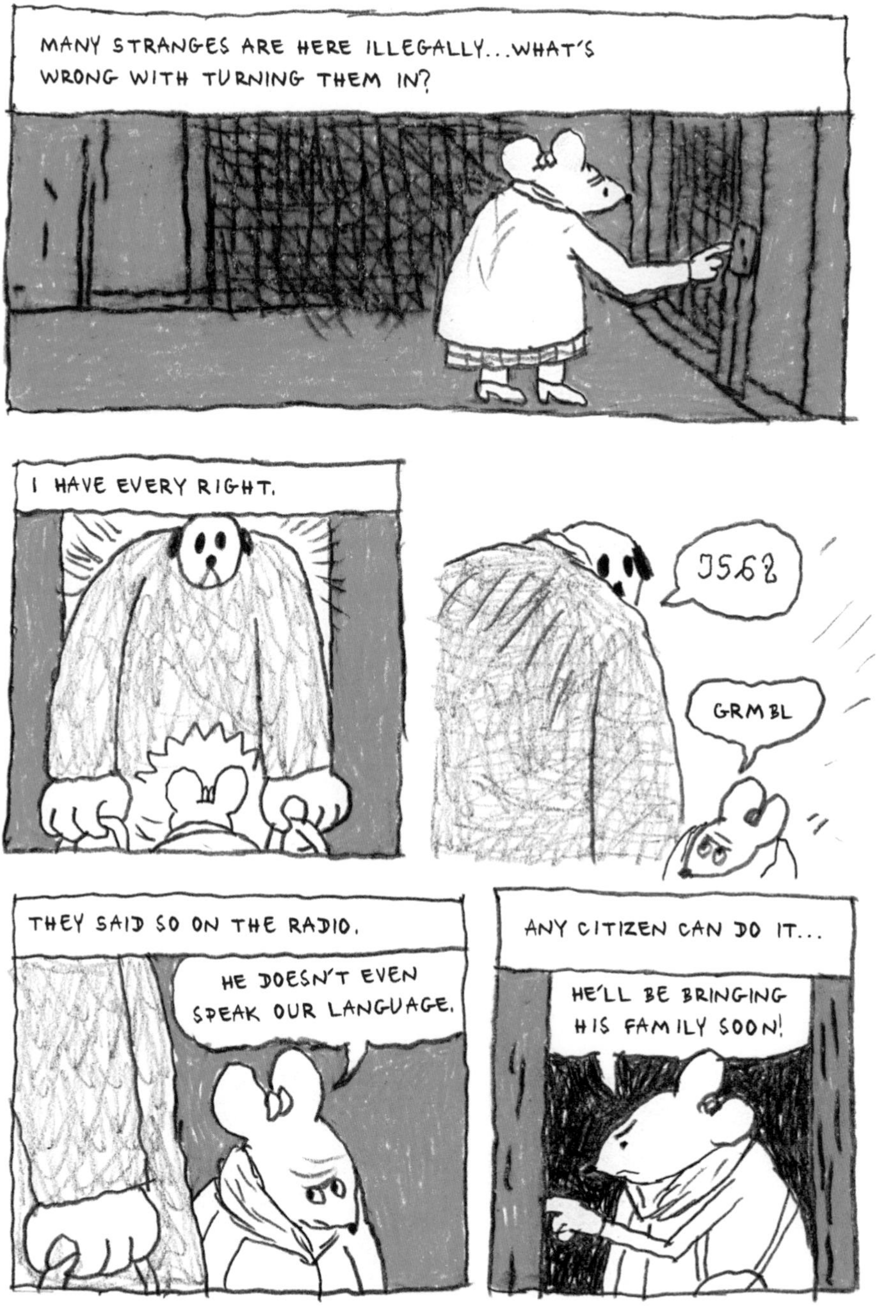
MANY STRANGES ARE HERE ILLEGALLY...WHAT'S WRONG WITH TURNING THEM IN?
I HAVE EVERY RIGHT.
GRMBL
THEY SAID SO ON THE RADIO.
HE DOESN'T EVEN SPEAK OUR LANGUAGE.
ANY CITIZEN CAN DO IT...
HE'LL BE BRINGING HIS FAMILY SOON!

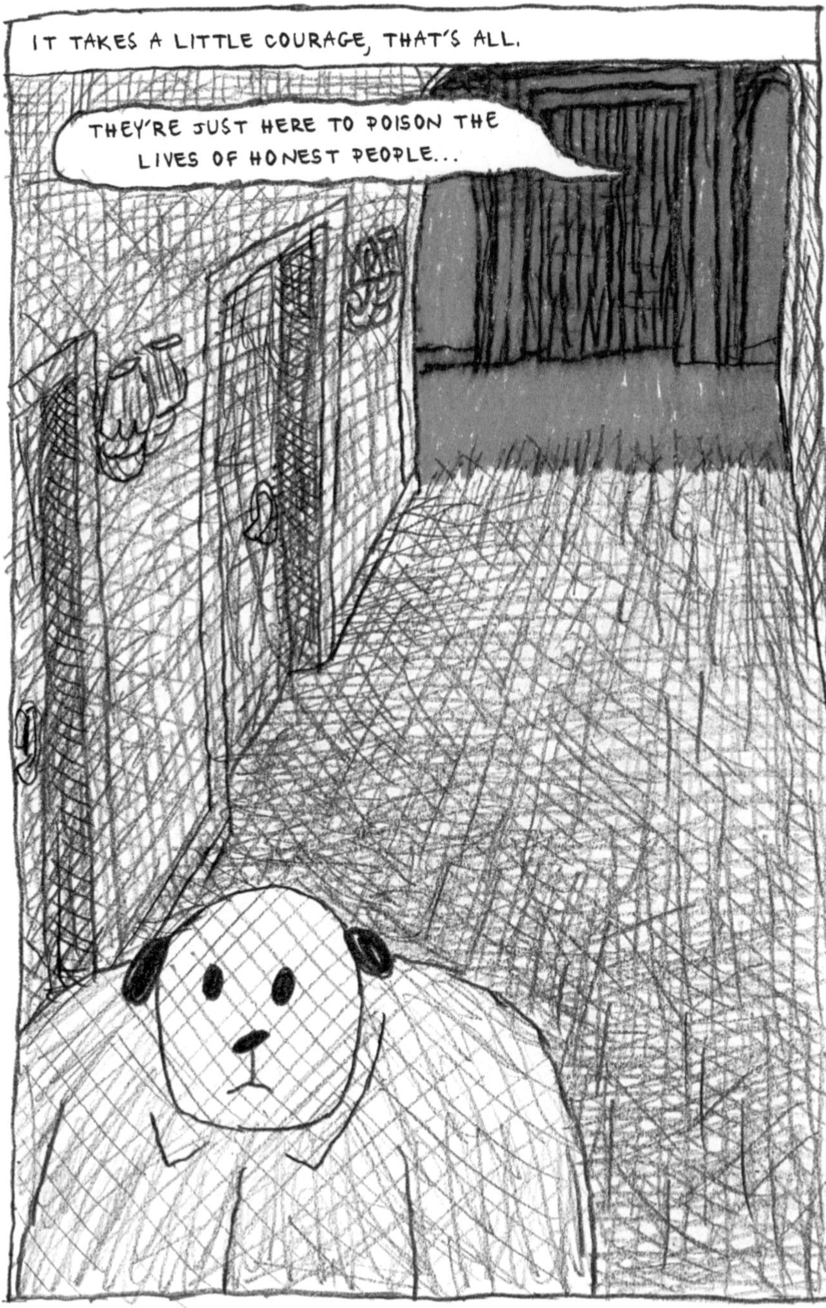
IT TAKES A LITTLE COURAGE, THAT'S ALL.
THEY'RE JUST HERE TO POISON THE LIVES OF HONEST PEOPLE...

Kader

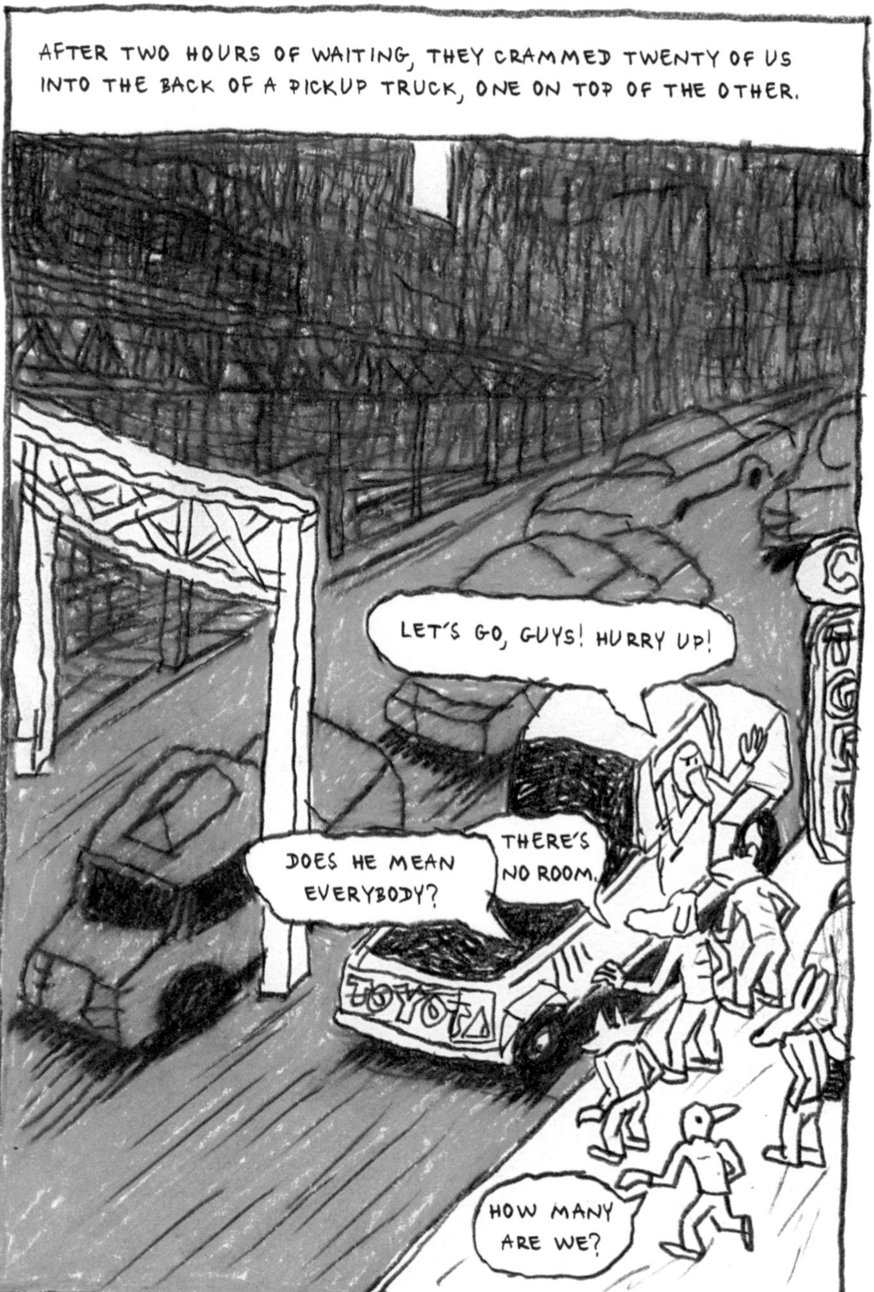
AFTER TWO HOURS OF WAITING, THEY CRAMMED TWENTY OF US INTO THE BACK OF A PICKUP TRUCK, ONE ON TOP OF THE OTHER.
LET'S GO, GUYS! HURRY UP!
DOES HE MEAN EVERYBODY?
THERE'S NO ROOM.
HOW MANY ARE WE?

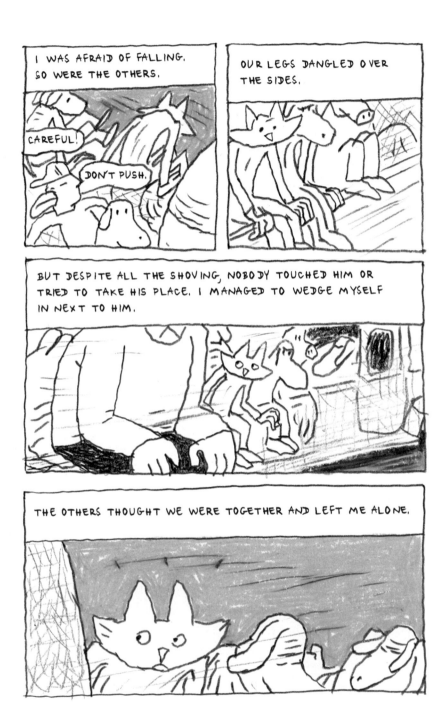

I WAS AFRAID OF FALLING, SO WERE THE OTHERS.

CAREFUL!

DON'T PUSH.

OUR LEGS DANGLED OVER THE SIDES.

BUT DESPITE ALL THE SHOVING, NOBODY TOUCHED HIM OR TRIED TO TAKE HIS PLACE. I MANAGED TO WEDGE MYSELF IN NEXT TO HIM.

THE OTHERS THOUGHT WE WERE TOGETHER AND LEFT ME ALONE.

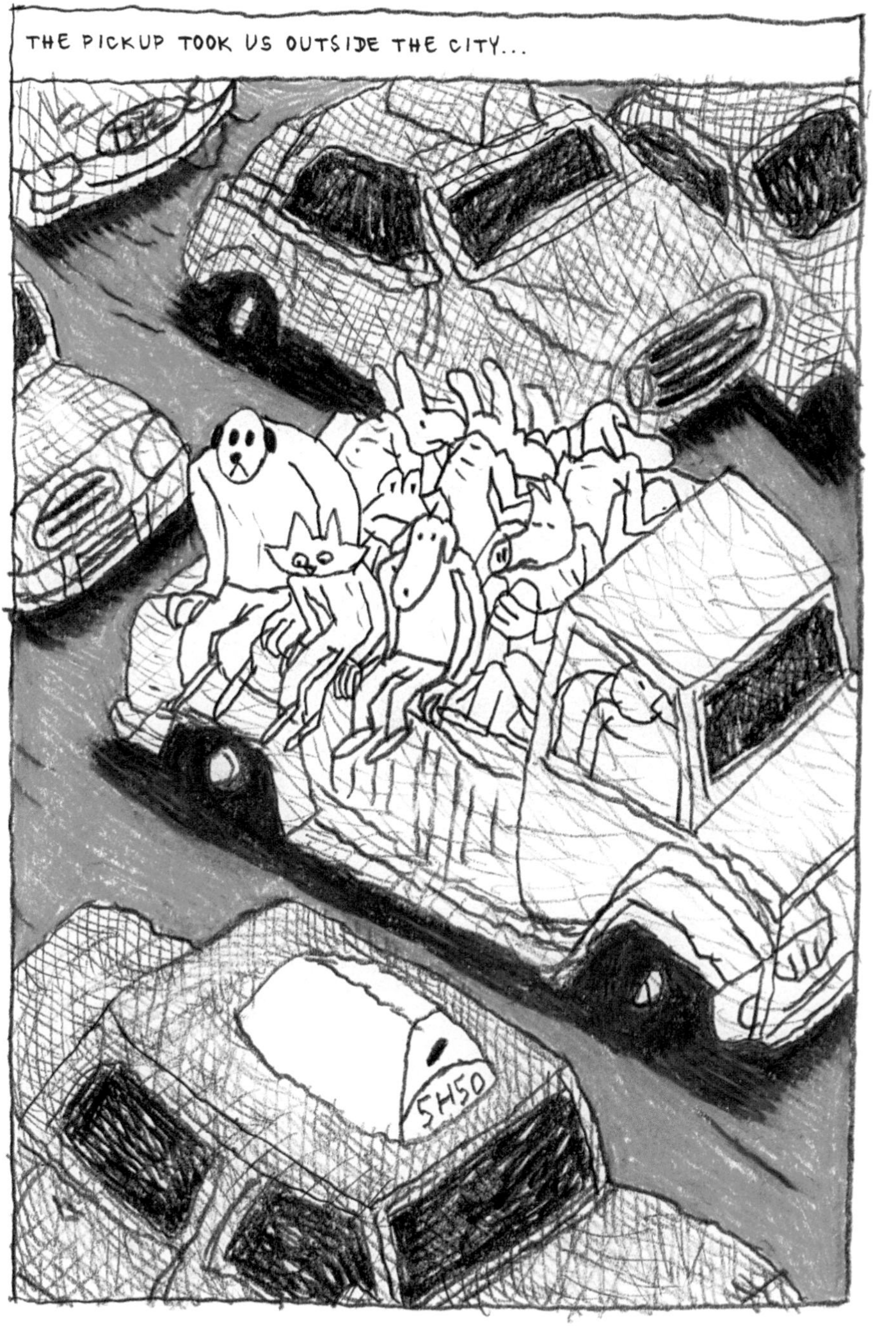
THE PICKUP TOOK US OUTSIDE THE CITY...
5H50

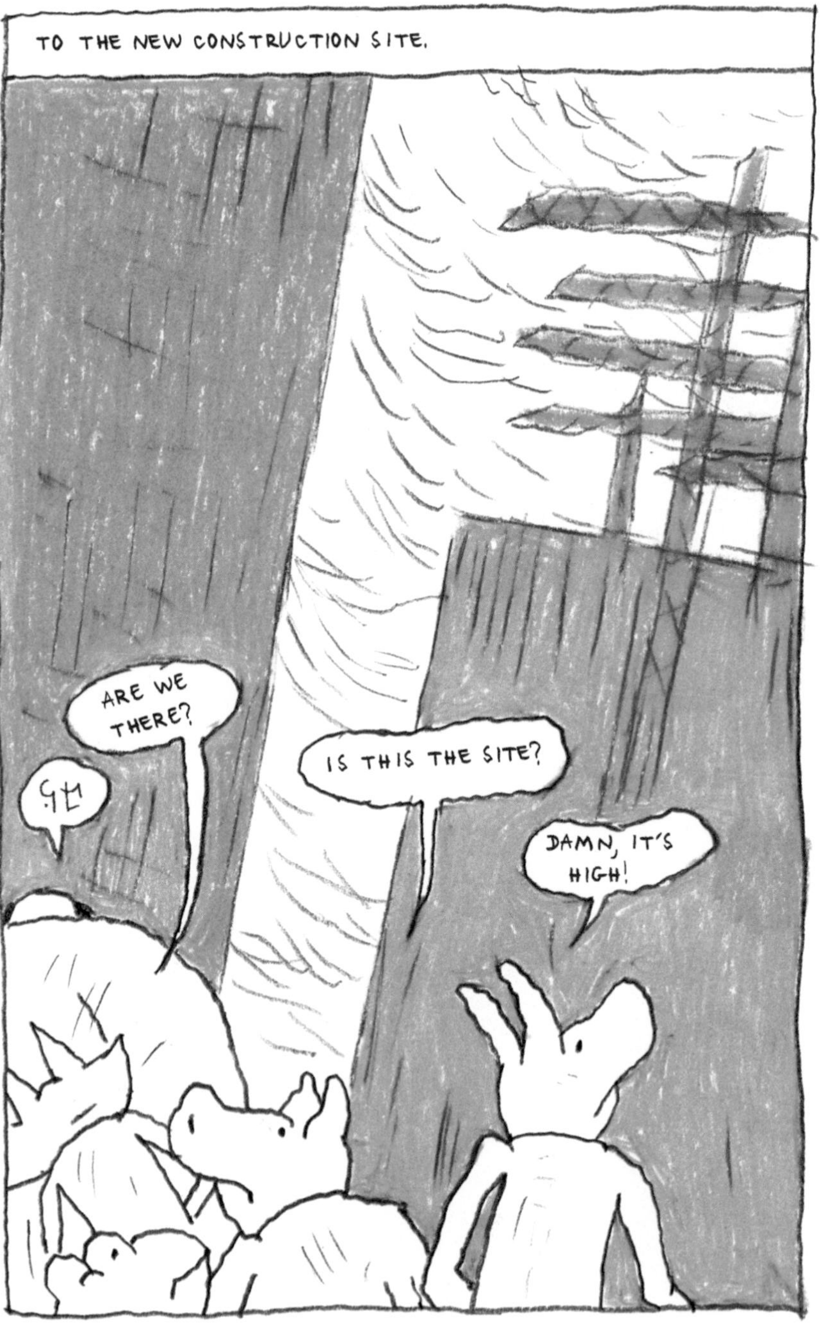
TO THE NEW CONSTRUCTION SITE.
ARE WE THERE?
IS THIS THE SITE?
DAMN, IT'S HIGH!

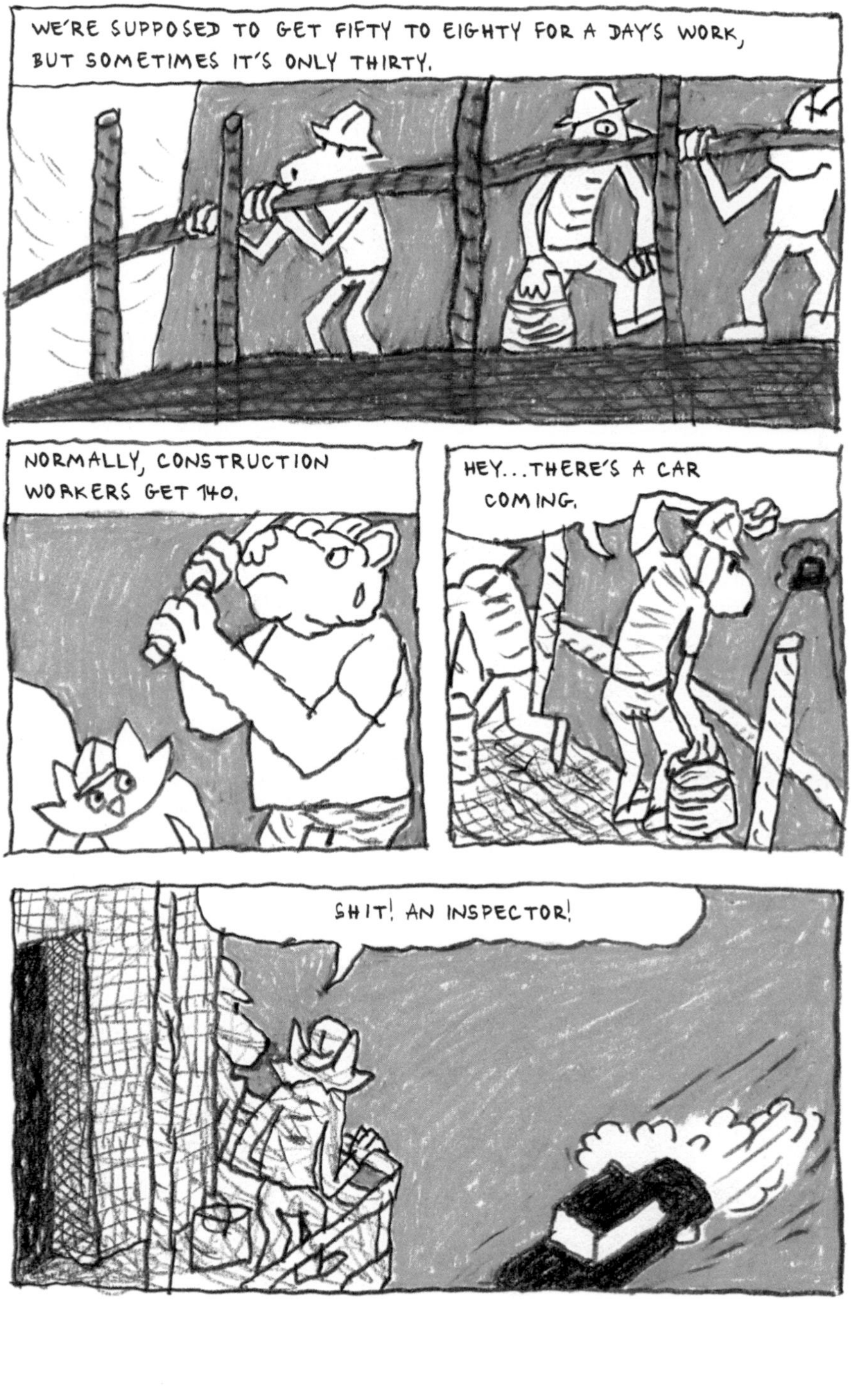
WE'RE SUPPOSED TO GET FIFTY TO EIGHTY FOR A DAY'S WORK, BUT SOMETIMES IT'S ONLY THIRTY.
NORMALLY, CONSTRUCTION WORKERS GET 140.
HEY... THERE'S A CAR COMING.
SHIT! AN INSPECTOR!

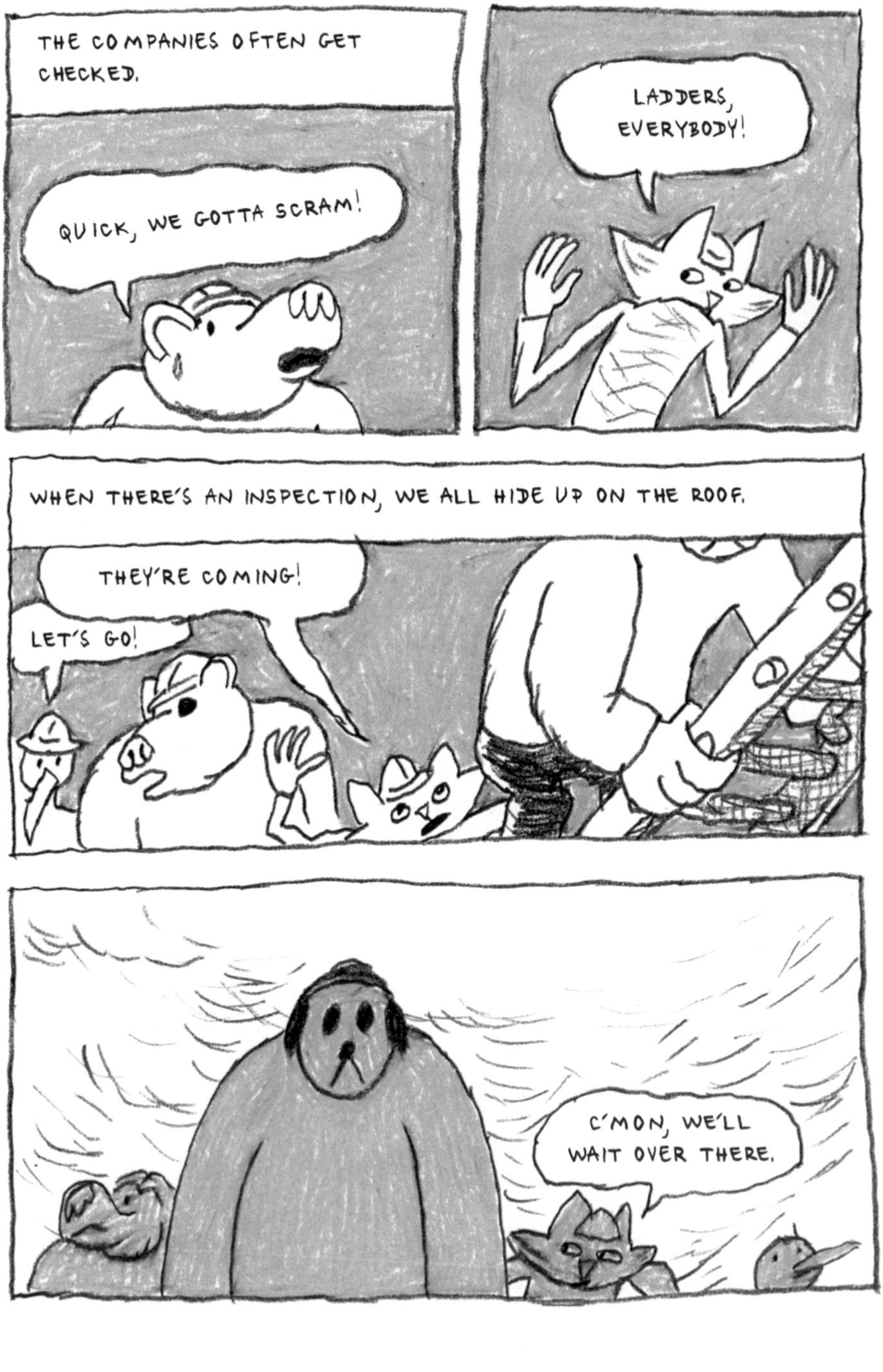
THE COMPANIES OFTEN GET CHECKED.
QUICK, WE GOTTA SCRAM!
LADDERS, EVERYBODY!
WHEN THERE'S AN INSPECTION, WE ALL HIDE UP ON THE ROOF.
THEY'RE COMING!
LET'S GO!
C'MON, WE'LL WAIT OVER THERE.

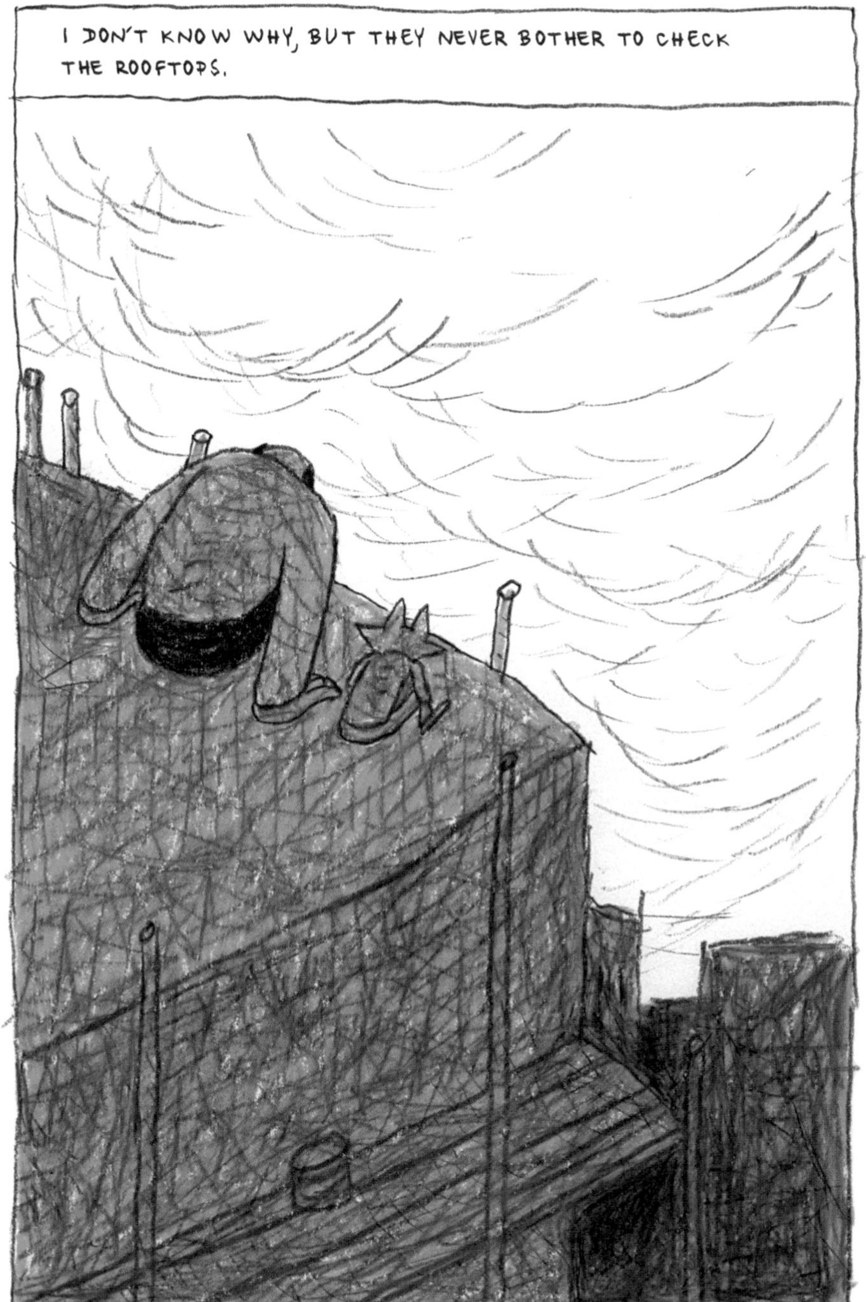
I DON'T KNOW WHY, BUT THEY NEVER BOTHER TO CHECK THE ROOFTOPS.

The boss

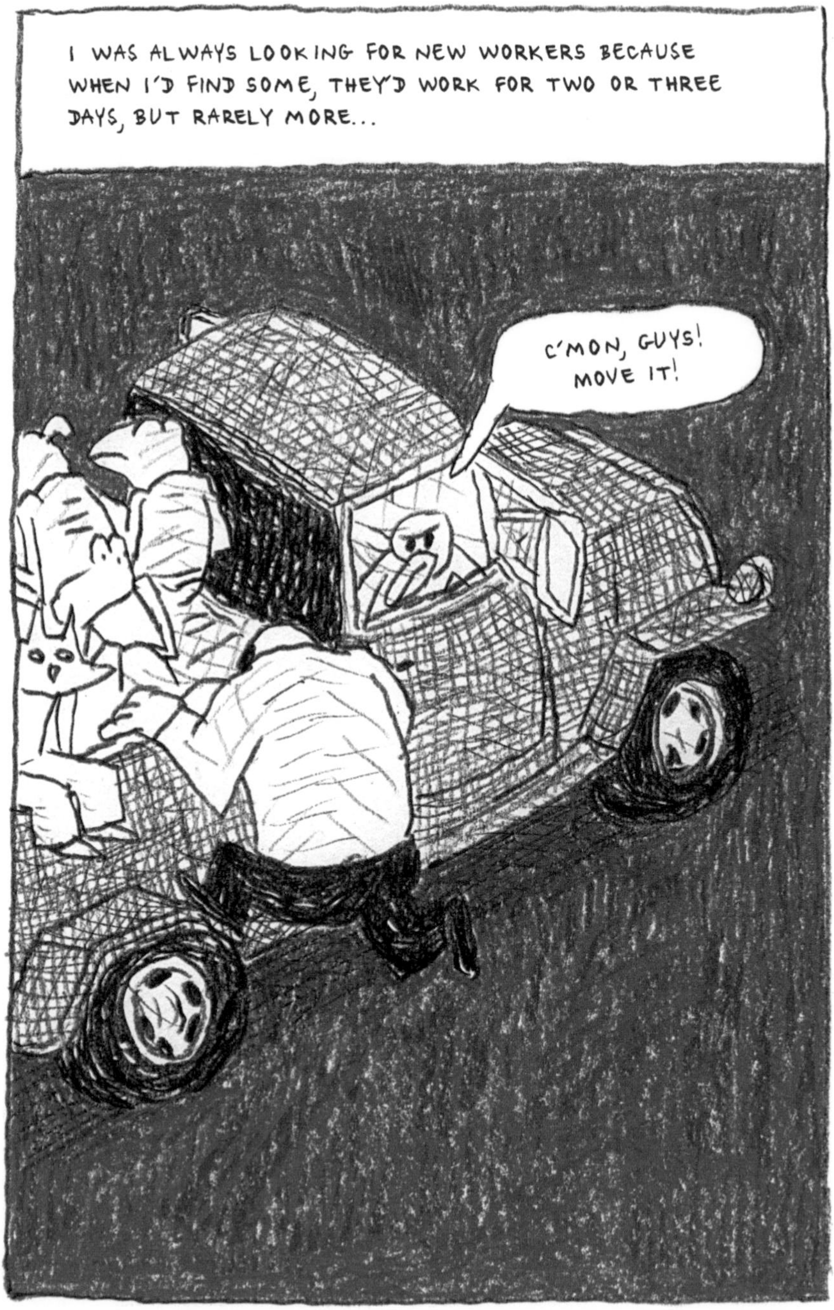
I WAS ALWAYS LOOKING FOR NEW WORKERS BECAUSE WHEN I'D FIND SOME, THEY'D WORK FOR TWO OR THREE DAYS, BUT RARELY MORE...
C'MON, GUYS! MOVE IT!

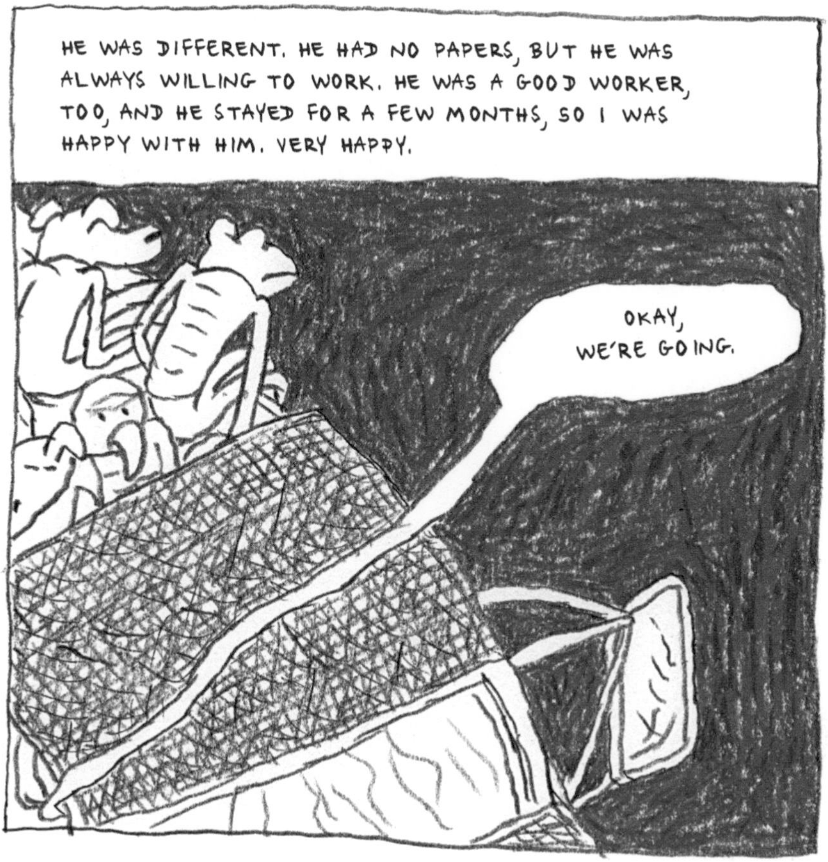
HE WAS DIFFERENT. HE HAD NO PAPERS, BUT HE WAS ALWAYS WILLING TO WORK. HE WAS A GOOD WORKER, TOO, AND HE STAYED FOR A FEW MONTHS, SO I WAS HAPPY WITH HIM. VERY HAPPY.
OKAY, WE'RE GOING.

The woman at the hostel

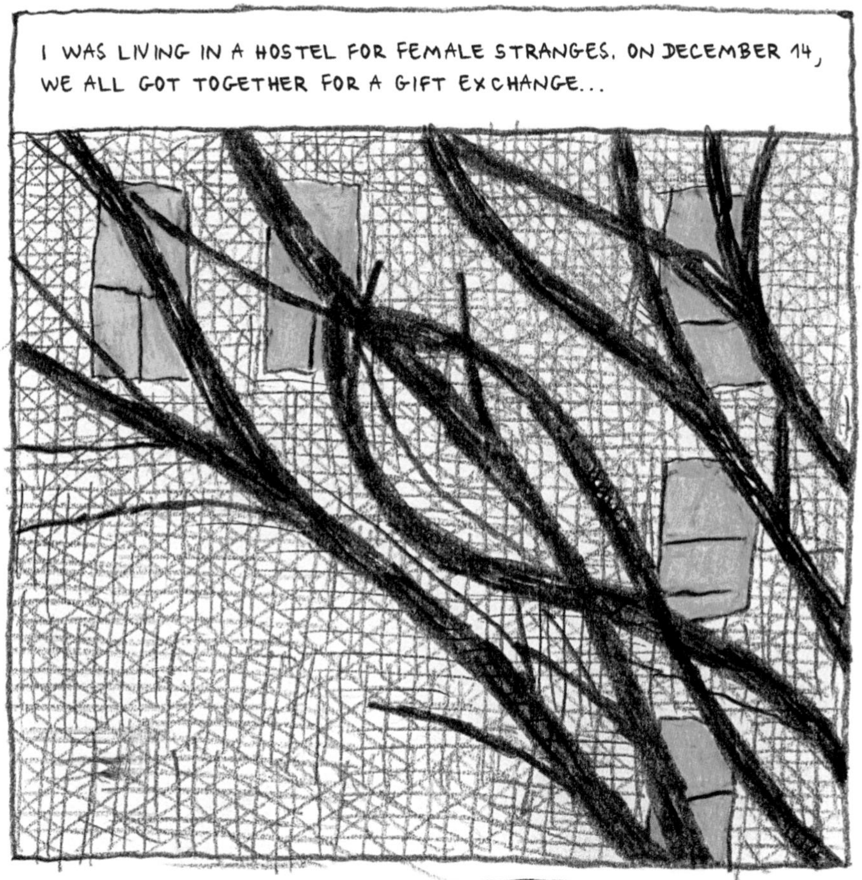
I WAS LIVING IN A HOSTEL FOR FEMALE STRANGES. ON DECEMBER 14, WE ALL GOT TOGETHER FOR A GIFT EXCHANGE...

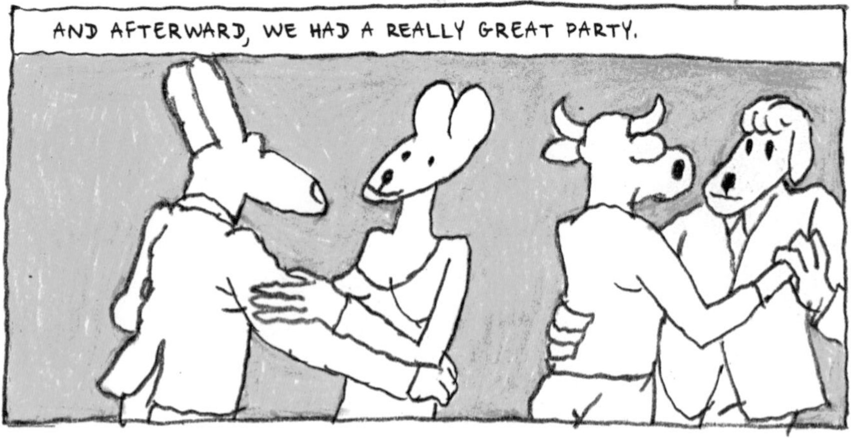
AND AFTERWARD, WE HAD A REALLY GREAT PARTY.

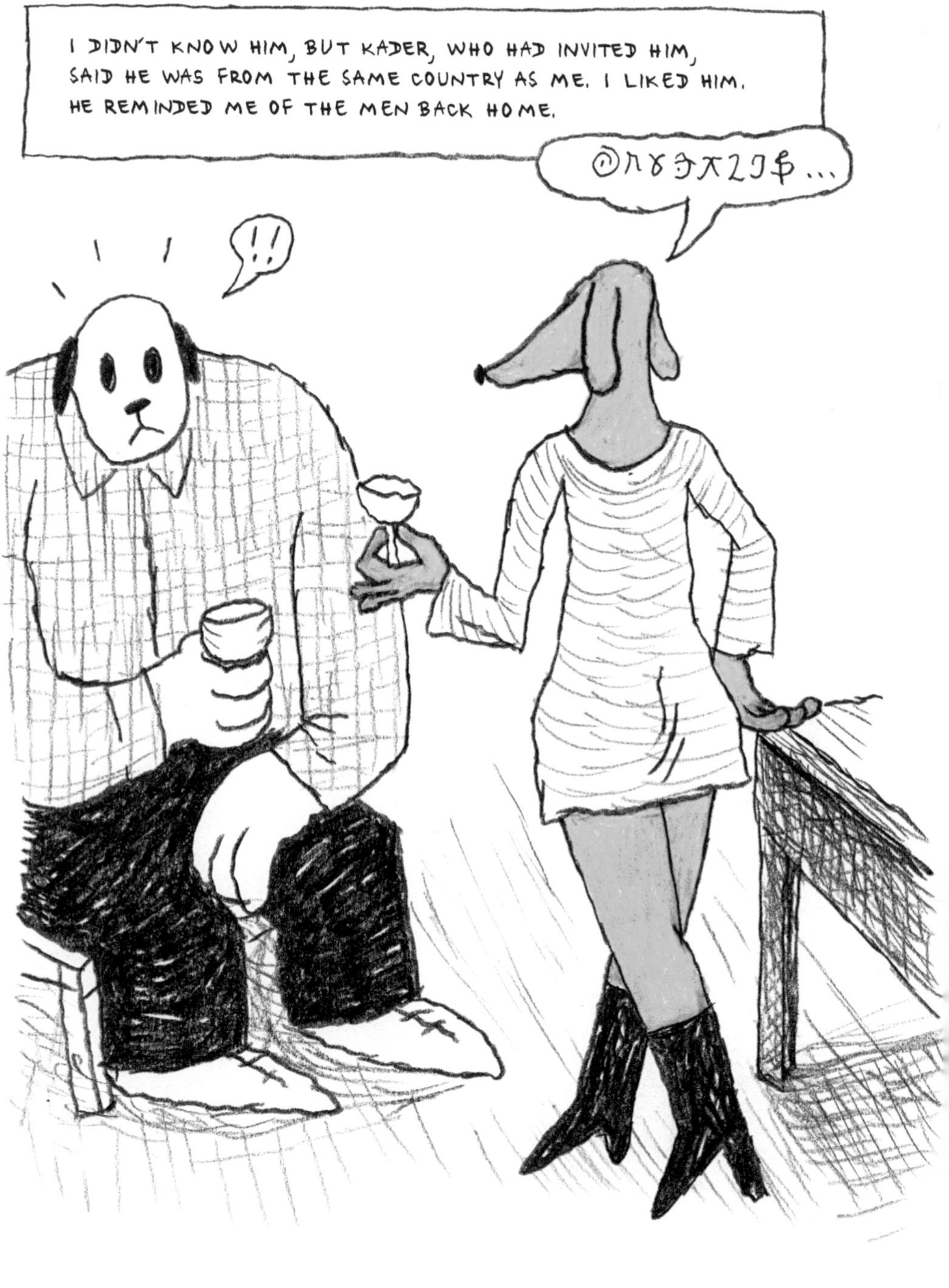
I DIDN'T KNOW HIM, BUT KADER, WHO HAD INVITED HIM, SAID HE WAS FROM THE SAME COUNTRY AS ME. I LIKED HIM. HE REMINDED ME OF THE MEN BACK HOME.
!!

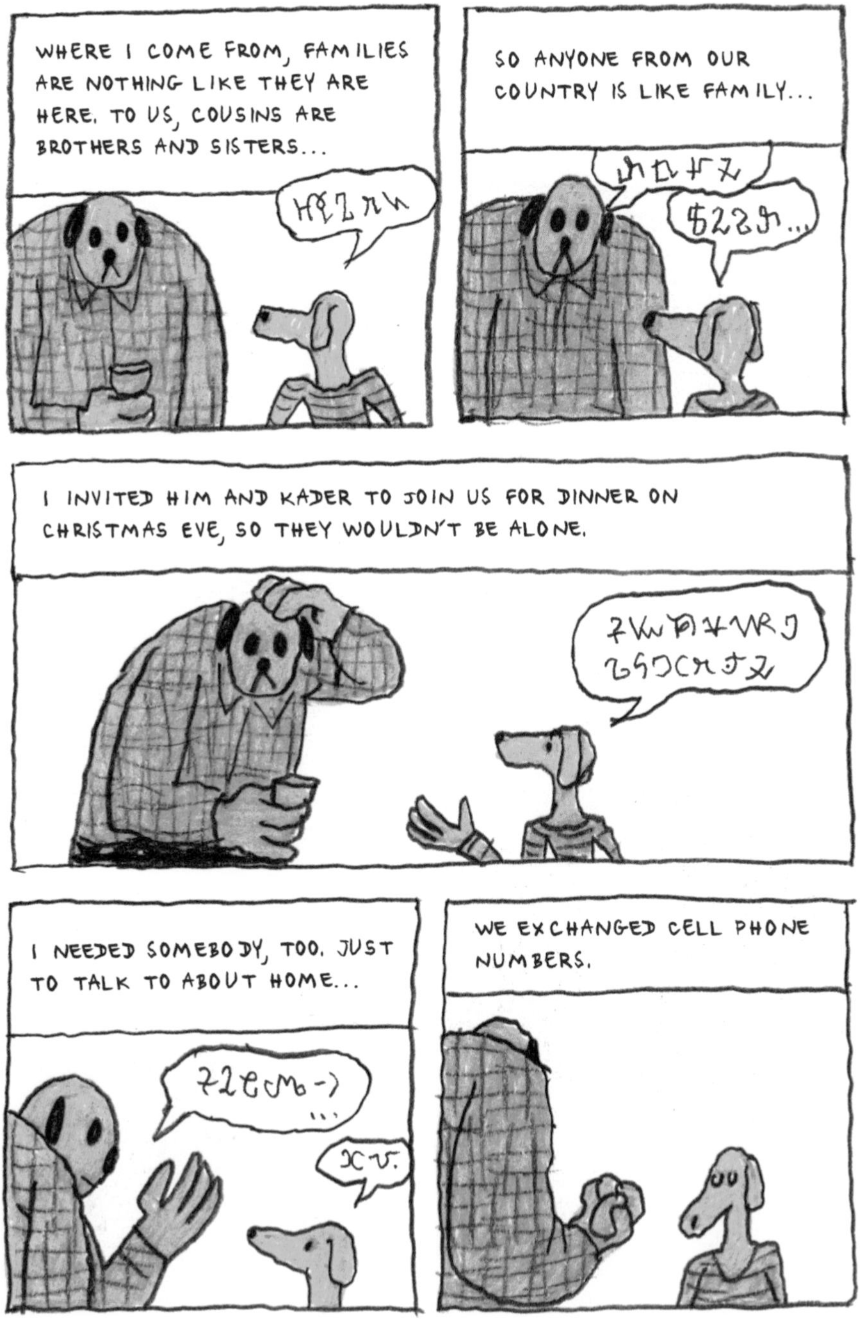
WHERE I COME FROM, FAMILIES ARE NOTHING LIKE THEY ARE HERE. TO US, COUSINS ARE BROTHERS AND SISTERS...
SO ANYONE FROM OUR COUNTRY IS LIKE FAMILY...
I INVITED HIM AND KADER TO JOIN US FOR DINNER ON CHRISTMAS EVE, SO THEY WOULDN'T BE ALONE.
I NEEDED SOMEBODY, TOO. JUST TO TALK TO ABOUT HOME...
WE EXCHANGED CELL PHONE NUMBERS.

THE PARTY WENT ON FOR A WHILE, BUT HE KEPT TO HIMSELF THE REST OF THE EVENING.

Mr. Robert

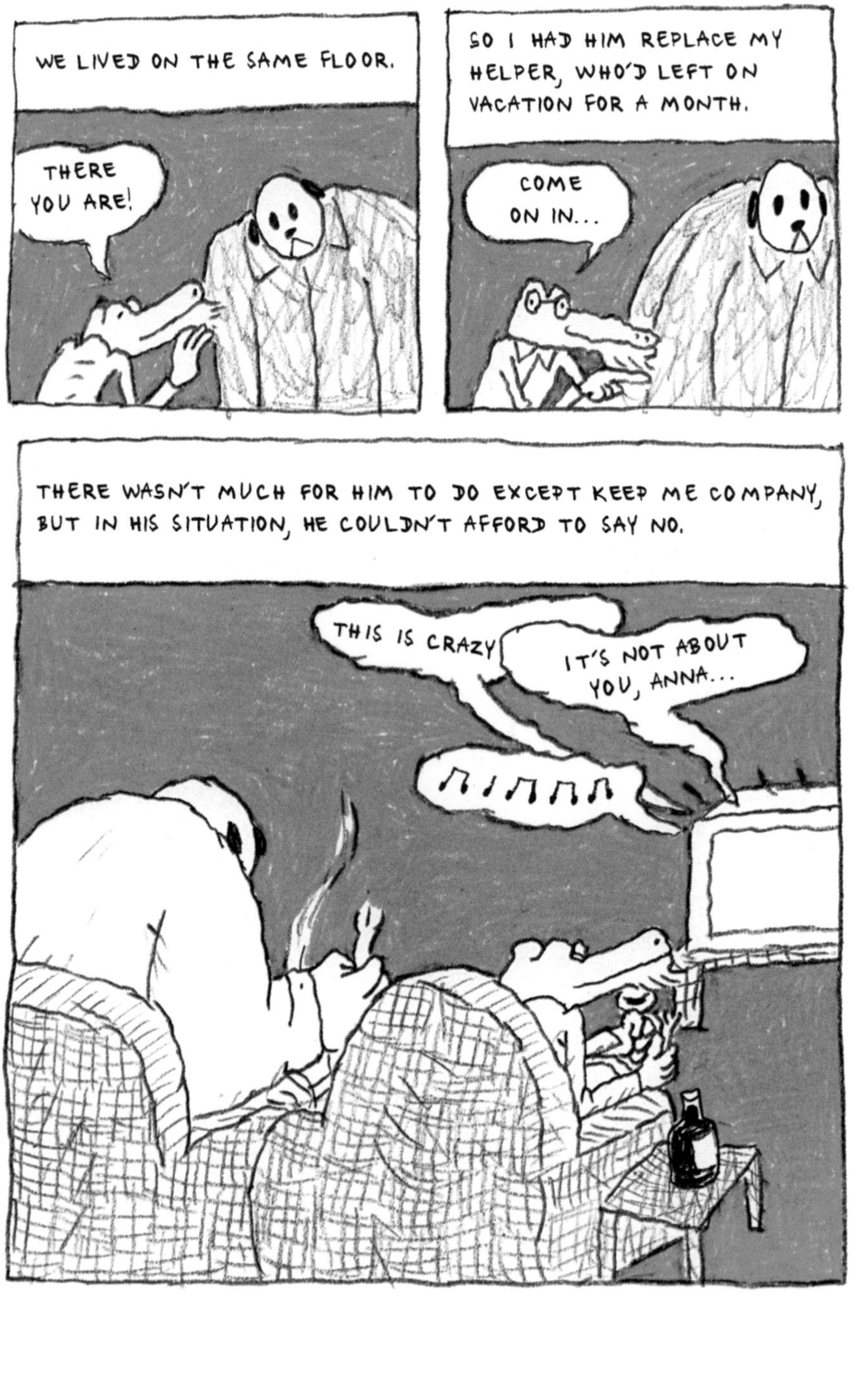
WE LIVED ON THE SAME FLOOR.
THERE YOU ARE!
SO I HAD HIM REPLACE MY HELPER, WHO'D LEFT ON VACATION FOR A MONTH.
COME ON IN...
THERE WASN'T MUCH FOR HIM TO DO EXCEPT KEEP ME COMPANY, BUT IN HIS SITUATION, HE COULDN'T AFFORD TO SAY NO.
THIS IS CRAZY
IT'S NOT ABOUT YOU, ANNA...

HE CAME EVERY EVENING AND LEFT IN THE MORNING.

SEE YOU TONIGHT.

HE SLEPT IN THE KITCHEN, ON A SHEET HE SPREAD OUT ON THE FLOOR.

GOOD NIGHT.

HE DIDN'T GET A PENNY AT THE END OF THE MONTH. WHY SHOULD HE? HE ATE FOR FREE THE WHOLE TIME.

The officer

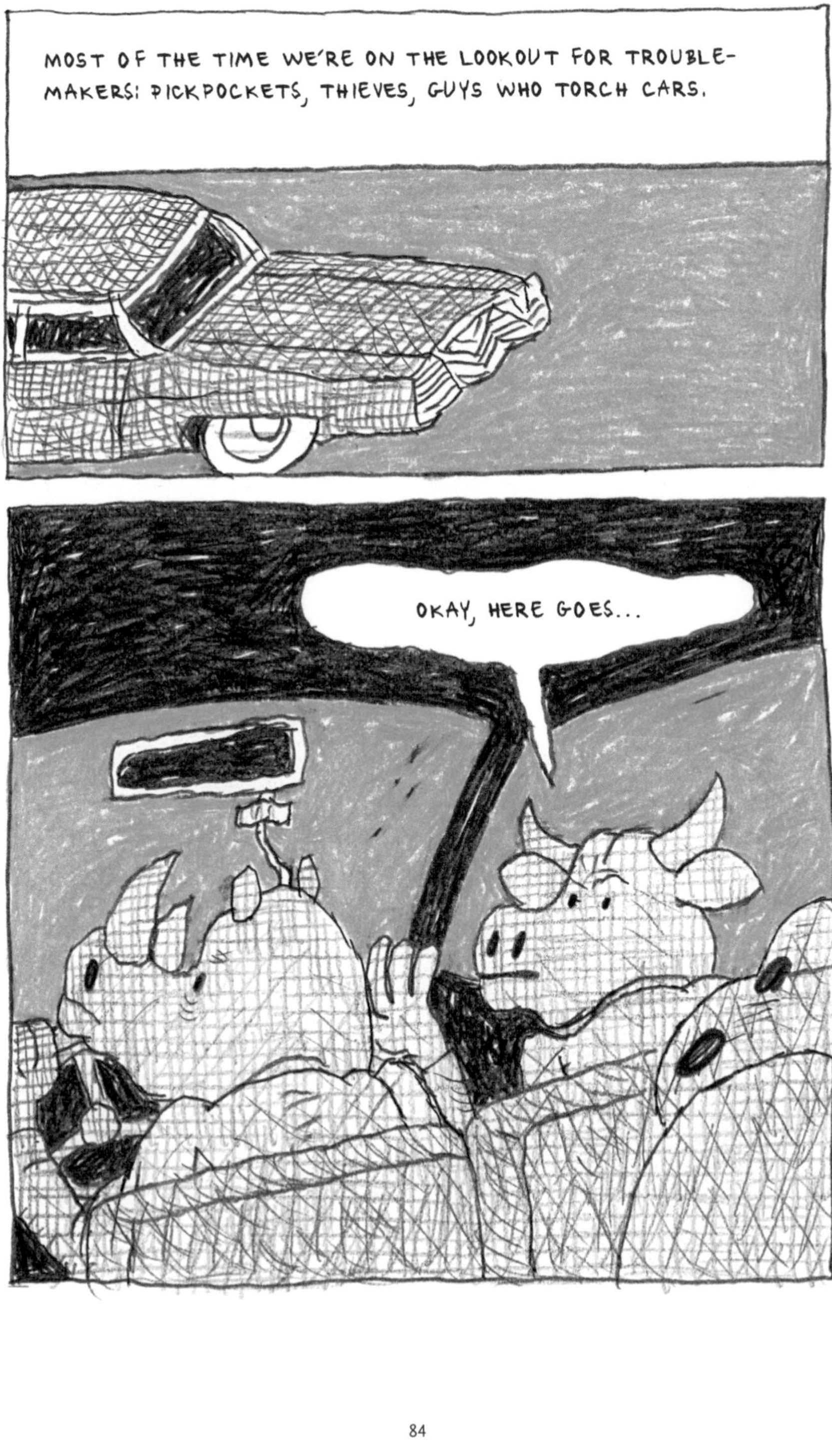
MOST OF THE TIME WE'RE ON THE LOOKOUT FOR TROUBLE-MAKERS: PICKPOCKETS, THIEVES, GUYS WHO TORCH CARS.
OKAY, HERE GOES...

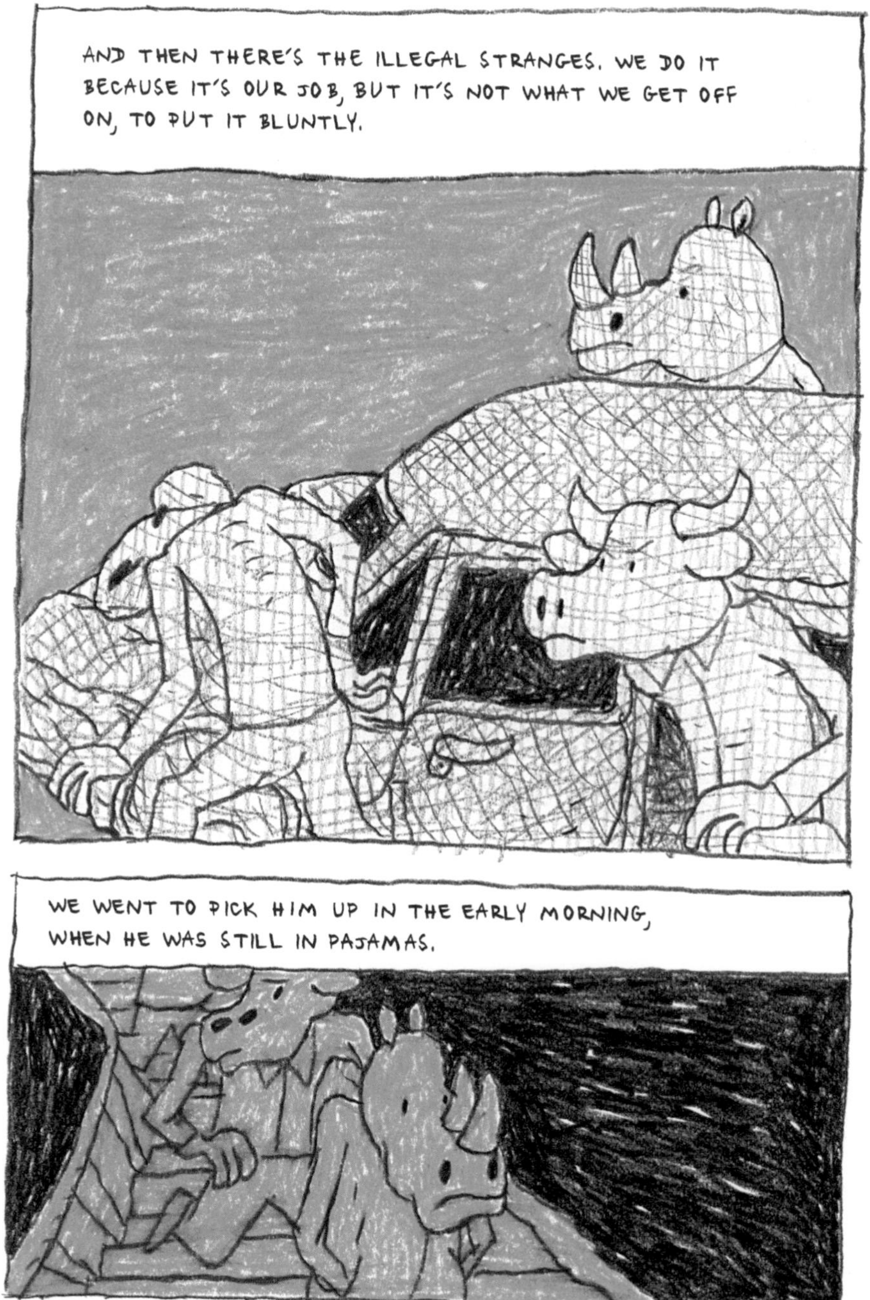
AND THEN THERE'S THE ILLEGAL STRANGES. WE DO IT BECAUSE IT'S OUR JOB, BUT IT'S NOT WHAT WE GET OFF ON, TO PUT IT BLUNTLY.
WE WENT TO PICK HIM UP IN THE EARLY MORNING, WHEN HE WAS STILL IN PAJAMAS.

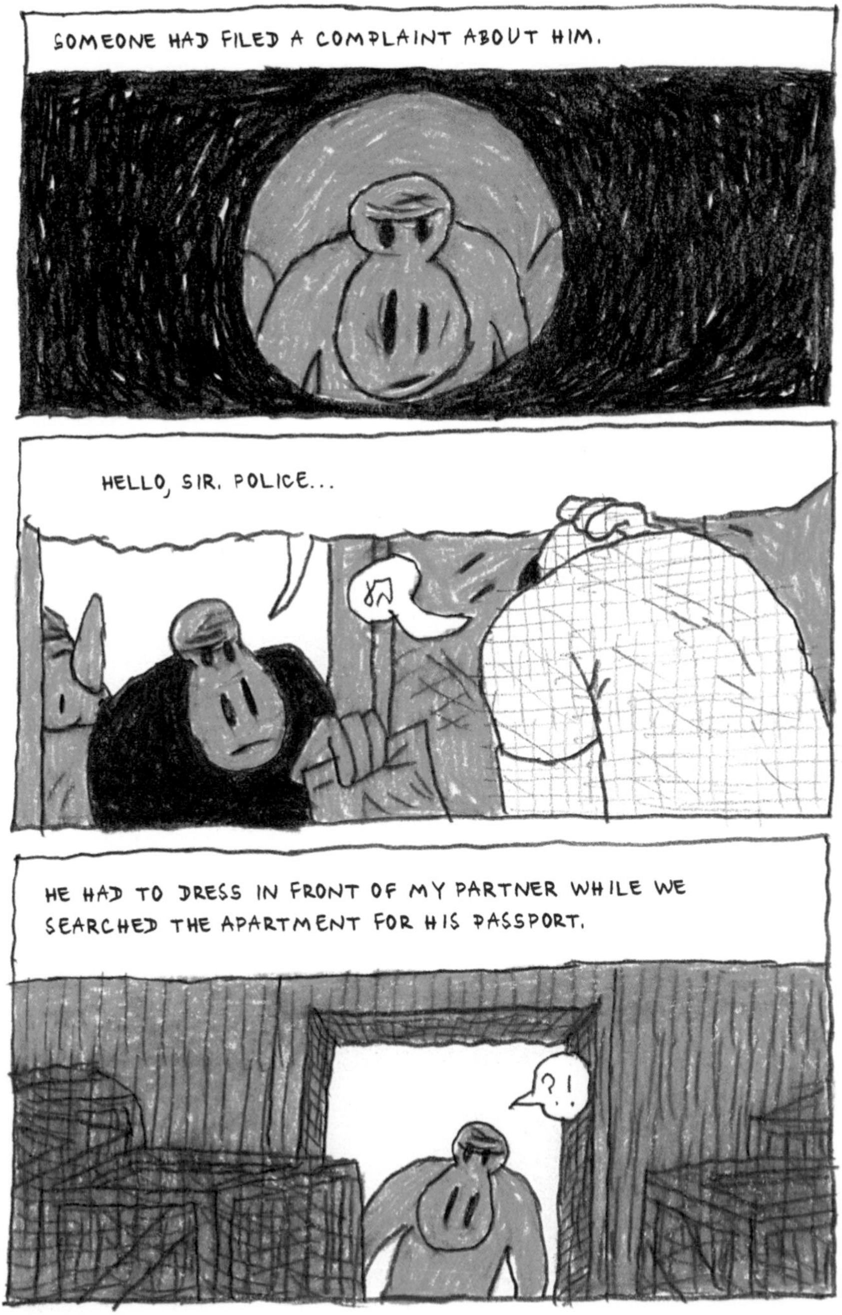
SOMEONE HAD FILED A COMPLAINT ABOUT HIM.
HELLO, SIR. POLICE...
HE HAD TO DRESS IN FRONT OF MY PARTNER WHILE WE SEARCHED THE APARTMENT FOR HIS PASSPORT.
?!

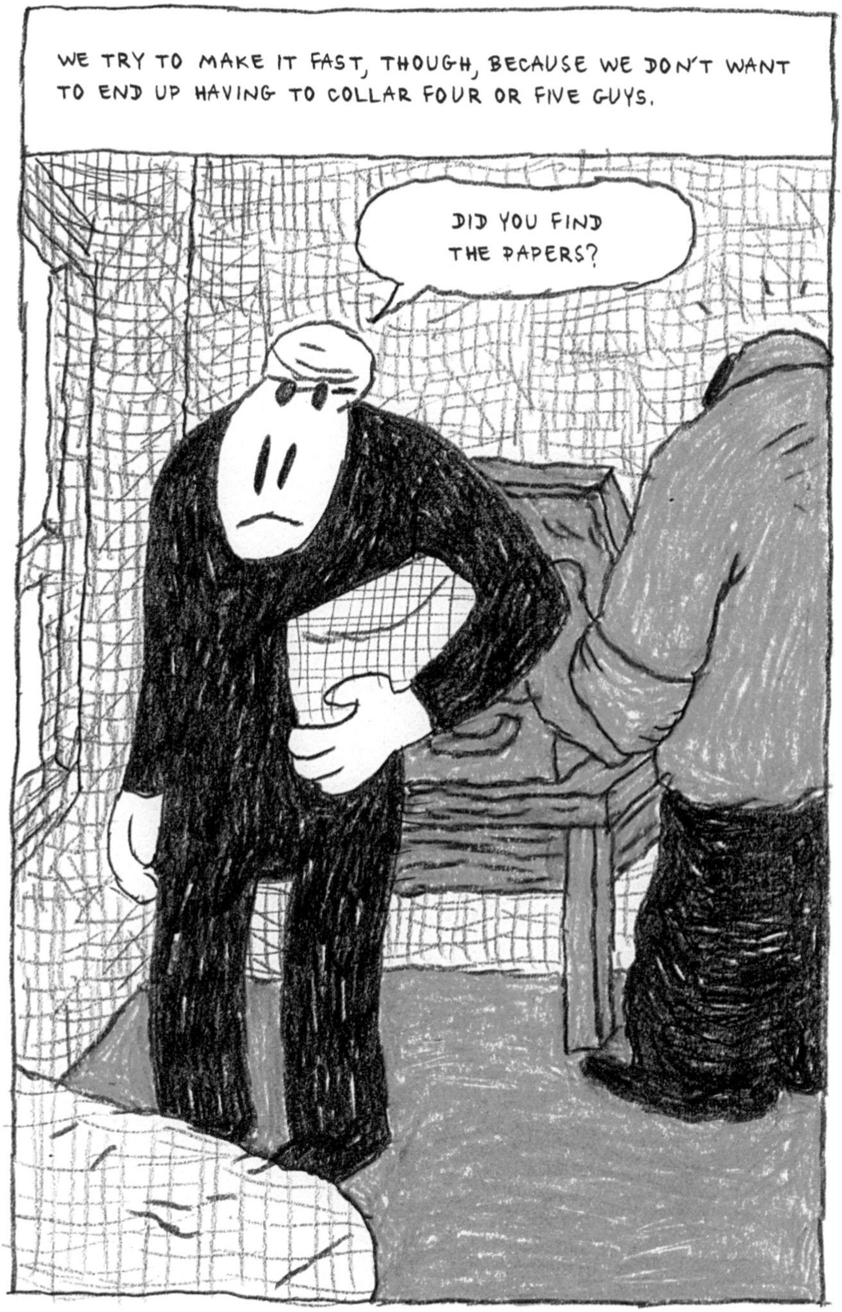
WE TRY TO MAKE IT FAST, THOUGH, BECAUSE WE DON'T WANT TO END UP HAVING TO COLLAR FOUR OR FIVE GUYS.
DID YOU FIND THE PAPERS?

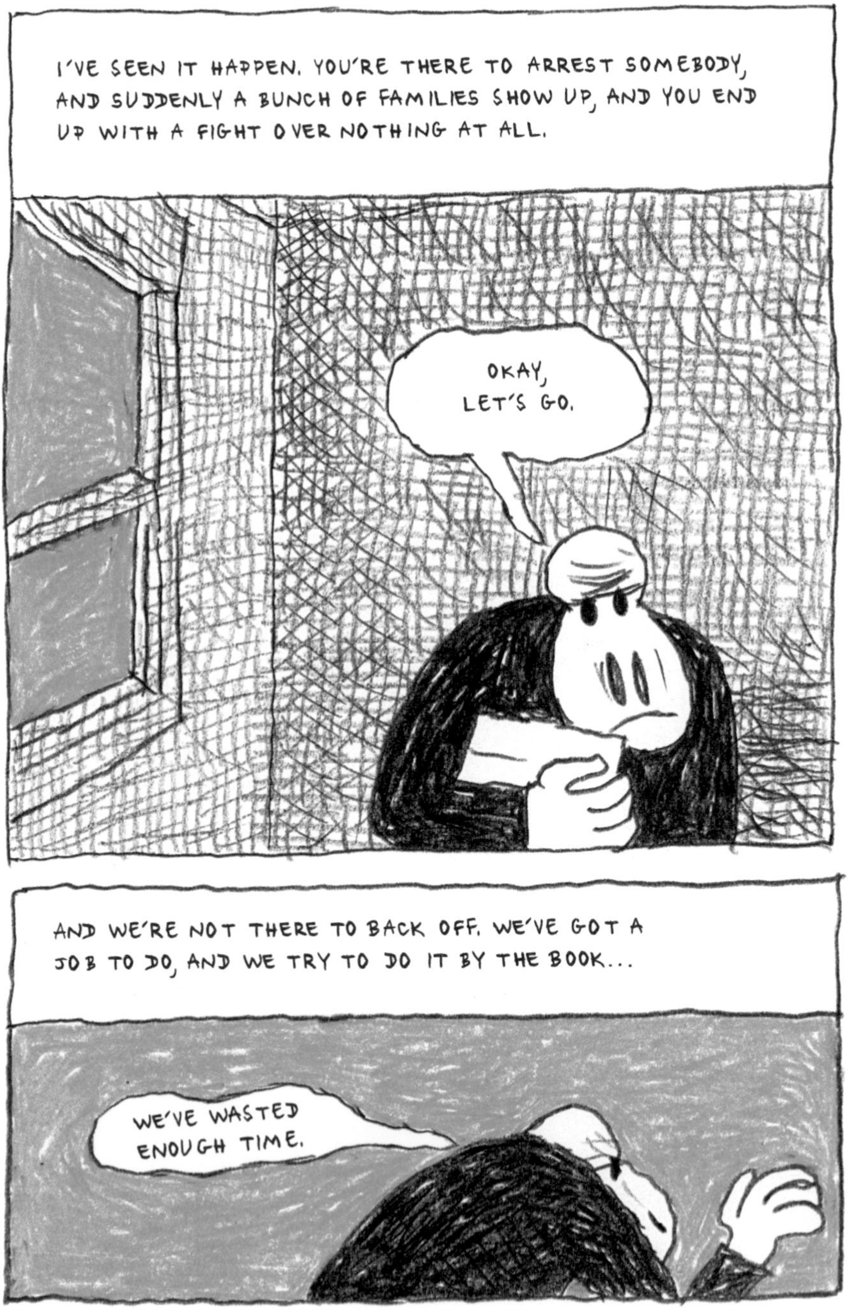
I'VE SEEN IT HAPPEN. YOU'RE THERE TO ARREST SOMEBODY, AND SUDDENLY A BUNCH OF FAMILIES SHOW UP, AND YOU END UP WITH A FIGHT OVER NOTHING AT ALL.
OKAY, LET'S GO.
AND WE'RE NOT THERE TO BACK OFF. WE'VE GOT A JOB TO DO, AND WE TRY TO DO IT BY THE BOOK...
WE'VE WASTED ENOUGH TIME.

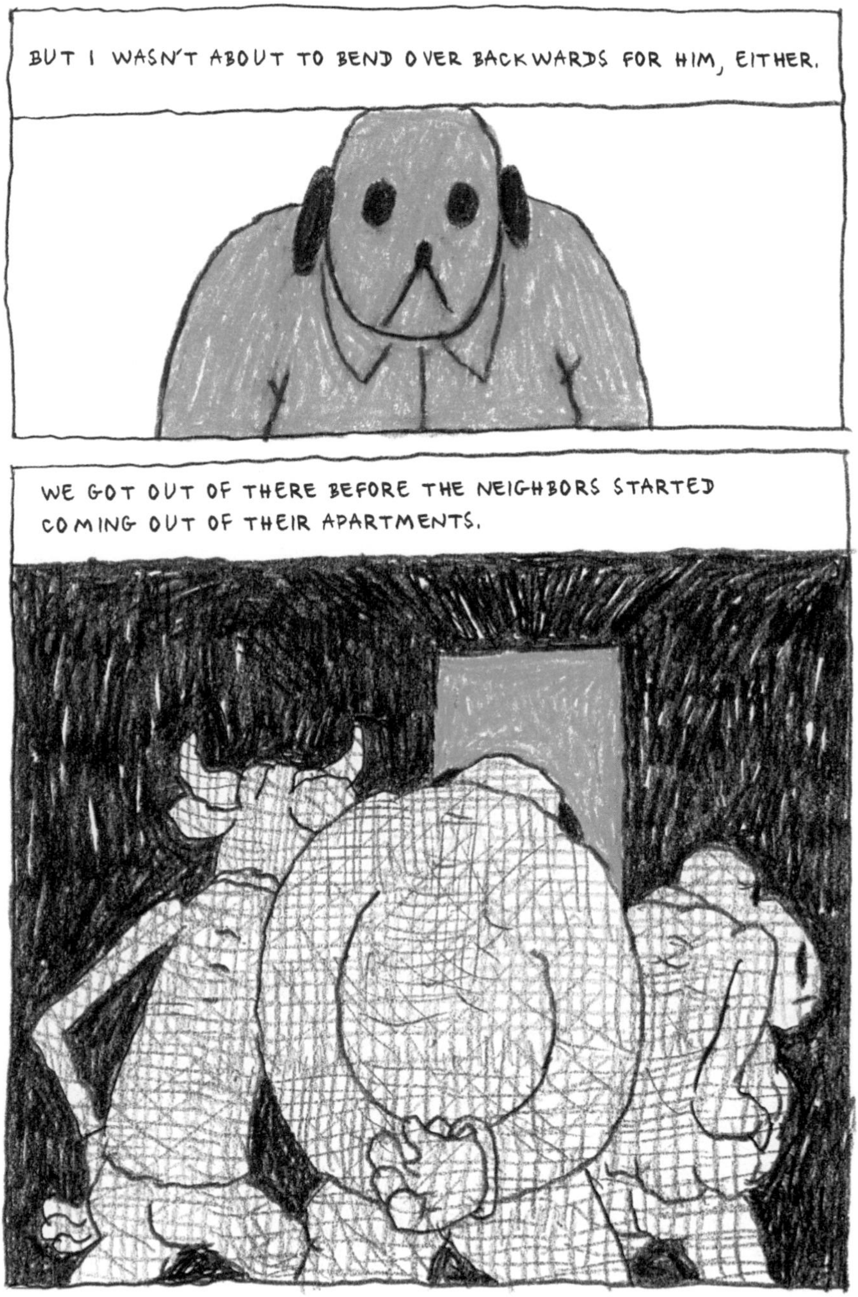
BUT I WASN'T ABOUT TO BEND OVER BACKWARDS FOR HIM, EITHER.
WE GOT OUT OF THERE BEFORE THE NEIGHBORS STARTED COMING OUT OF THEIR APARTMENTS.

Christine

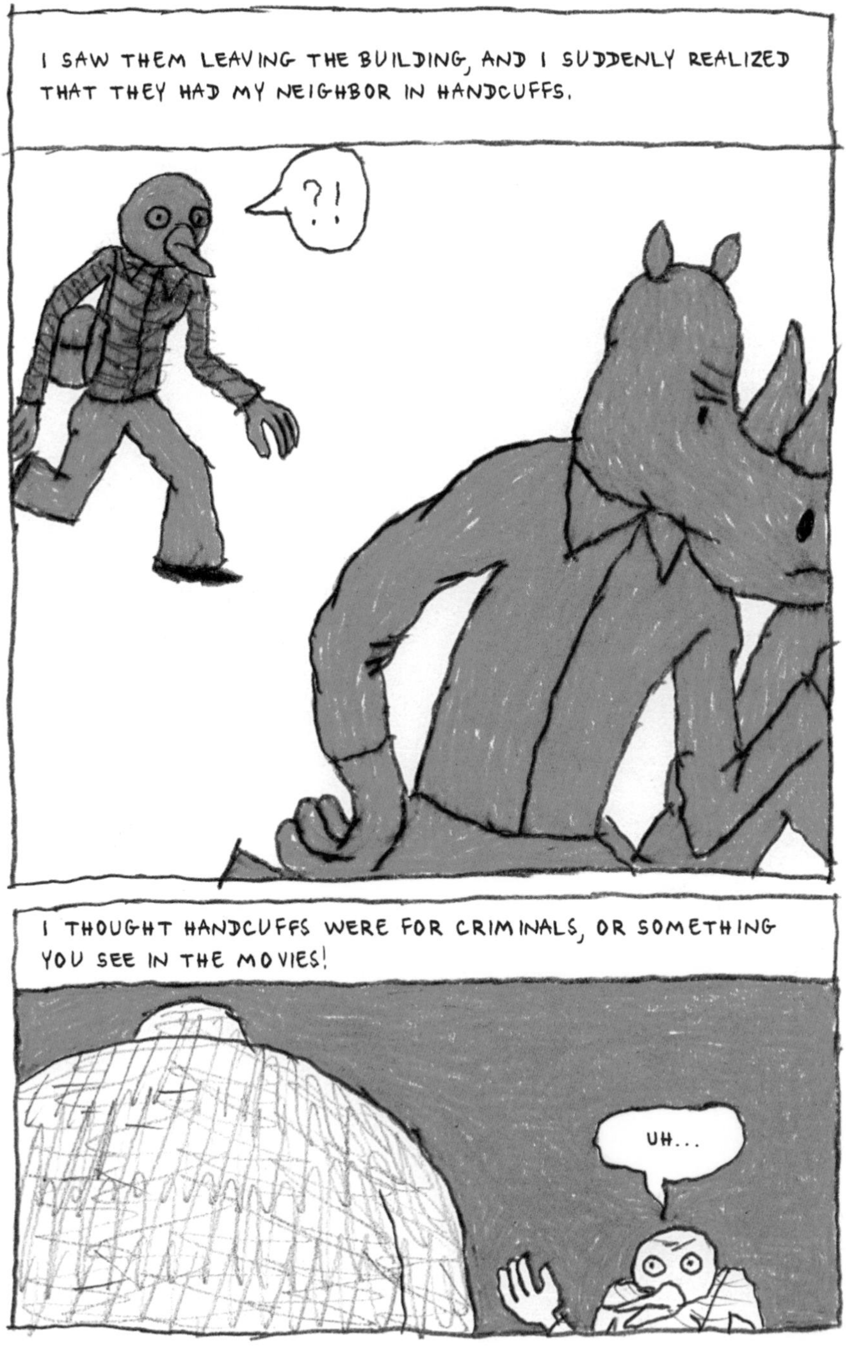
I SAW THEM LEAVING THE BUILDING, AND I SUDDENLY REALIZED THAT THEY HAD MY NEIGHBOR IN HANDCUFFS.
?!
I THOUGHT HANDCUFFS WERE FOR CRIMINALS, OR SOMETHING YOU SEE IN THE MOVIES!
UH...

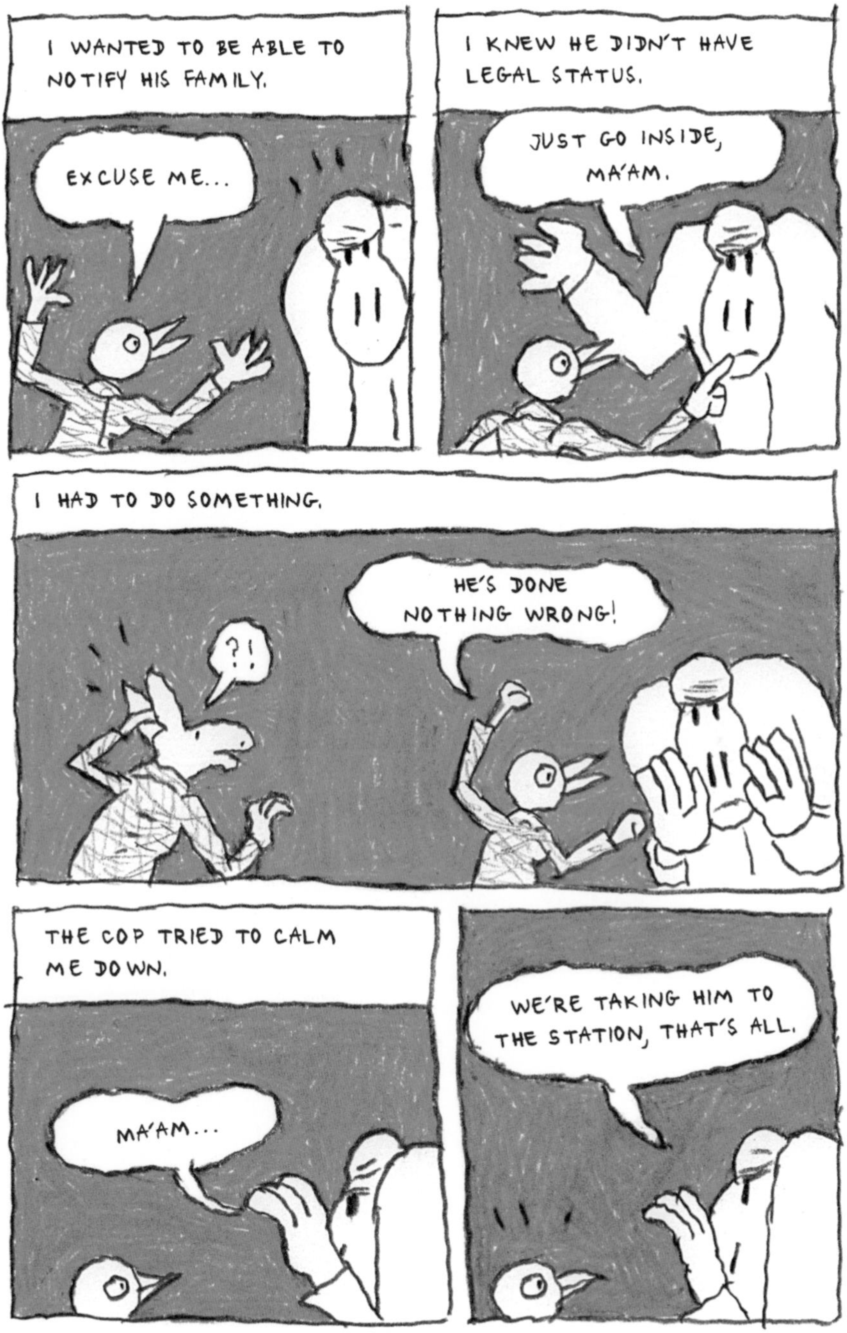
I WANTED TO BE ABLE TO NOTIFY HIS FAMILY.
EXCUSE ME...
I KNEW HE DIDN'T HAVE LEGAL STATUS.
JUST GO INSIDE, MA'AM.
I HAD TO DO SOMETHING.
?!
HE'S DONE NOTHING WRONG!
THE COP TRIED TO CALM ME DOWN.
MA'AM...
WE'RE TAKING HIM TO THE STATION, THAT'S ALL.

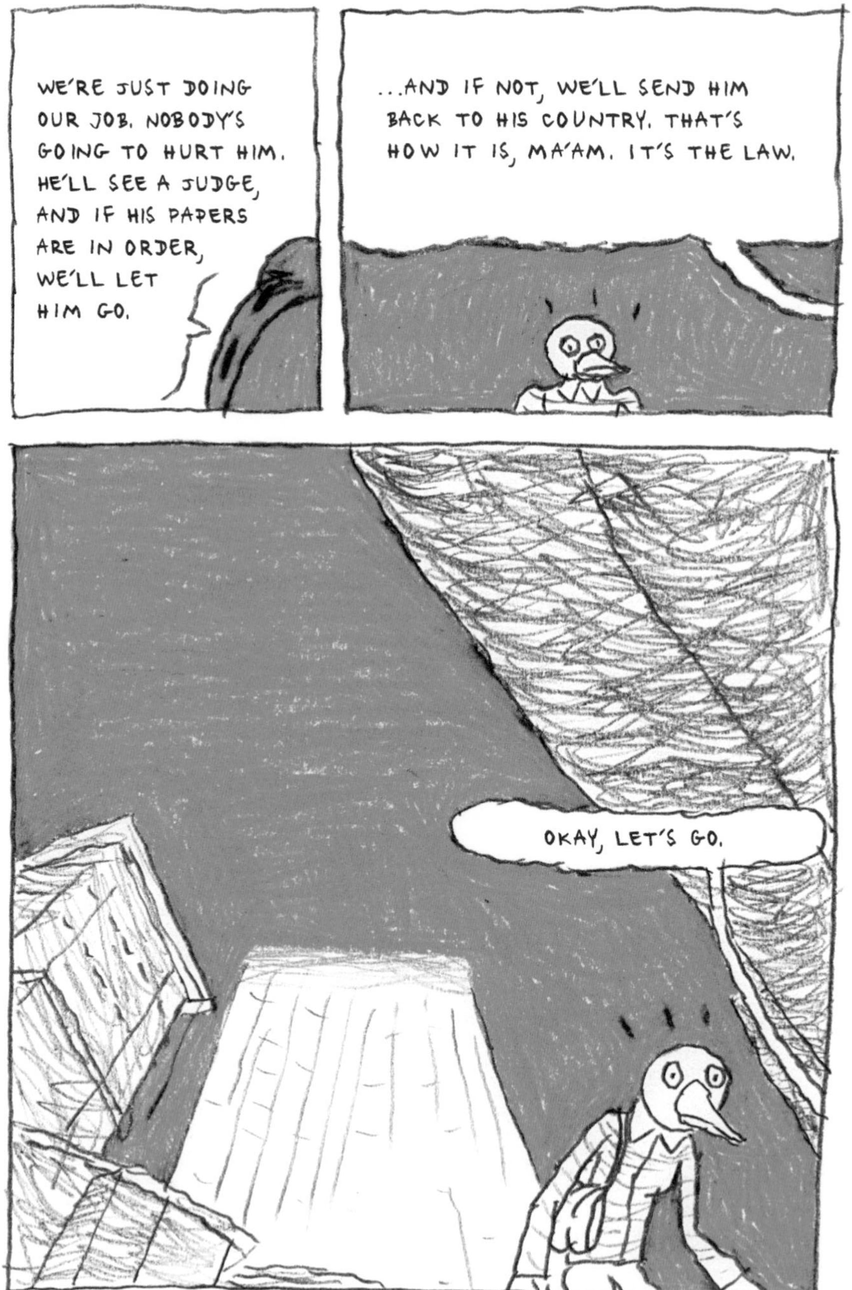

WE'RE JUST DOING OUR JOB. NOBODY'S GOING TO HURT HIM. HE'LL SEE A JUDGE, AND IF HIS PAPERS ARE IN ORDER, WE'LL LET HIM GO.
...AND IF NOT, WE'LL SEND HIM BACK TO HIS COUNTRY. THAT'S HOW IT IS, MA'AM. IT'S THE LAW.
OKAY, LET'S GO.

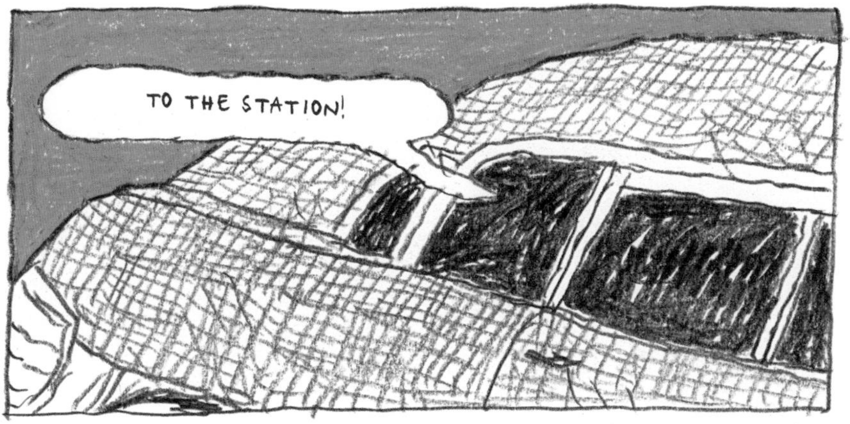
TO THE STATION!

Bernard

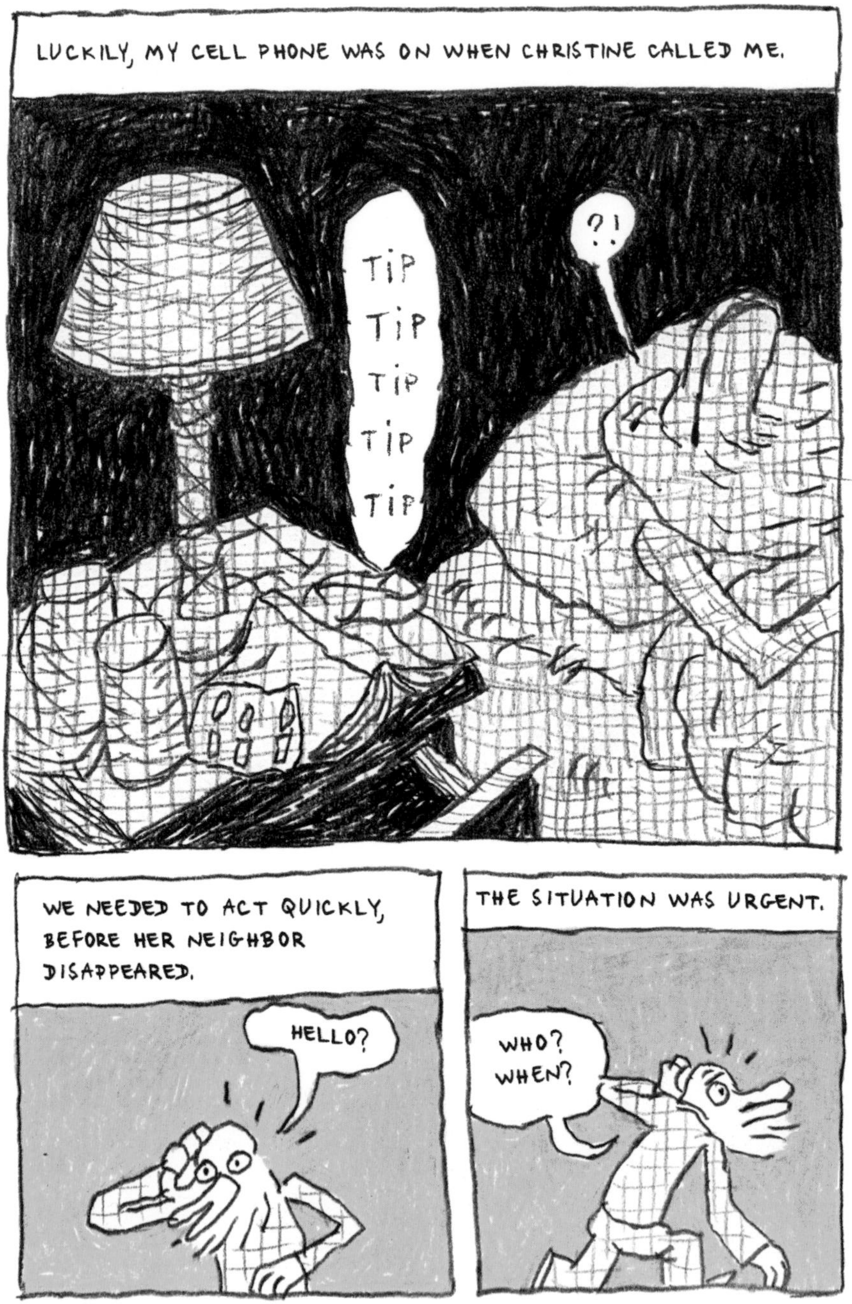
LUCKILY, MY CELL PHONE WAS ON WHEN CHRISTINE CALLED ME.
TIP TIP TIP TIP TIP
?!
WE NEEDED TO ACT QUICKLY, BEFORE HER NEIGHBOR DISAPPEARED.
HELLO?
THE SITUATION WAS URGENT.
WHO? WHEN?

SO I CALLED SUSIE IMMEDIATELY, EVEN THOUGH IT WAS STILL EARLY.

HELLO, SUSIE?

Susie

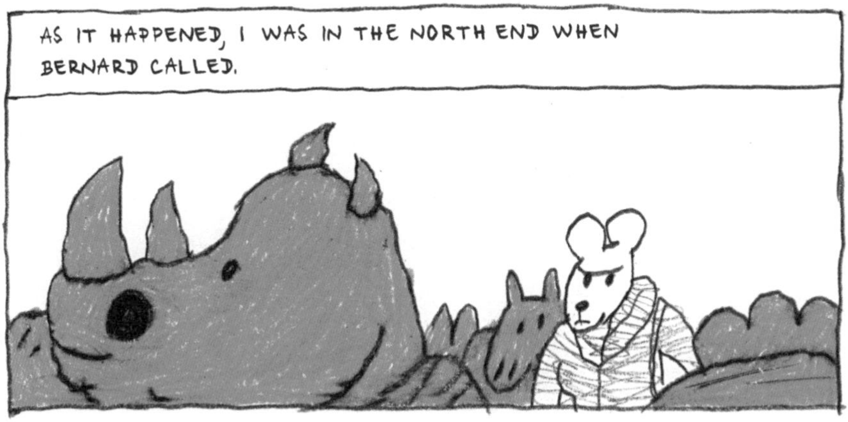
AS IT HAPPENED, I WAS IN THE NORTH END WHEN BERNARD CALLED.

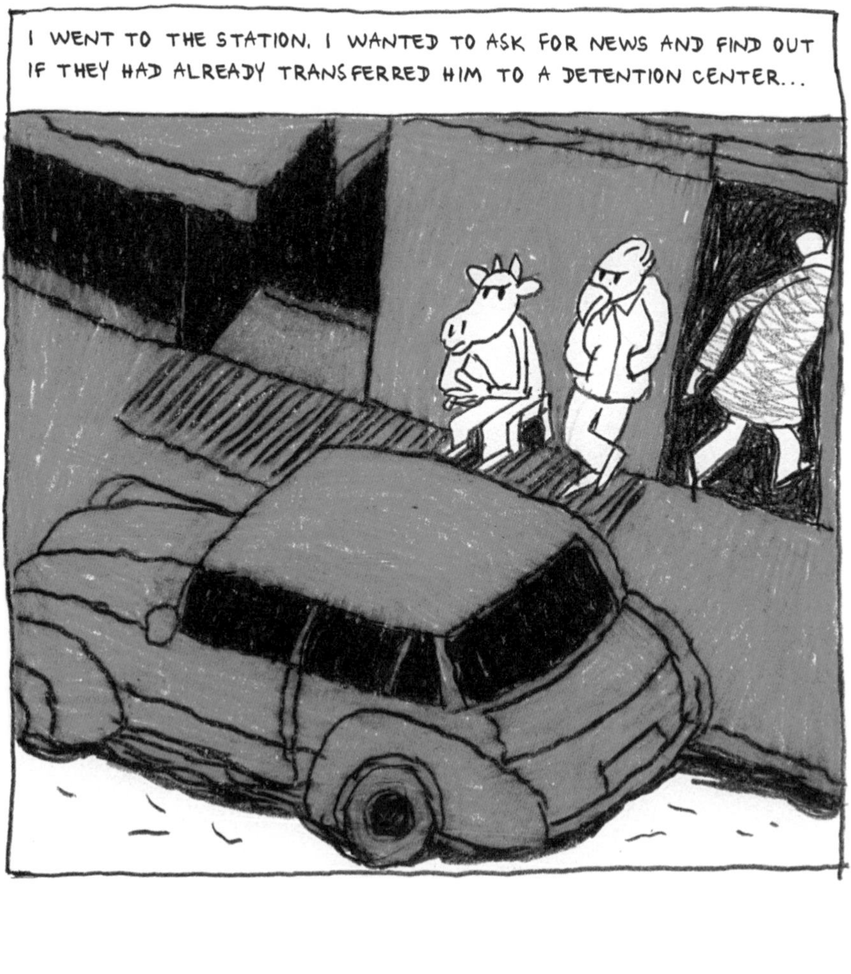
I WENT TO THE STATION. I WANTED TO ASK FOR NEWS AND FIND OUT IF THEY HAD ALREADY TRANSFERRED HIM TO A DETENTION CENTER...

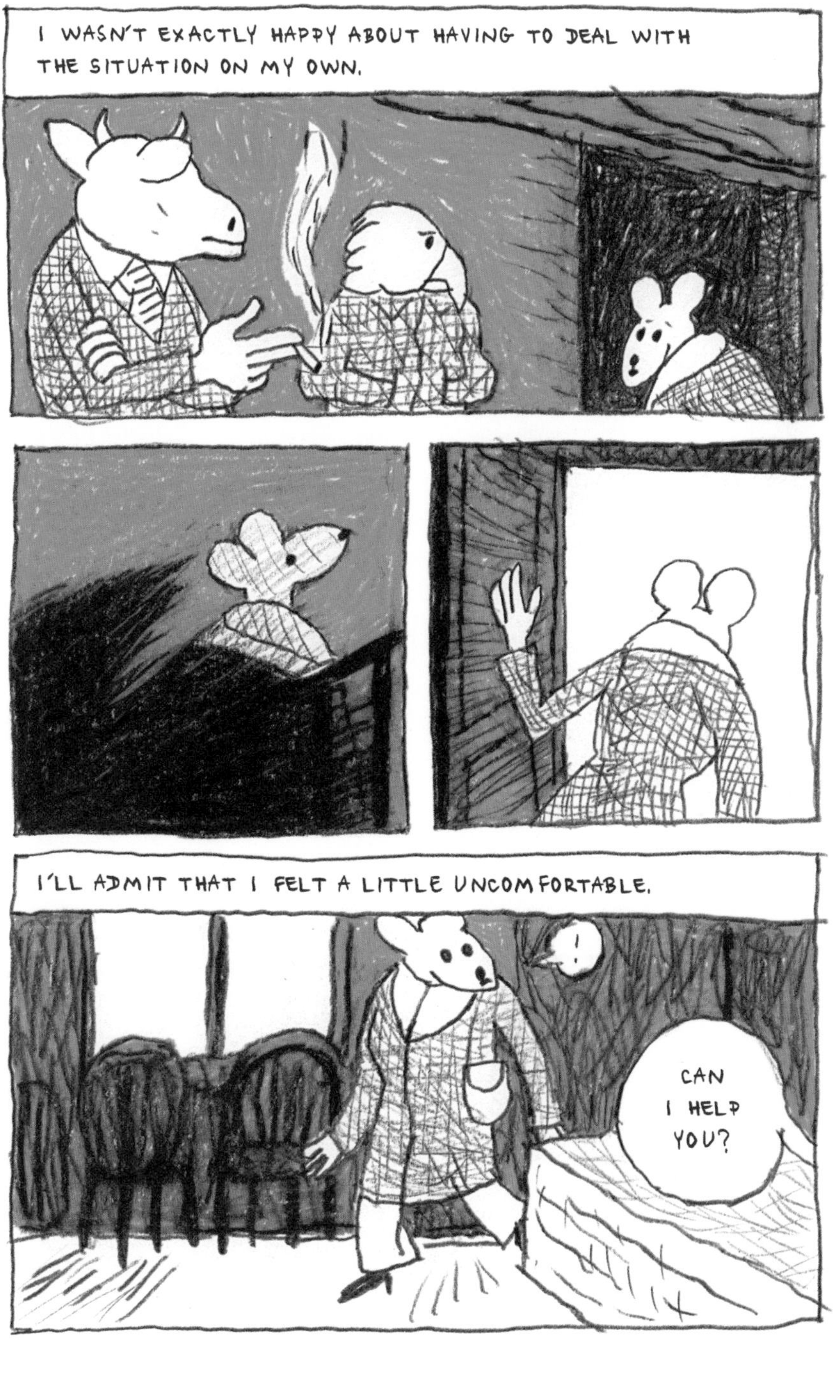
I WASN'T EXACTLY HAPPY ABOUT HAVING TO DEAL WITH THE SITUATION ON MY OWN.
I'LL ADMIT THAT I FELT A LITTLE UNCOMFORTABLE.
CAN I HELP YOU?

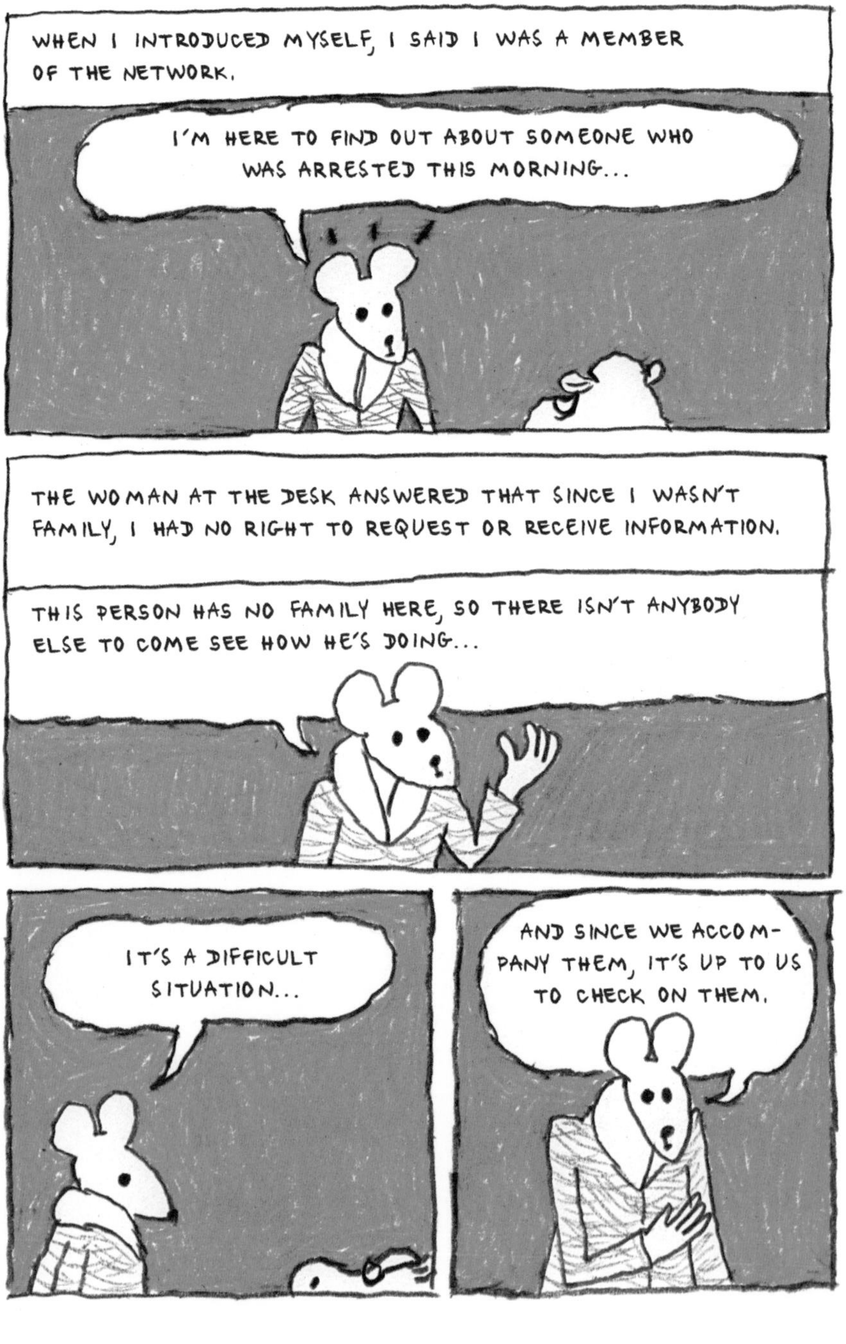
WHEN I INTRODUCED MYSELF, I SAID I WAS A MEMBER OF THE NETWORK.
I'M HERE TO FIND OUT ABOUT SOMEONE WHO WAS ARRESTED THIS MORNING...
THE WOMAN AT THE DESK ANSWERED THAT SINCE I WASN'T FAMILY, I HAD NO RIGHT TO REQUEST OR RECEIVE INFORMATION.
THIS PERSON HAS NO FAMILY HERE, SO THERE ISN'T ANYBODY ELSE TO COME SEE HOW HE'S DOING...
IT'S A DIFFICULT SITUATION...
AND SINCE WE ACCOMPANY THEM, IT'S UP TO US TO CHECK ON THEM.

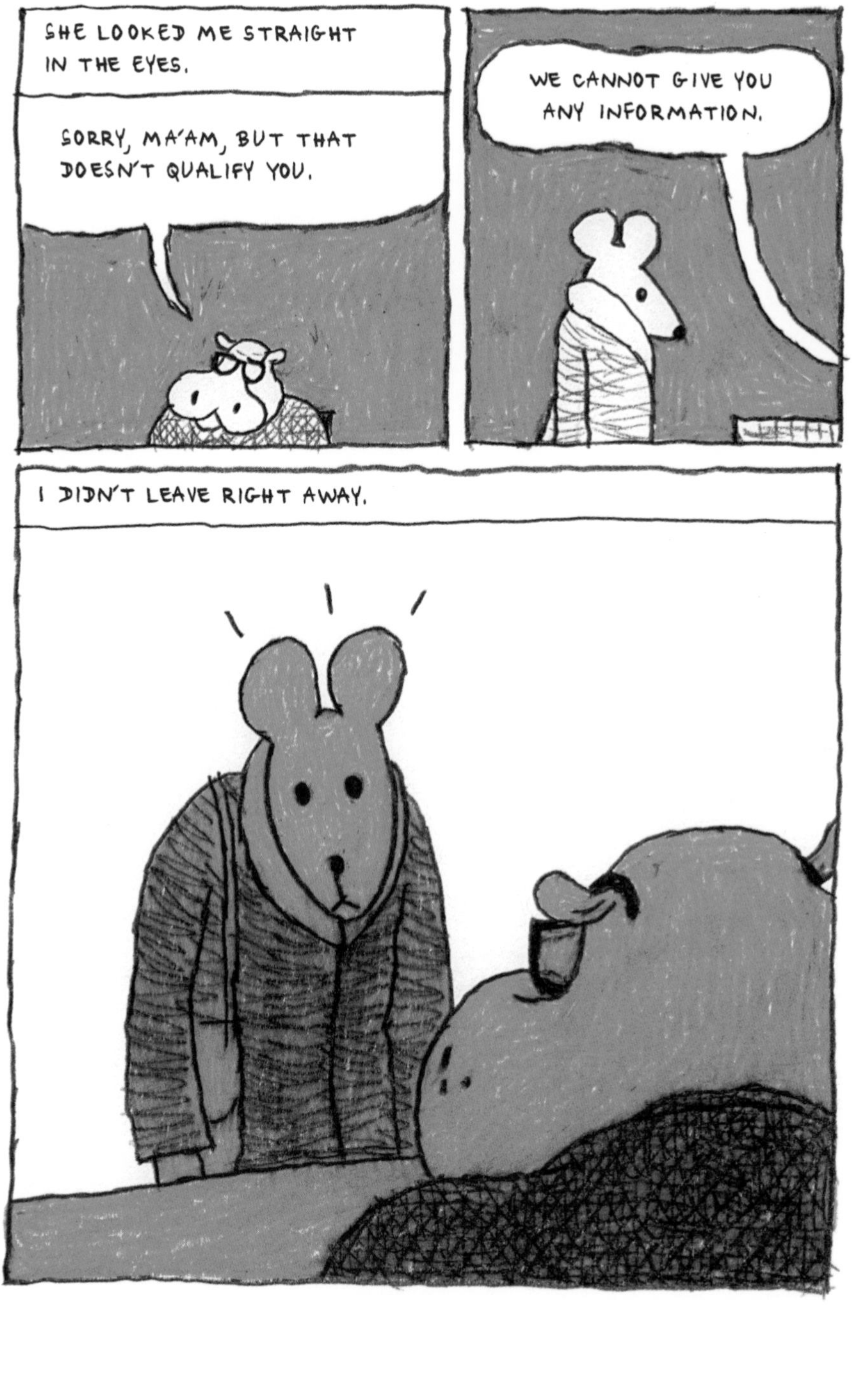
SHE LOOKED ME STRAIGHT IN THE EYES.
SORRY, MA'AM, BUT THAT DOESN'T QUALIFY YOU.
WE CANNOT GIVE YOU ANY INFORMATION.
I DIDN'T LEAVE RIGHT AWAY.

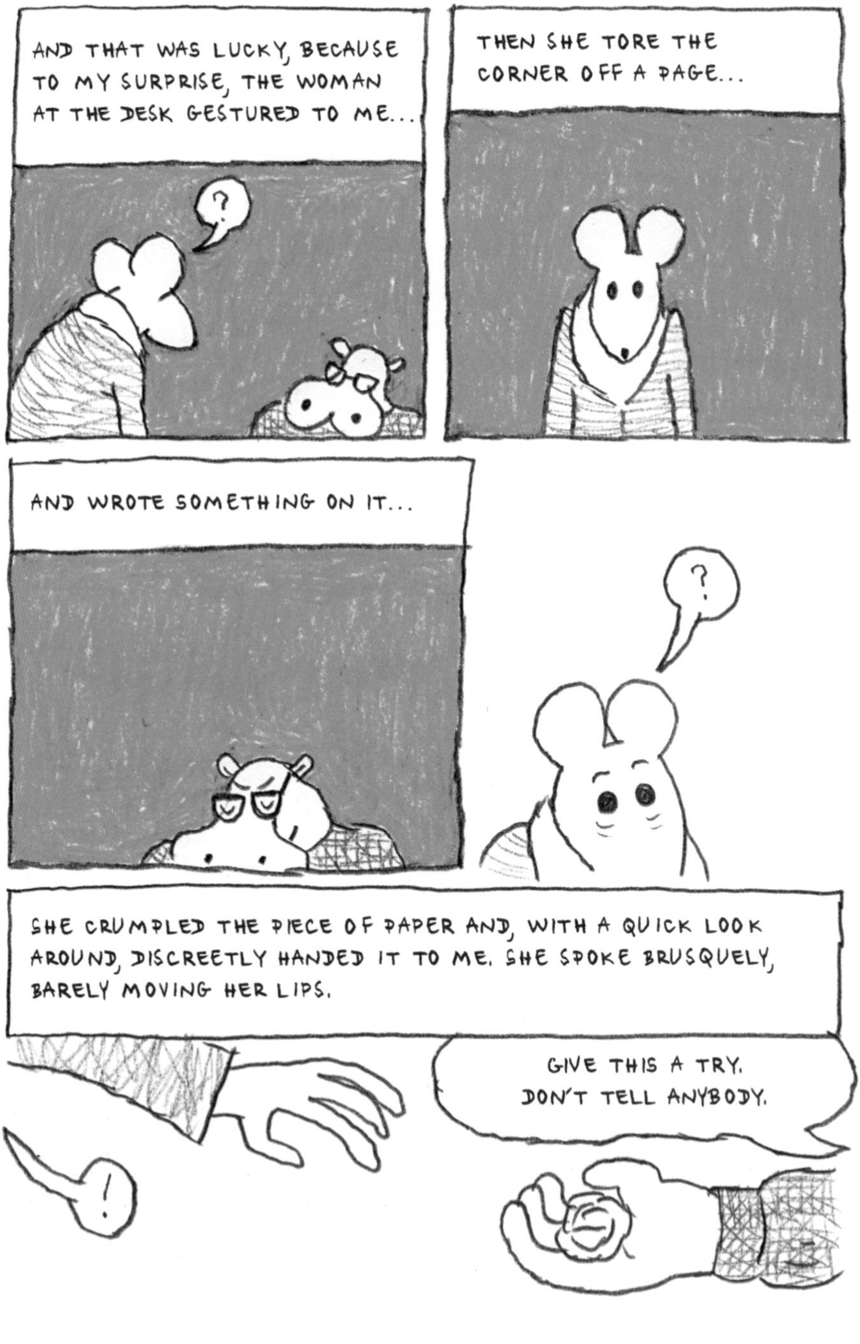
AND THAT WAS LUCKY, BECAUSE TO MY SURPRISE, THE WOMAN AT THE DESK GESTURED TO ME...
?
THEN SHE TORE THE CORNER OFF A PAGE...
AND WROTE SOMETHING ON IT...
?
SHE CRUMPLED THE PIECE OF PAPER AND, WITH A QUICK LOOK AROUND, DISCREETLY HANDED IT TO ME. SHE SPOKE BRUSQUELY, BARELY MOVING HER LIPS.
GIVE THIS A TRY. DON'T TELL ANYBODY.
!

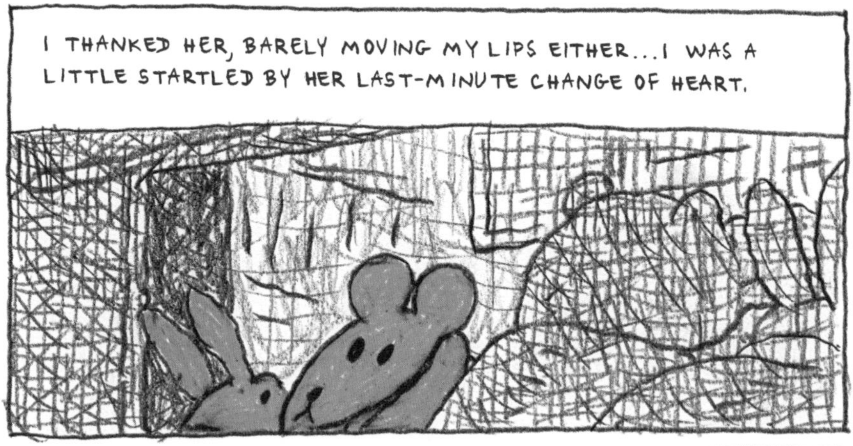
I THANKED HER, BARELY MOVING MY LIPS EITHER... I WAS A LITTLE STARTLED BY HER LAST-MINUTE CHANGE OF HEART.

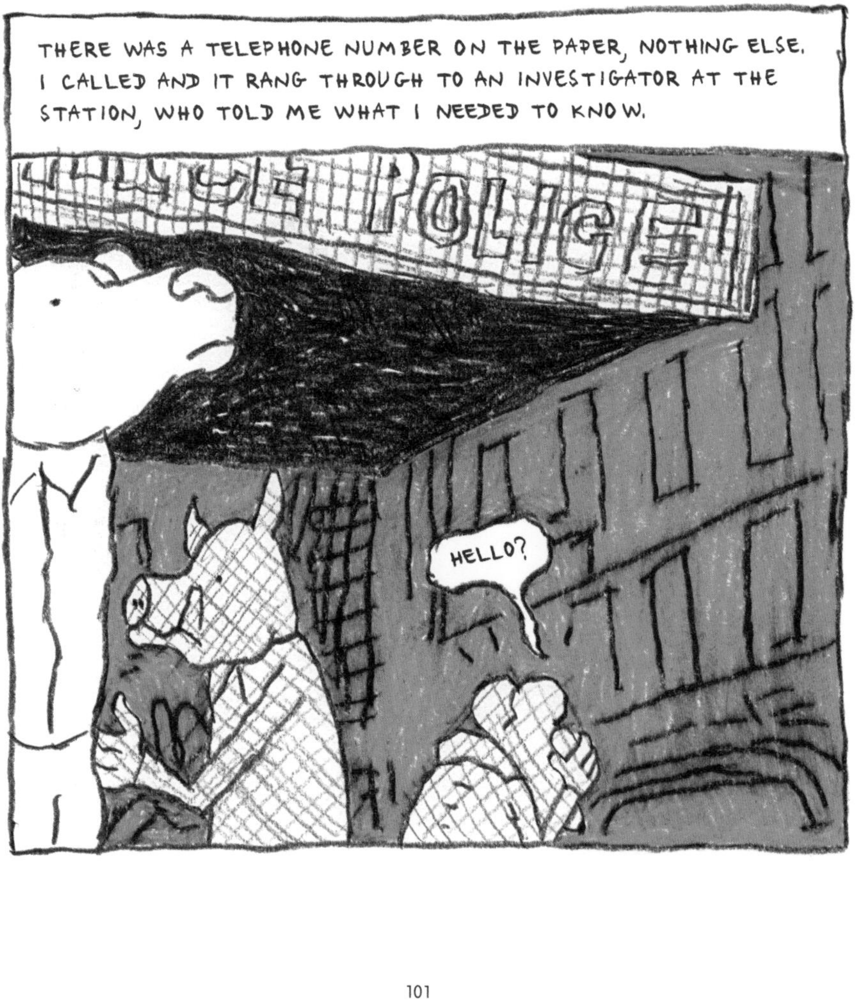
THERE WAS A TELEPHONE NUMBER ON THE PAPER, NOTHING ELSE. I CALLED AND IT RANG THROUGH TO AN INVESTIGATOR AT THE STATION, WHO TOLD ME WHAT I NEEDED TO KNOW.
POLICE
HELLO?

Kader

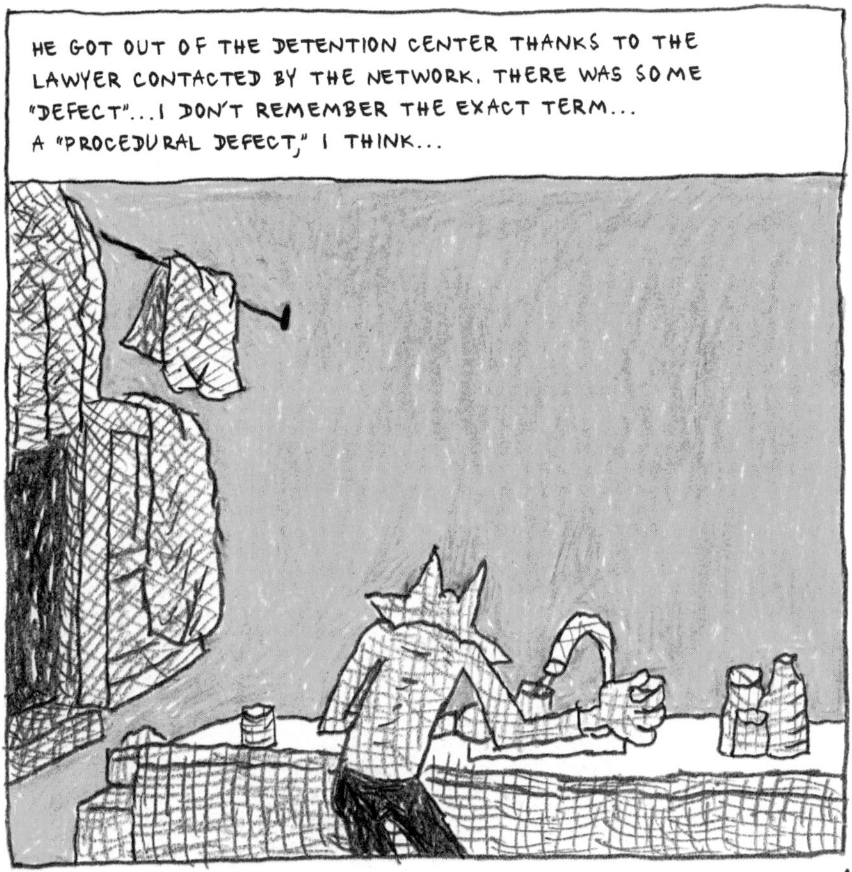
HE GOT OUT OF THE DETENTION CENTER THANKS TO THE LAWYER CONTACTED BY THE NETWORK. THERE WAS SOME "DEFECT"...I DON'T REMEMBER THE EXACT TERM... A "PROCEDURAL DEFECT," I THINK...

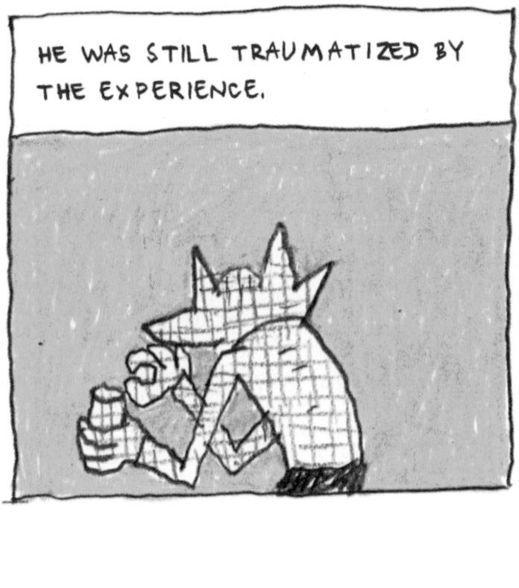
HE WAS STILL TRAUMATIZED BY THE EXPERIENCE.

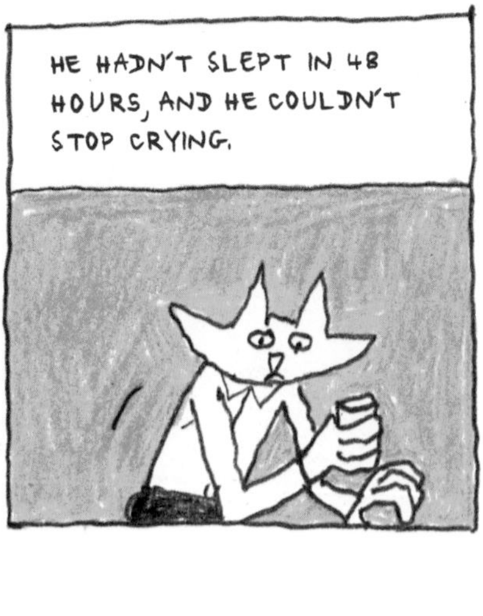
HE HADN'T SLEPT IN 48 HOURS, AND HE COULDN'T STOP CRYING.

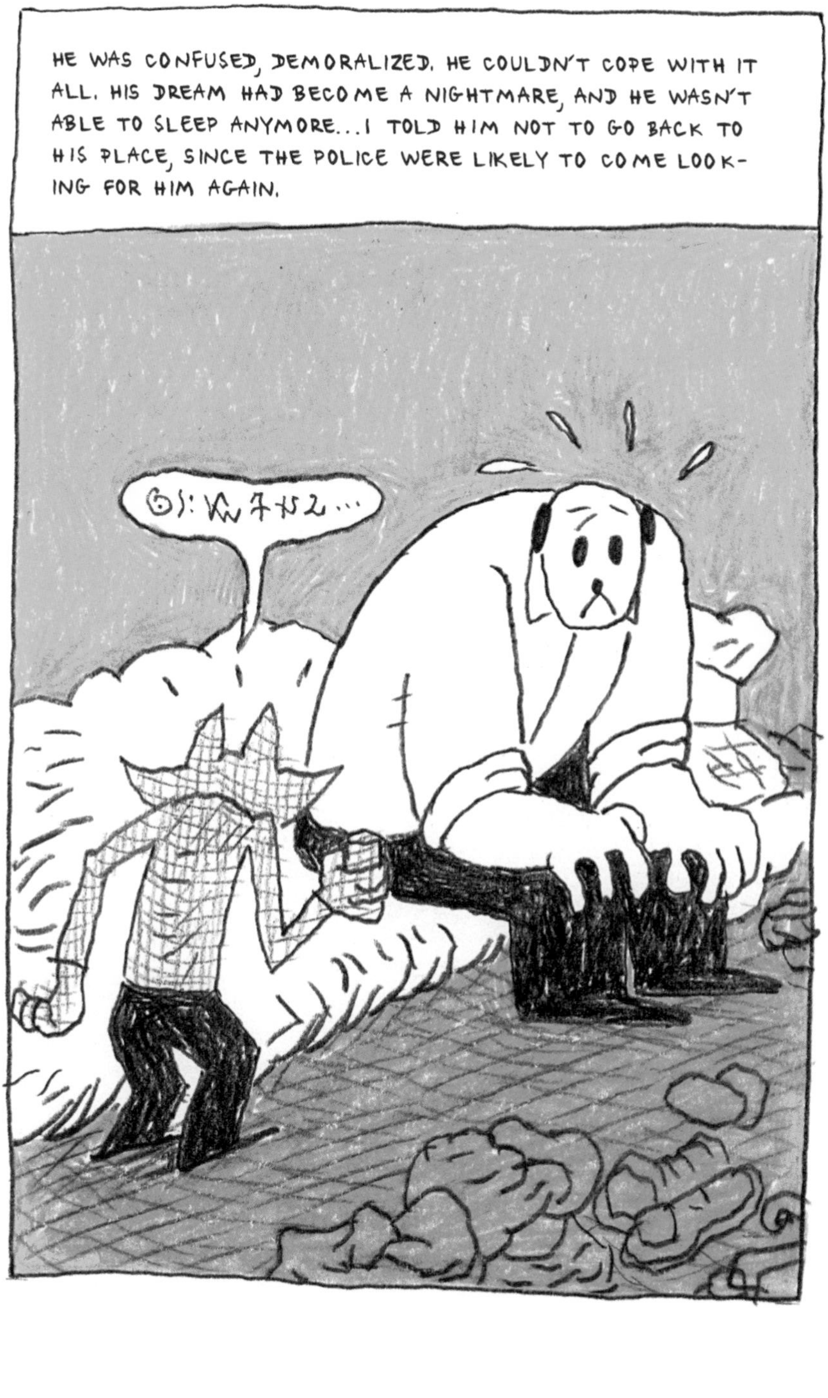
HE WAS CONFUSED, DEMORALIZED. HE COULDN'T COPE WITH IT ALL. HIS DREAM HAD BECOME A NIGHTMARE, AND HE WASN'T ABLE TO SLEEP ANYMORE... I TOLD HIM NOT TO GO BACK TO HIS PLACE, SINCE THE POLICE WERE LIKELY TO COME LOOKING FOR HIM AGAIN.

The customer

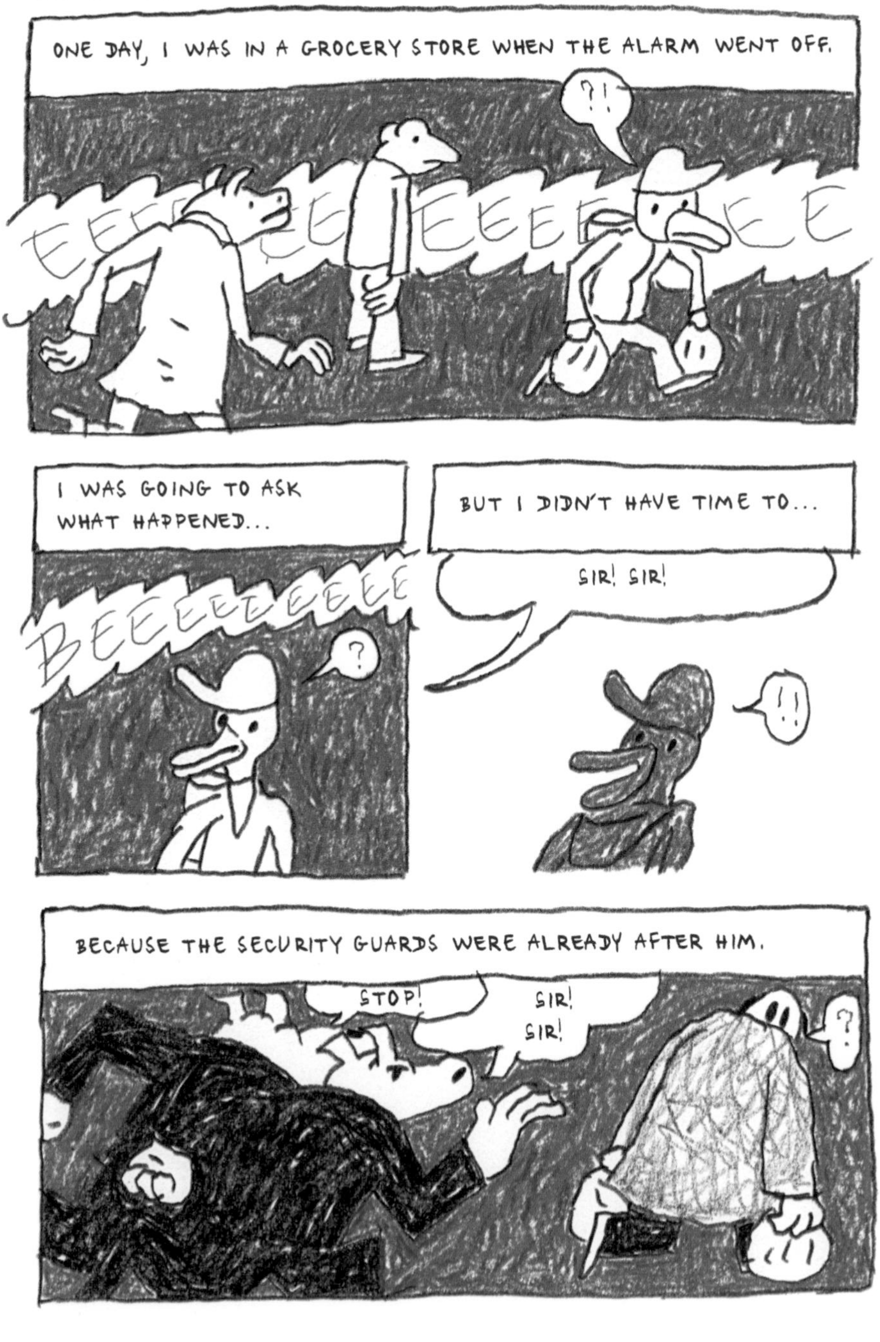
ONE DAY, I WAS IN A GROCERY STORE WHEN THE ALARM WENT OFF.
?!
I WAS GOING TO ASK WHAT HAPPENED...
?
BUT I DIDN'T HAVE TIME TO...
SIR! SIR!
!!
BECAUSE THE SECURITY GUARDS WERE ALREADY AFTER HIM.
STOP!
SIR! SIR!
?

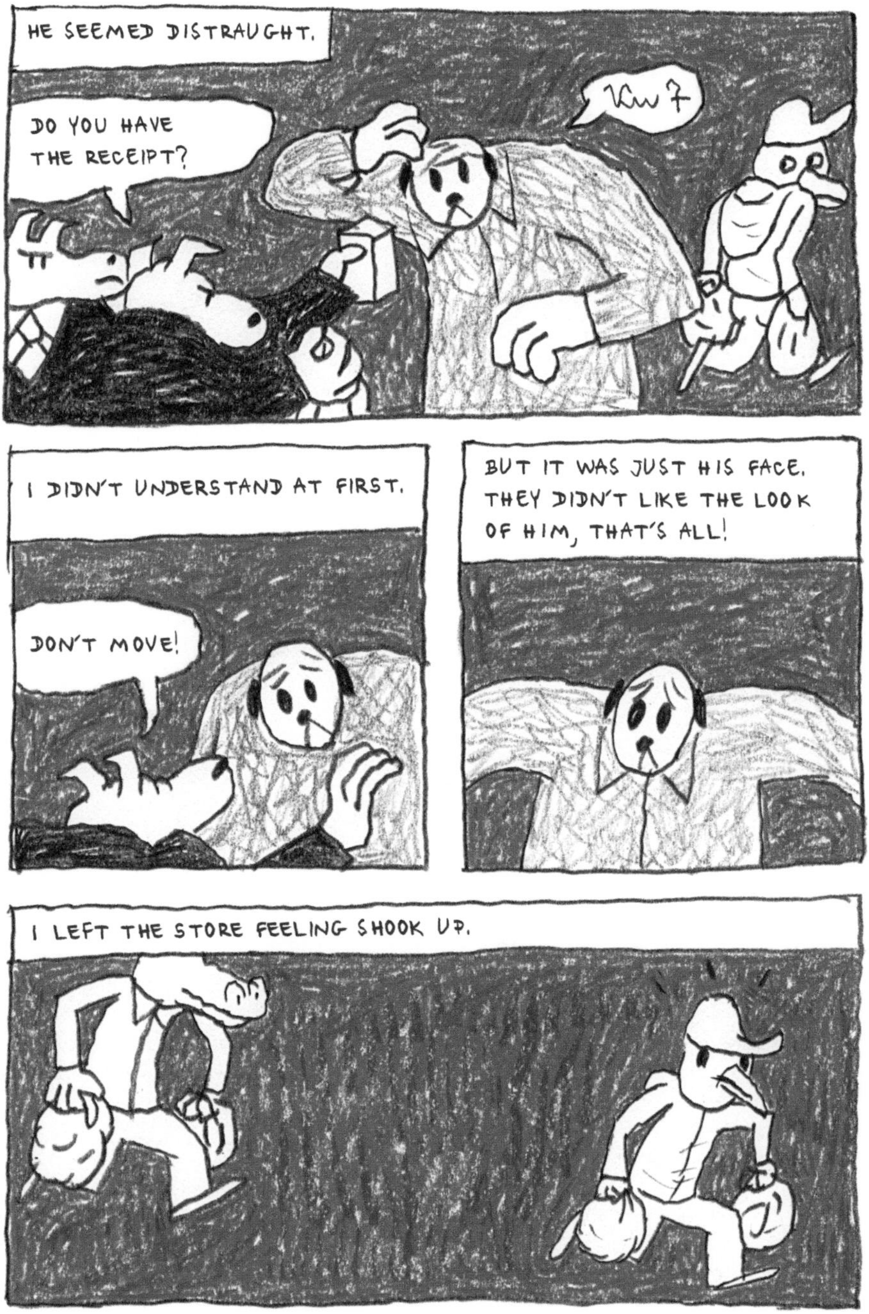
HE SEEMED DISTRAUGHT.
DO YOU HAVE THE RECEIPT?
I DIDN'T UNDERSTAND AT FIRST.
DON'T MOVE!
BUT IT WAS JUST HIS FACE. THEY DIDN'T LIKE THE LOOK OF HIM, THAT'S ALL!
I LEFT THE STORE FEELING SHOOK UP.

The crow

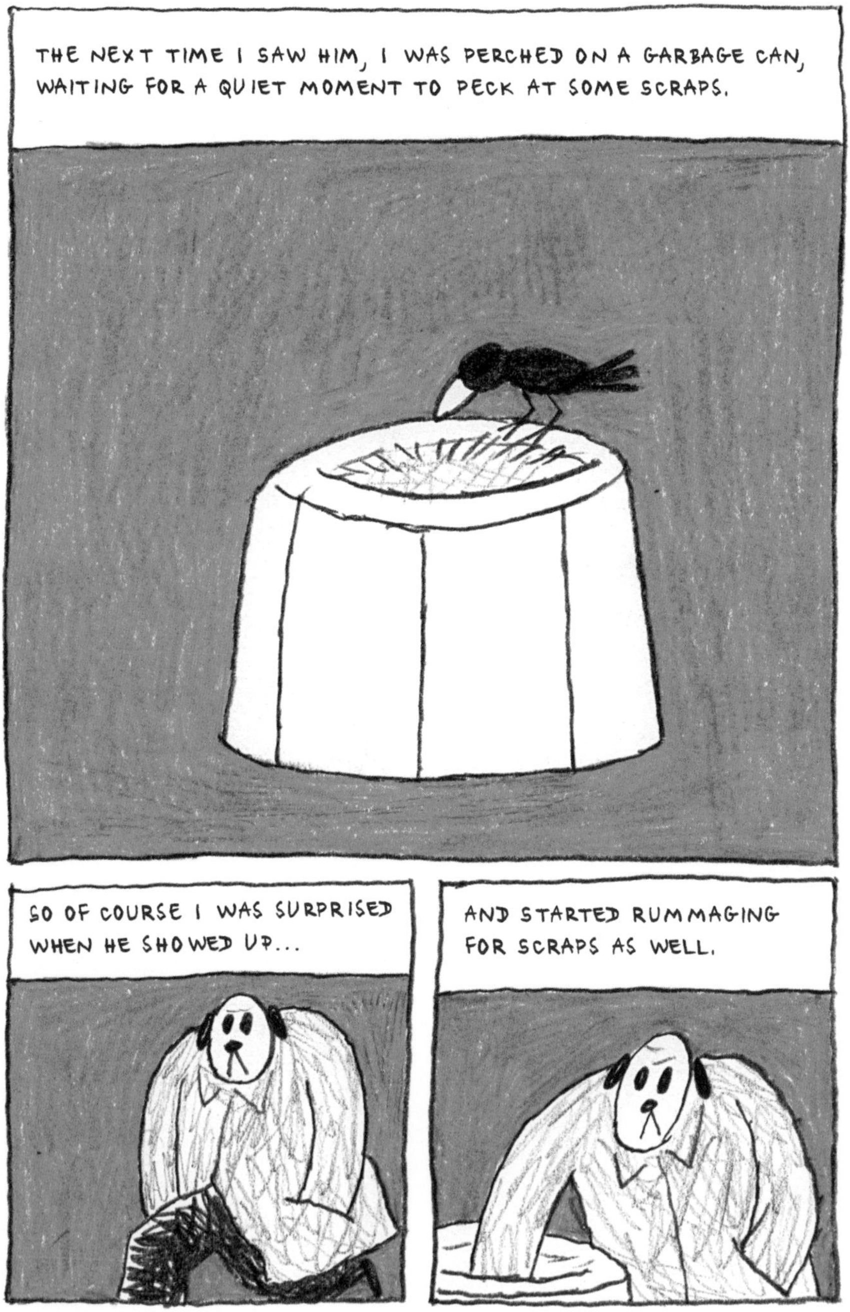
THE NEXT TIME I SAW HIM, I WAS PERCHED ON A GARBAGE CAN, WAITING FOR A QUIET MOMENT TO PECK AT SOME SCRAPS.
SO OF COURSE I WAS SURPRISED WHEN HE SHOWED UP...
AND STARTED RUMMAGING FOR SCRAPS AS WELL.

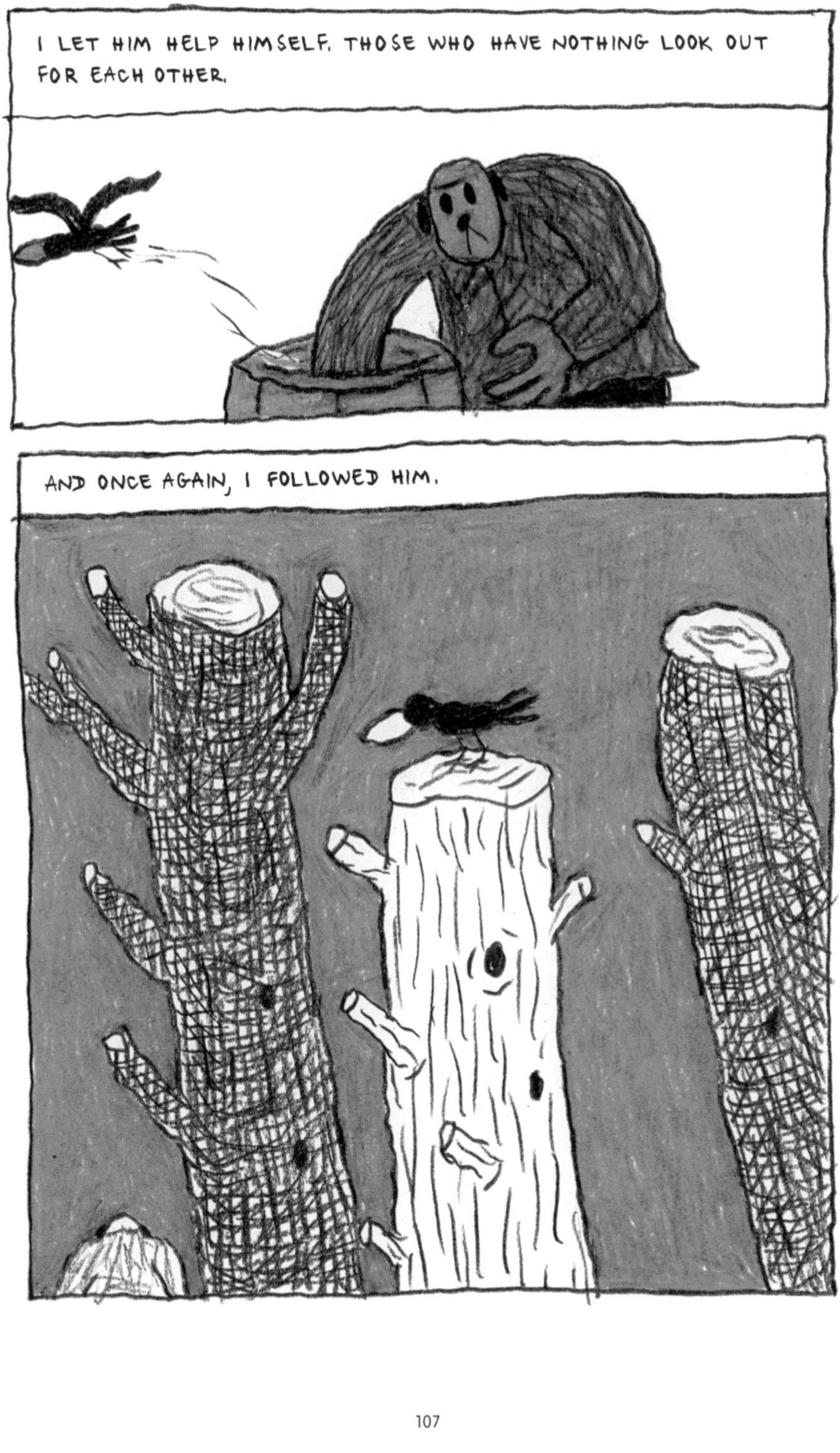
I LET HIM HELP HIMSELF. THOSE WHO HAVE NOTHING LOOK OUT FOR EACH OTHER.
AND ONCE AGAIN, I FOLLOWED HIM.

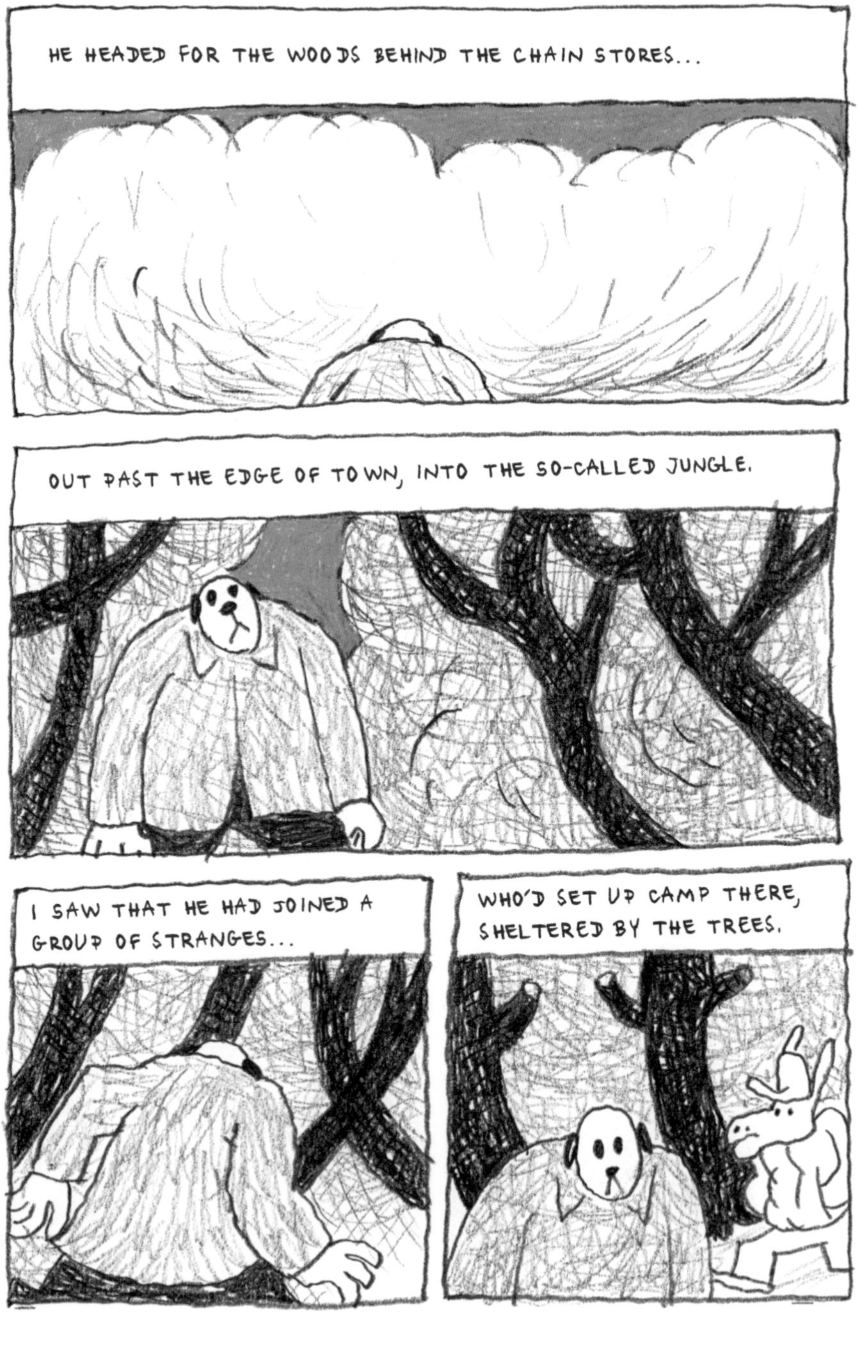
HE HEADED FOR THE WOODS BEHIND THE CHAIN STORES...
OUT PAST THE EDGE OF TOWN, INTO THE SO-CALLED JUNGLE.
I SAW THAT HE HAD JOINED A GROUP OF STRANGES...
WHO'D SET UP CAMP THERE, SHELTERED BY THE TREES.

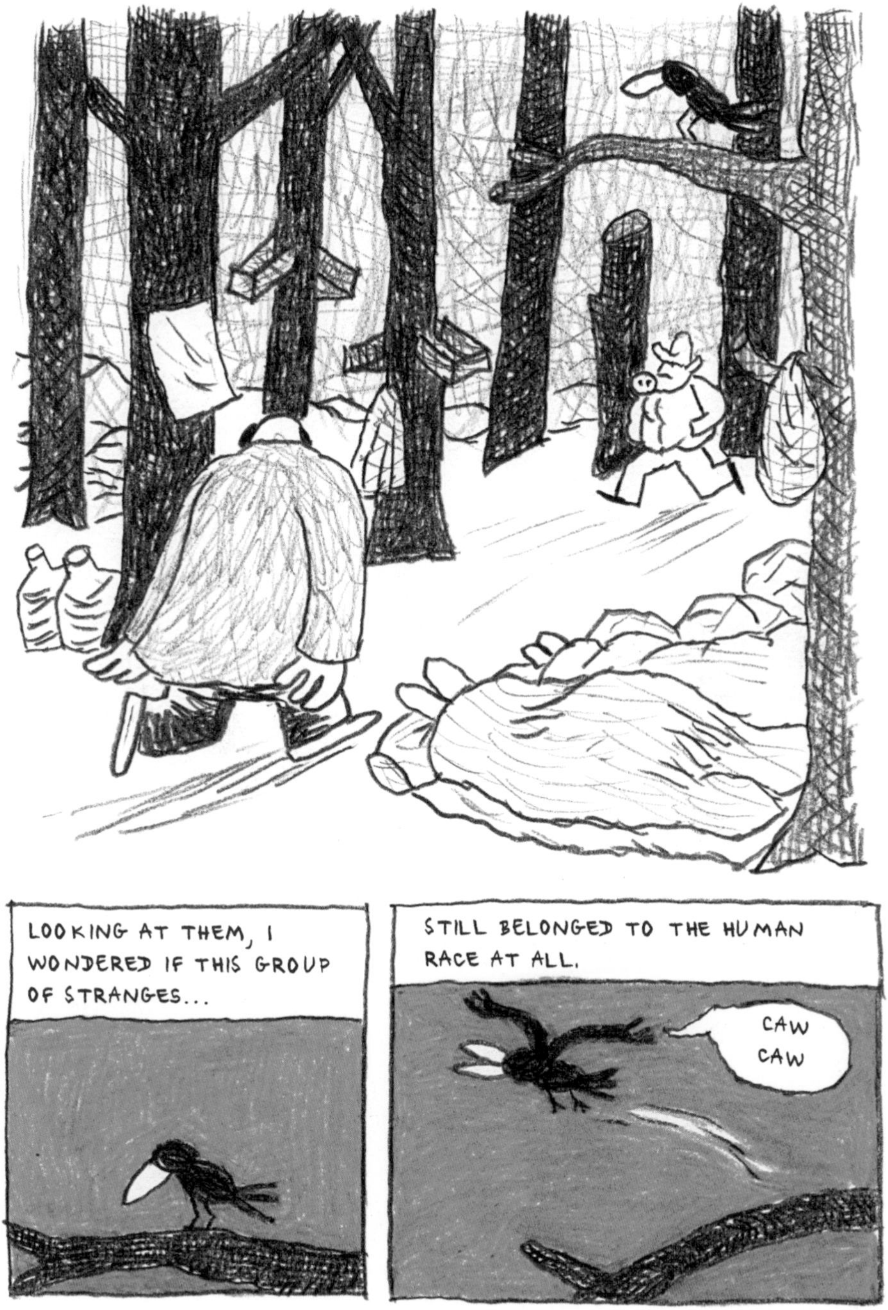
LOOKING AT THEM, I WONDERED IF THIS GROUP OF STRANGES...
STILL BELONGED TO THE HUMAN RACE AT ALL.
CAW CAW

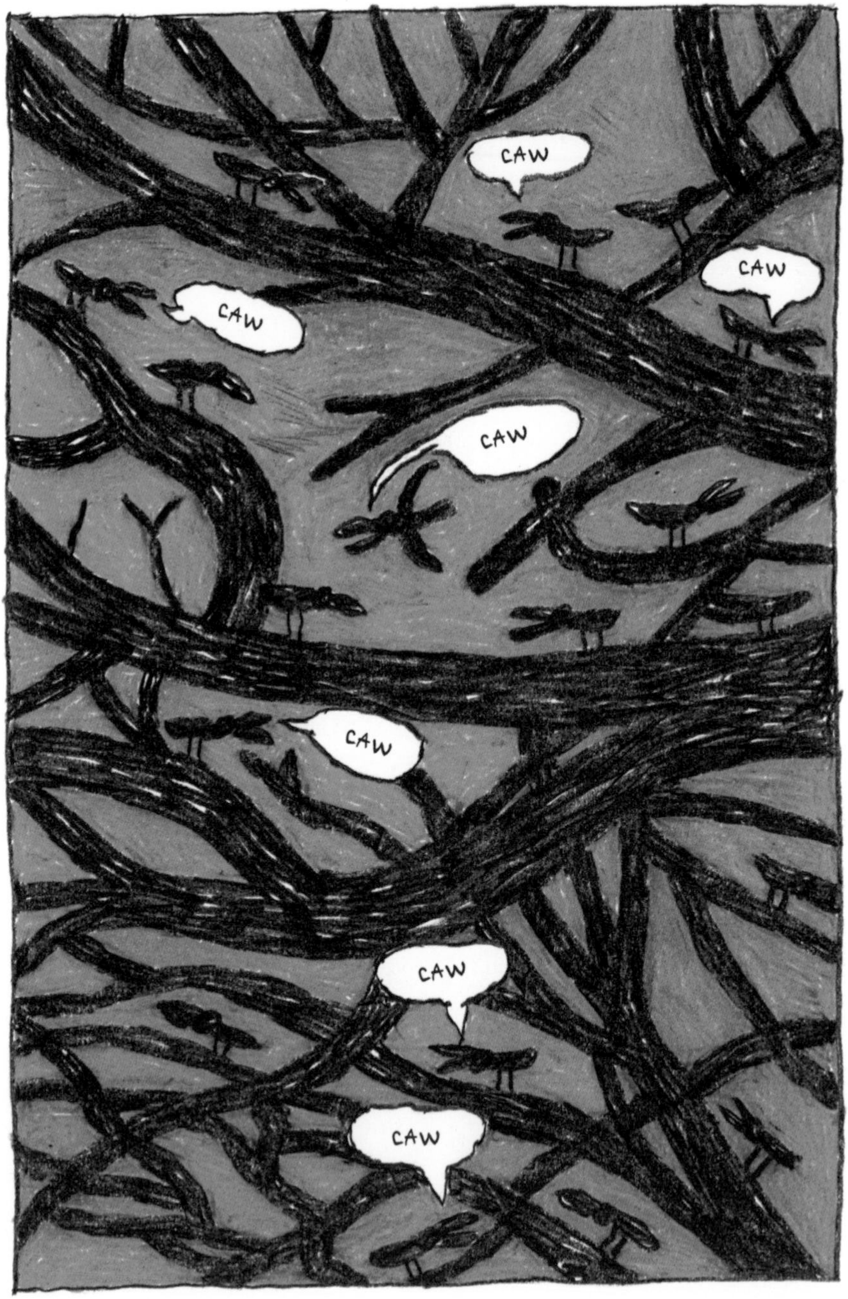
CAW
CAW
CAW
CAW
CAW
CAW
CAW

The Patriarch

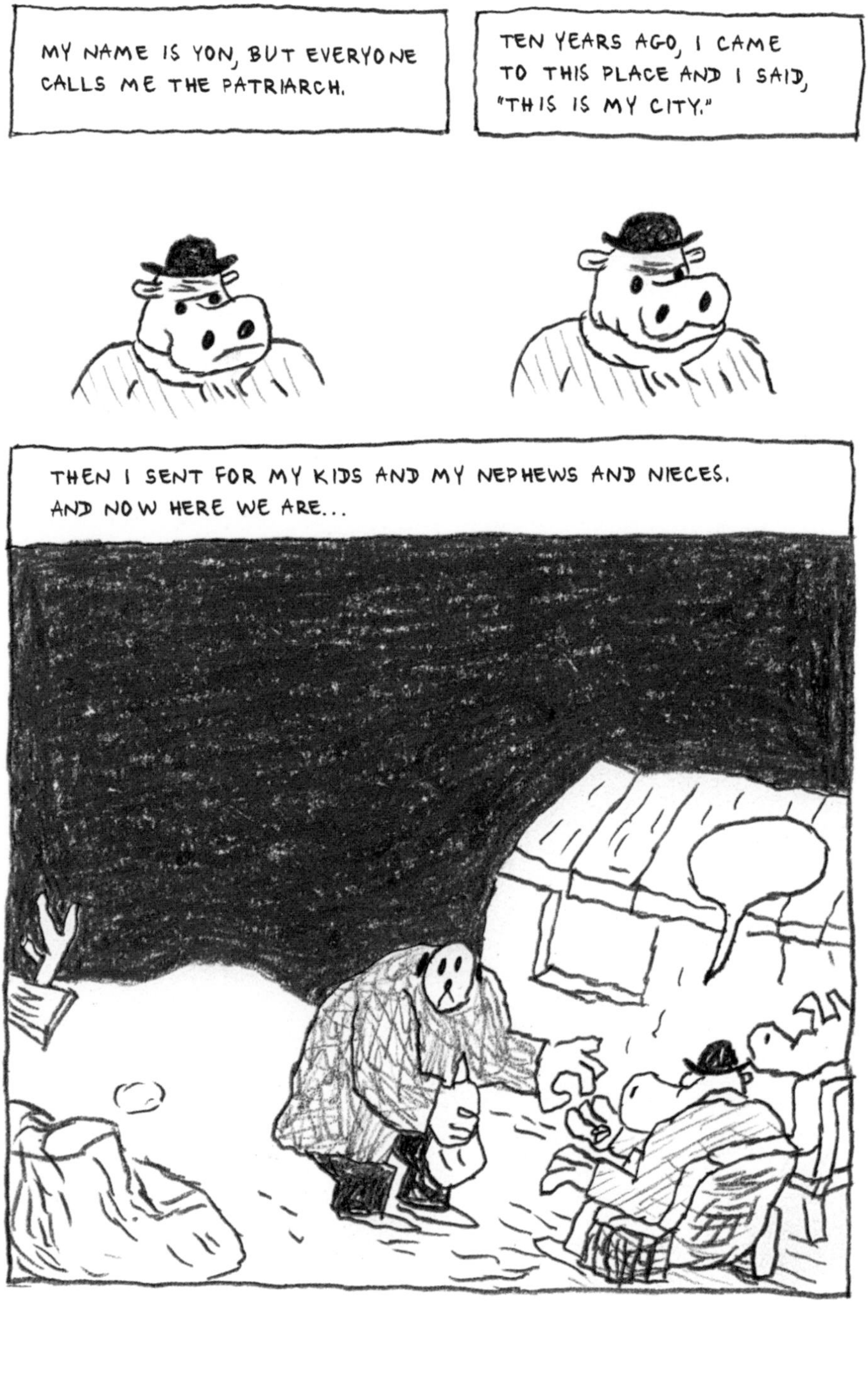
MY NAME IS YON, BUT EVERYONE CALLS ME THE PATRIARCH.
TEN YEARS AGO, I CAME TO THIS PLACE AND I SAID, "THIS IS MY CITY."
THEN I SENT FOR MY KIDS AND MY NEPHEWS AND NIECES. AND NOW HERE WE ARE...

WHEN HE CAME TO THE CAMP,
HE WAS LOOKING FOR PROTEC-
TION FROM THE STREETS.

I CHARGED HIM FIVE
A DAY, LIKE THE FAMILY
MEMBERS I HAVE
LIVING HERE...

BUT HE QUICKLY FELL ILL.

Cornelia

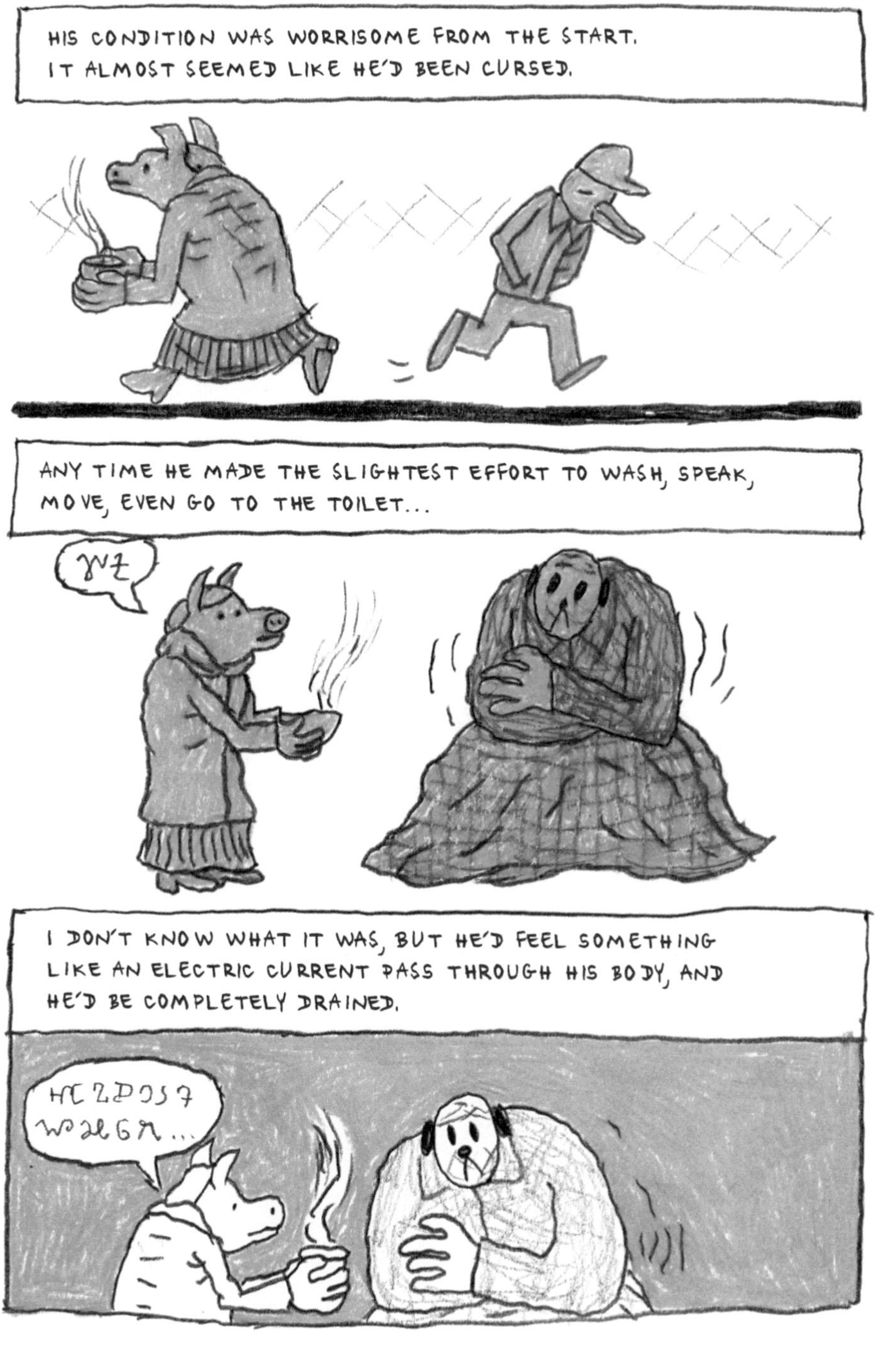
HIS CONDITION WAS WORRISOME FROM THE START. IT ALMOST SEEMED LIKE HE'D BEEN CURSED.
ANY TIME HE MADE THE SLIGHTEST EFFORT TO WASH, SPEAK, MOVE, EVEN GO TO THE TOILET...
I DON'T KNOW WHAT IT WAS, BUT HE'D FEEL SOMETHING LIKE AN ELECTRIC CURRENT PASS THROUGH HIS BODY, AND HE'D BE COMPLETELY DRAINED.

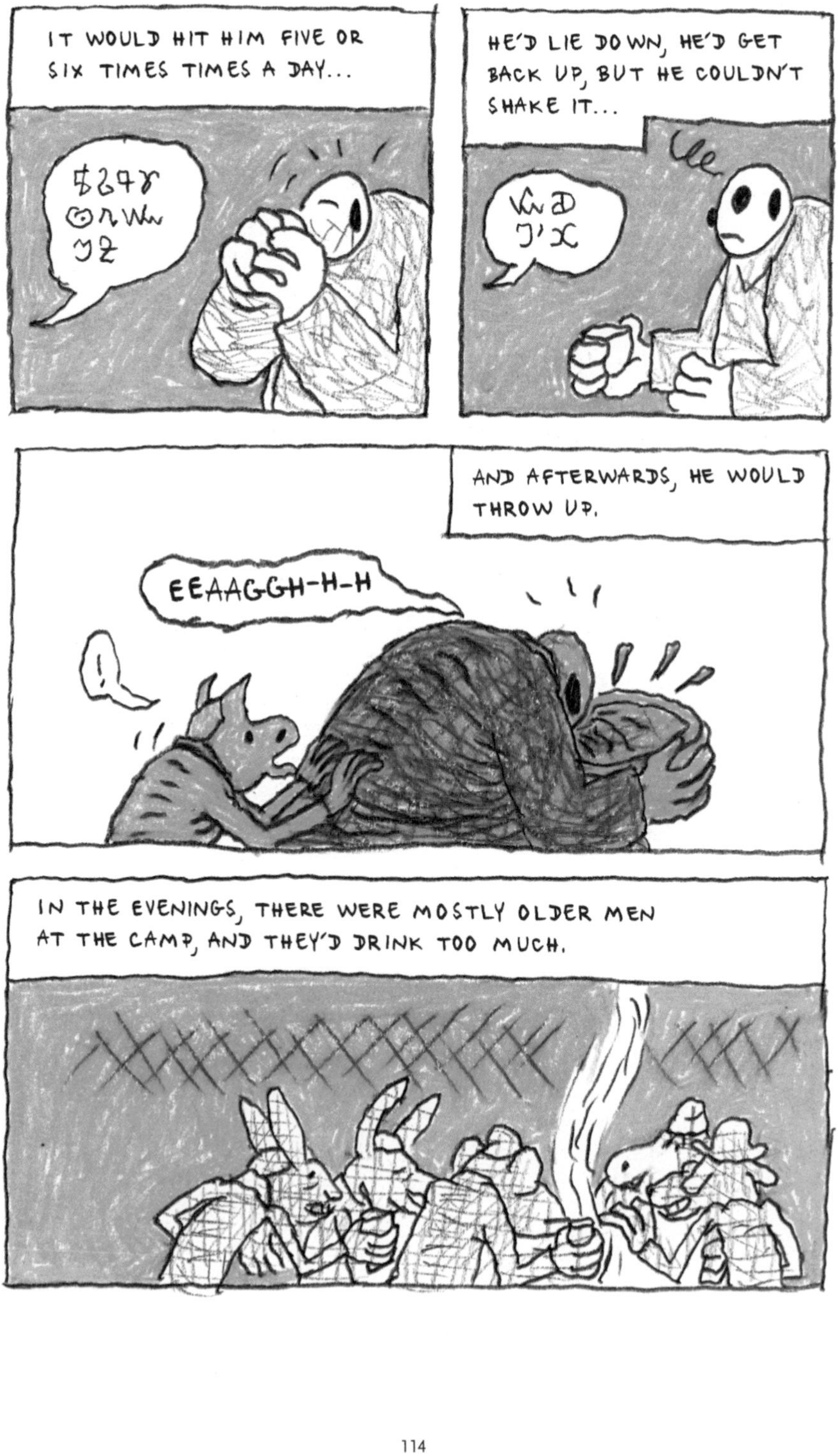
IT WOULD HIT HIM FIVE OR SIX TIMES TIMES A DAY...
HE'D LIE DOWN, HE'D GET BACK UP, BUT HE COULDN'T SHAKE IT...
AND AFTERWARDS, HE WOULD THROW UP.
EEAAGGH-H-H
!
IN THE EVENINGS, THERE WERE MOSTLY OLDER MEN AT THE CAMP, AND THEY'D DRINK TOO MUCH.

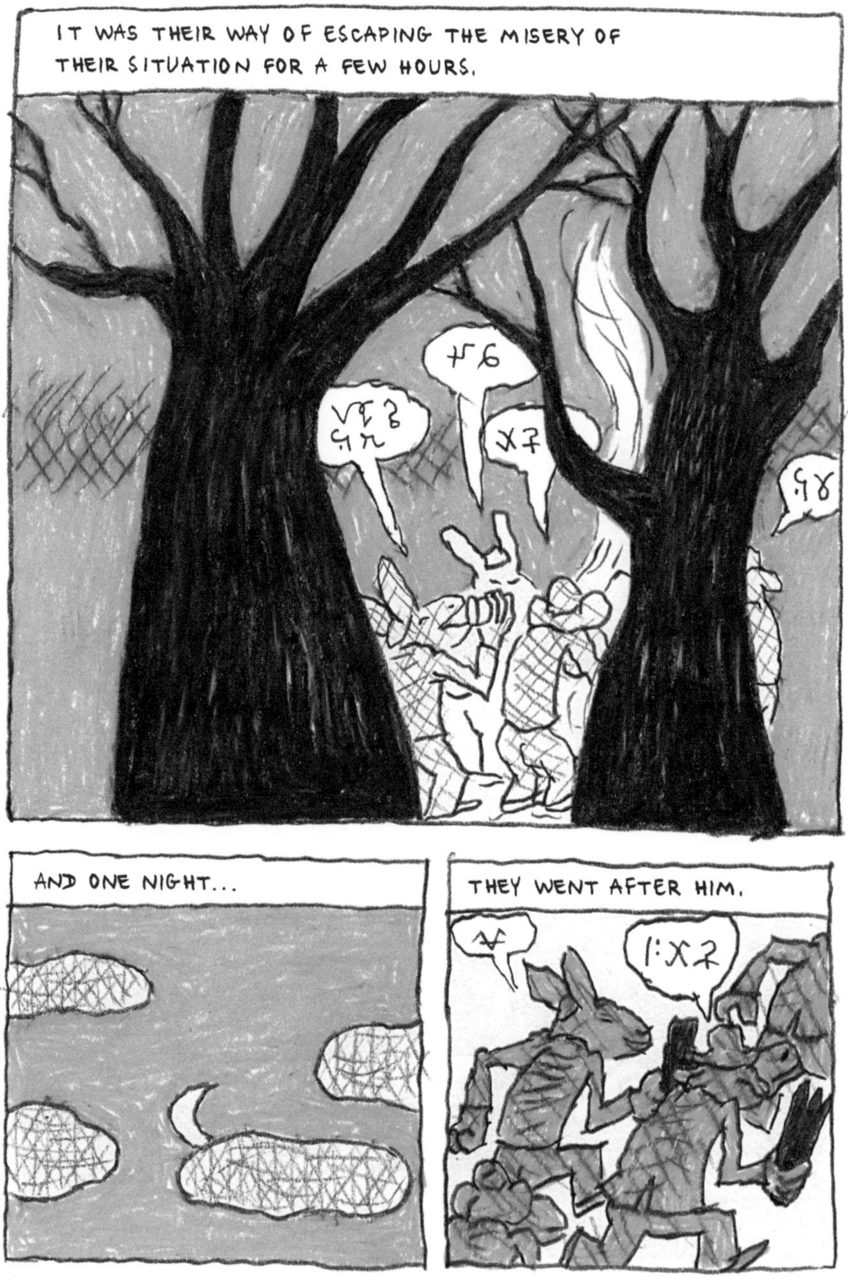
IT WAS THEIR WAY OF ESCAPING THE MISERY OF THEIR SITUATION FOR A FEW HOURS.
AND ONE NIGHT...
THEY WENT AFTER HIM.

I WANTED TO GET HIM TO SAFETY, AWAY FROM WHAT WAS HAP-
PENING HERE, SO I CALLED THE WOMAN FROM THE NETWORK.

HELLO, CORNELIA HERE...

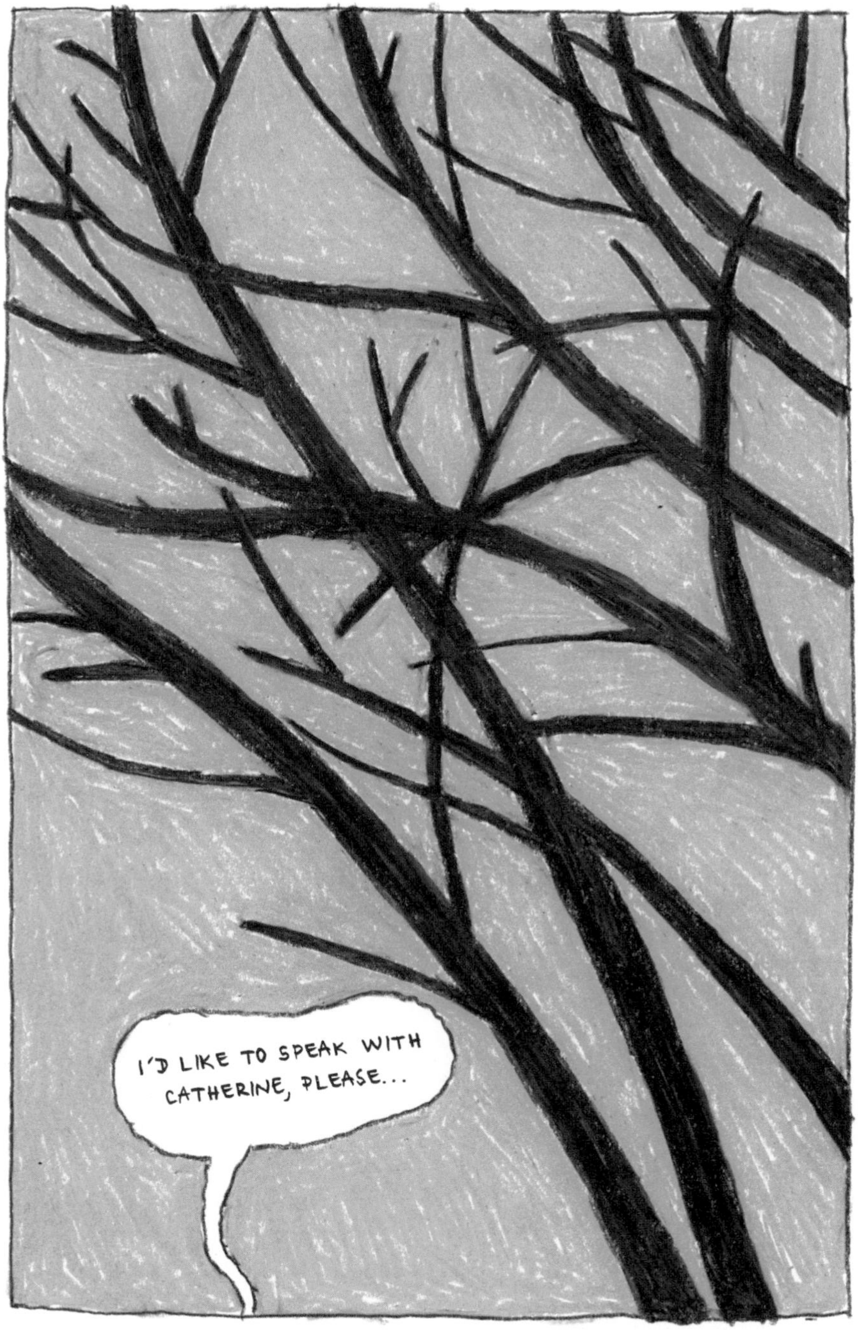
I'D LIKE TO SPEAK WITH CATHERINE, PLEASE...

"YOU'VE HAD ENOUGH OF THESE GANGS OF THUGS?
WELL, WE'LL GET RID OF THEM FOR YOU!"

Catherine

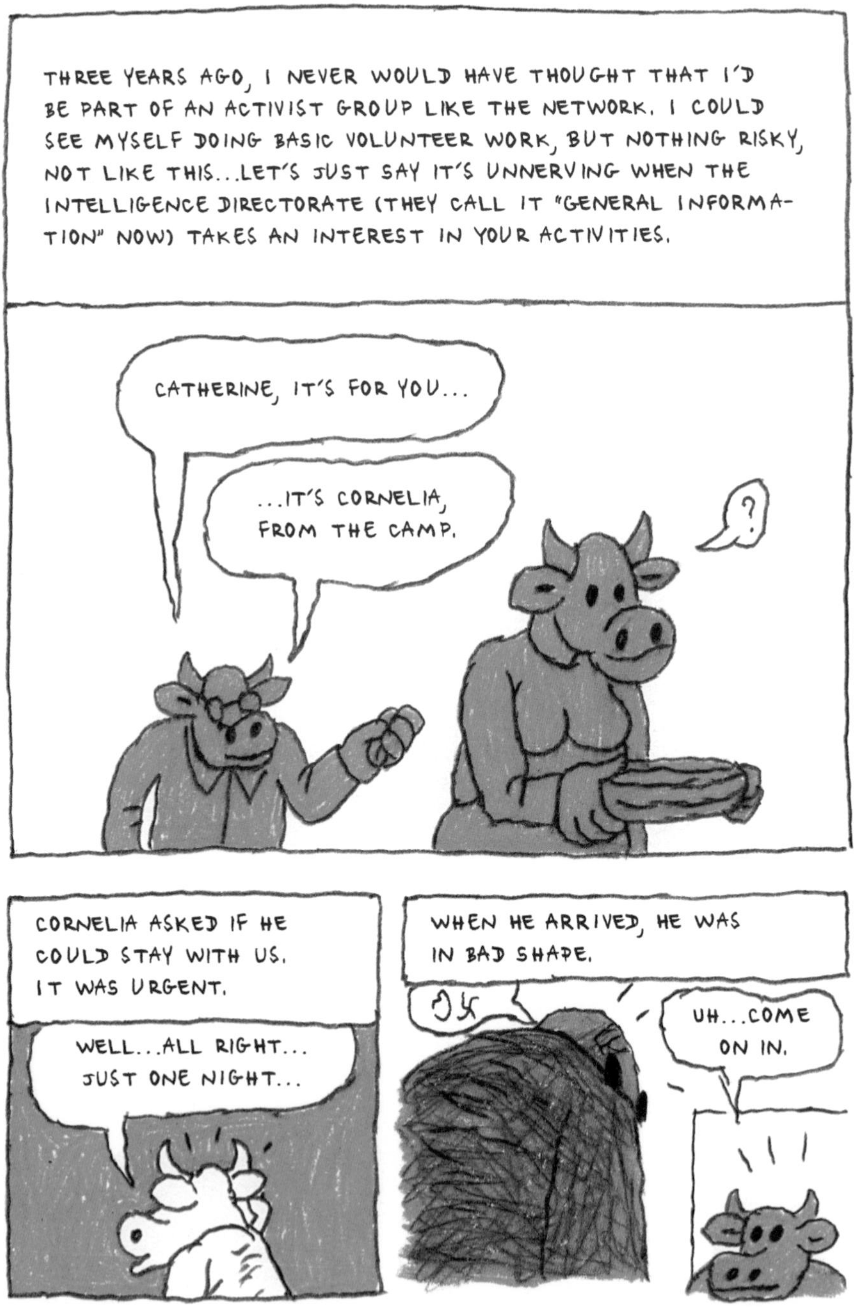

THREE YEARS AGO, I NEVER WOULD HAVE THOUGHT THAT I'D BE PART OF AN ACTIVIST GROUP LIKE THE NETWORK. I COULD SEE MYSELF DOING BASIC VOLUNTEER WORK, BUT NOTHING RISKY, NOT LIKE THIS...LET'S JUST SAY IT'S UNNERVING WHEN THE INTELLIGENCE DIRECTORATE (THEY CALL IT "GENERAL INFORMATION" NOW) TAKES AN INTEREST IN YOUR ACTIVITIES.
CATHERINE, IT'S FOR YOU...
...IT'S CORNELIA, FROM THE CAMP.
?
CORNELIA ASKED IF HE COULD STAY WITH US. IT WAS URGENT.
WELL...ALL RIGHT... JUST ONE NIGHT...
WHEN HE ARRIVED, HE WAS IN BAD SHAPE.
UH...COME ON IN.

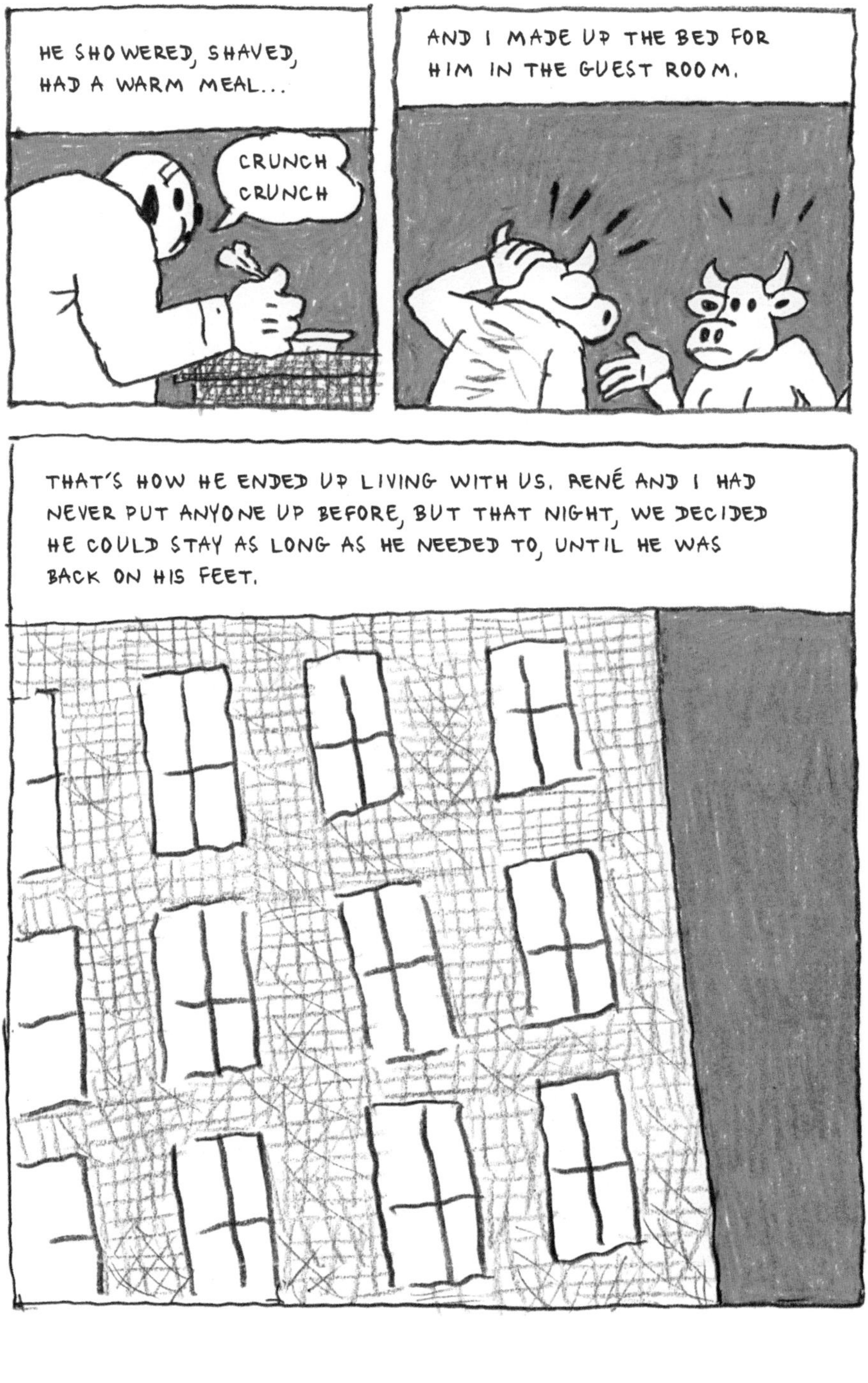
HE SHOWERED, SHAVED, HAD A WARM MEAL...
CRUNCH CRUNCH
AND I MADE UP THE BED FOR HIM IN THE GUEST ROOM.
THAT'S HOW HE ENDED UP LIVING WITH US. RENÉ AND I HAD NEVER PUT ANYONE UP BEFORE, BUT THAT NIGHT, WE DECIDED HE COULD STAY AS LONG AS HE NEEDED TO, UNTIL HE WAS BACK ON HIS FEET.

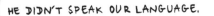
HE DIDN'T SPEAK OUR LANGUAGE.

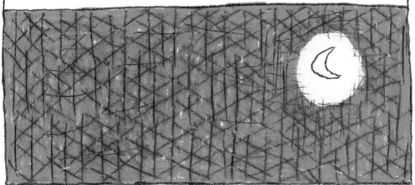

HE HAD LIVED IN HIDING SINCE HIS ARRIVAL...

AND HE NEVER LEFT HOME EXCEPT TO WORK. SO HE HADN'T MET MANY PEOPLE FROM HERE AND ONLY EVER SPOKE HIS OWN LANGUAGE.

ONE EVENING, HE REMINDED ME OF MY EIGHTY-YEAR-OLD GRANDFATHER, THAT'S HOW OLD AND STOOPED HE LOOKED.

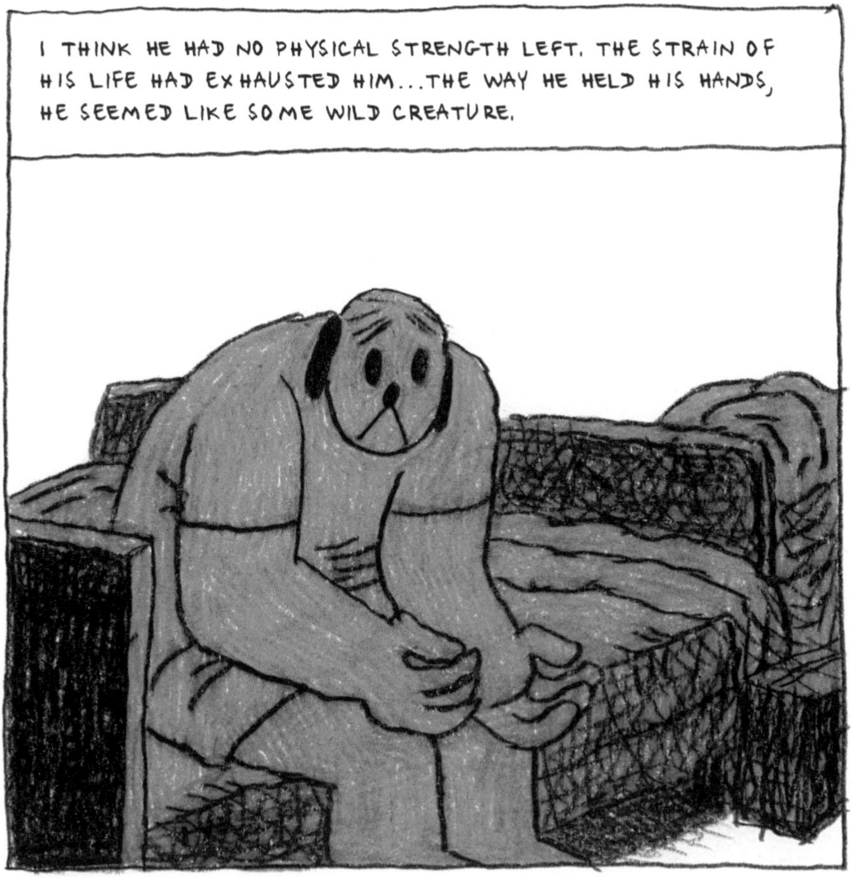
I THINK HE HAD NO PHYSICAL STRENGTH LEFT. THE STRAIN OF HIS LIFE HAD EXHAUSTED HIM...THE WAY HE HELD HIS HANDS, HE SEEMED LIKE SOME WILD CREATURE.

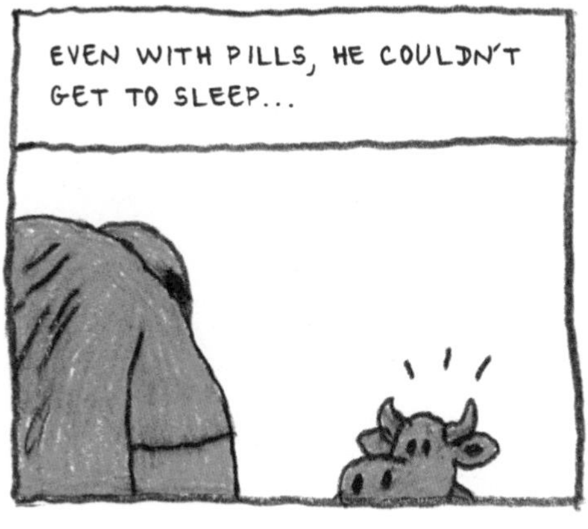
EVEN WITH PILLS, HE COULDN'T GET TO SLEEP...

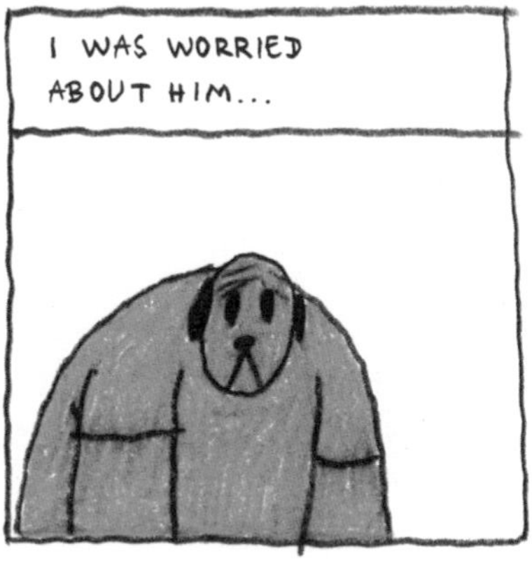
I WAS WORRIED ABOUT HIM...

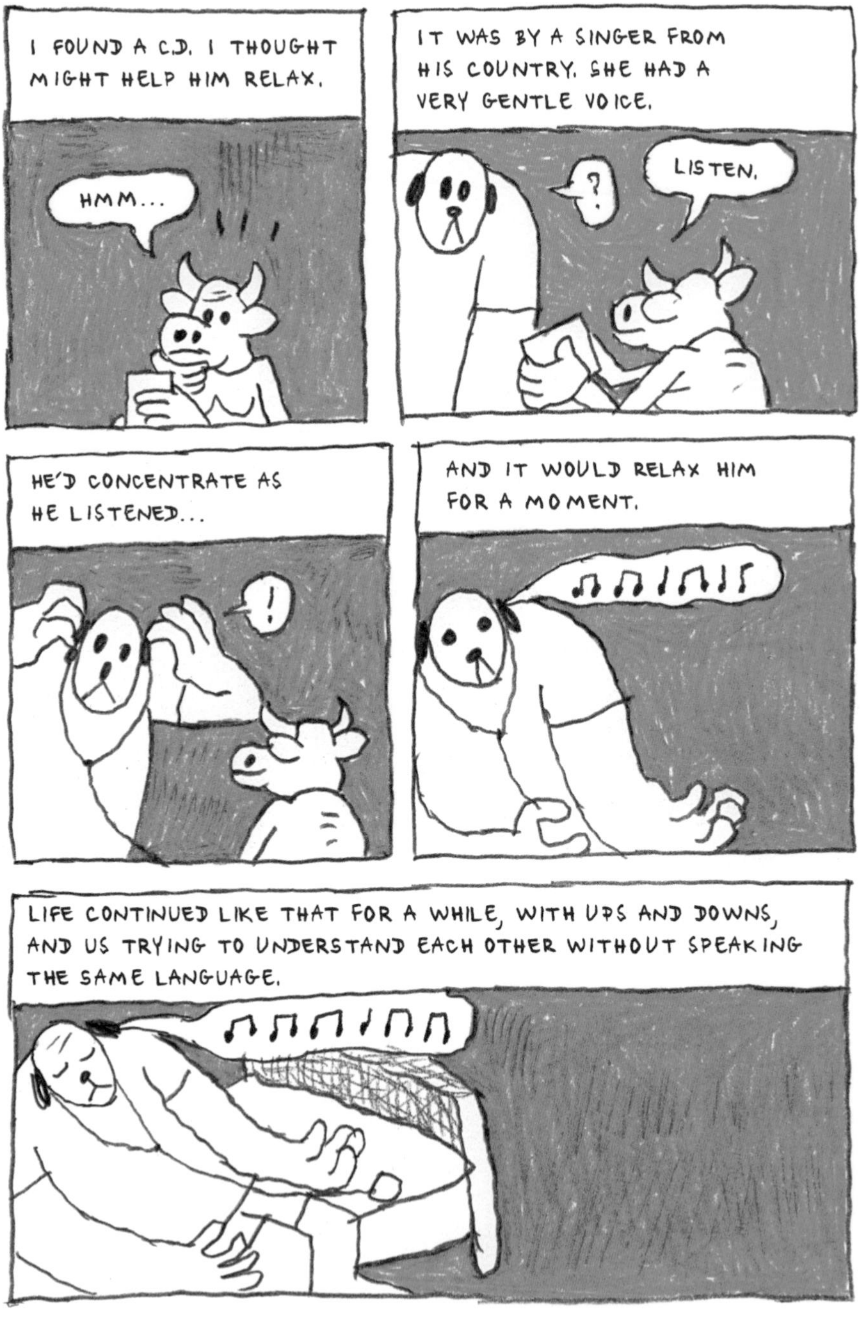
I FOUND A C.D. I THOUGHT MIGHT HELP HIM RELAX.
HMM...
IT WAS BY A SINGER FROM HIS COUNTRY. SHE HAD A VERY GENTLE VOICE.
?
LISTEN.
HE'D CONCENTRATE AS HE LISTENED...
!
AND IT WOULD RELAX HIM FOR A MOMENT.
LIFE CONTINUED LIKE THAT FOR A WHILE, WITH UPS AND DOWNS, AND US TRYING TO UNDERSTAND EACH OTHER WITHOUT SPEAKING THE SAME LANGUAGE.

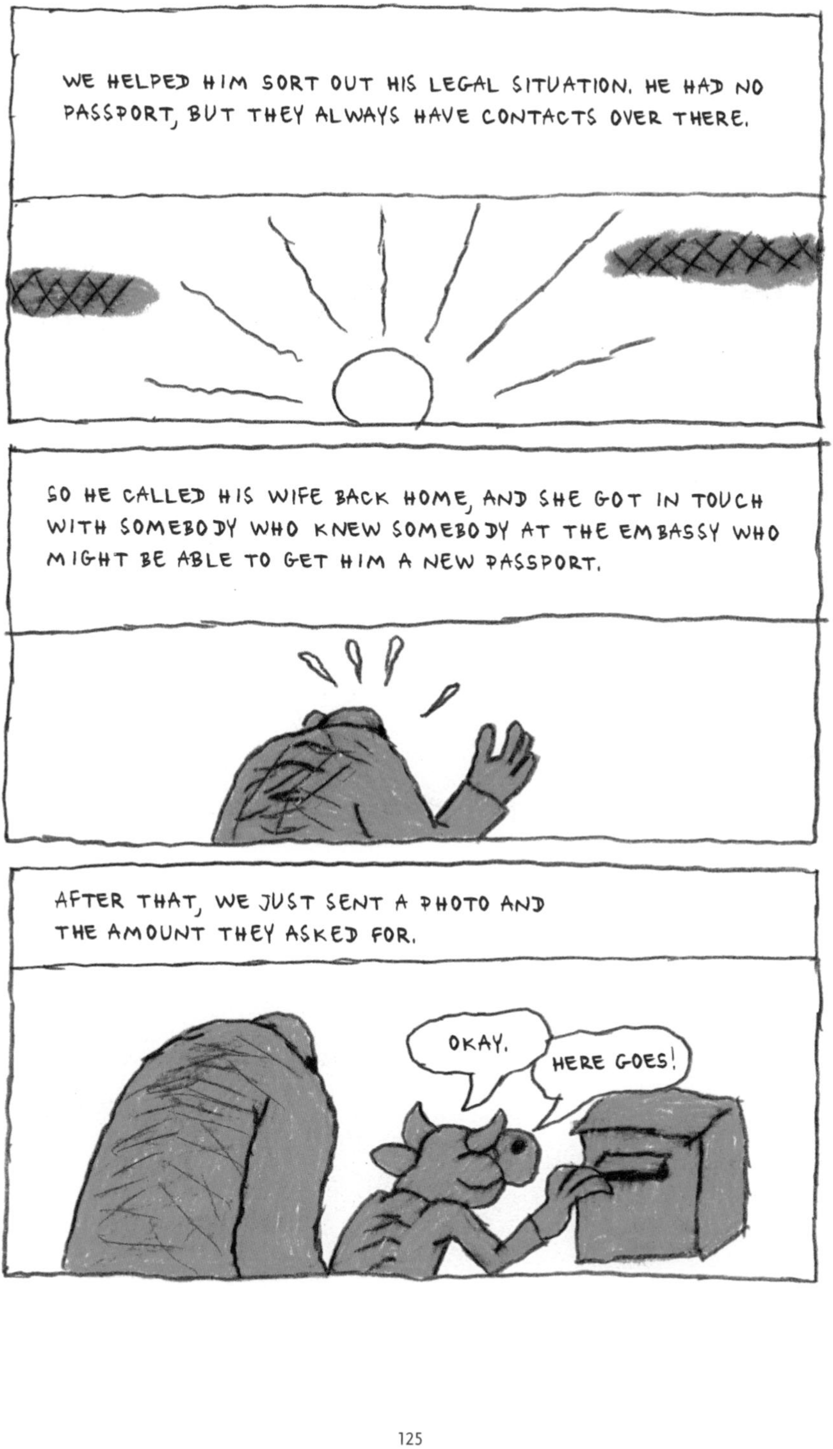
WE HELPED HIM SORT OUT HIS LEGAL SITUATION. HE HAD NO PASSPORT, BUT THEY ALWAYS HAVE CONTACTS OVER THERE.
SO HE CALLED HIS WIFE BACK HOME, AND SHE GOT IN TOUCH WITH SOMEBODY WHO KNEW SOMEBODY AT THE EMBASSY WHO MIGHT BE ABLE TO GET HIM A NEW PASSPORT.
AFTER THAT, WE JUST SENT A PHOTO AND THE AMOUNT THEY ASKED FOR.
OKAY.
HERE GOES!

AND ONE DAY WE GOT A CALL. WE HAD TO COME PICK UP THE
NEW PASSPORT. AT THE TRAIN STATION. A SMUGGLER HAD
BROUGHT IT, AND THE GUY WOULD BE IN TOWN FOR NO MORE
THAN TWENTY-FOUR HOURS. ONLY THEN WERE WE ABLE TO
START THE RESIDENCE PERMIT PROCESS WITH THE NETWORK—
BECAUSE WE FINALLY HAD "VALID" PAPERS!

IT'S TOTALLY ABSURD!

The crow

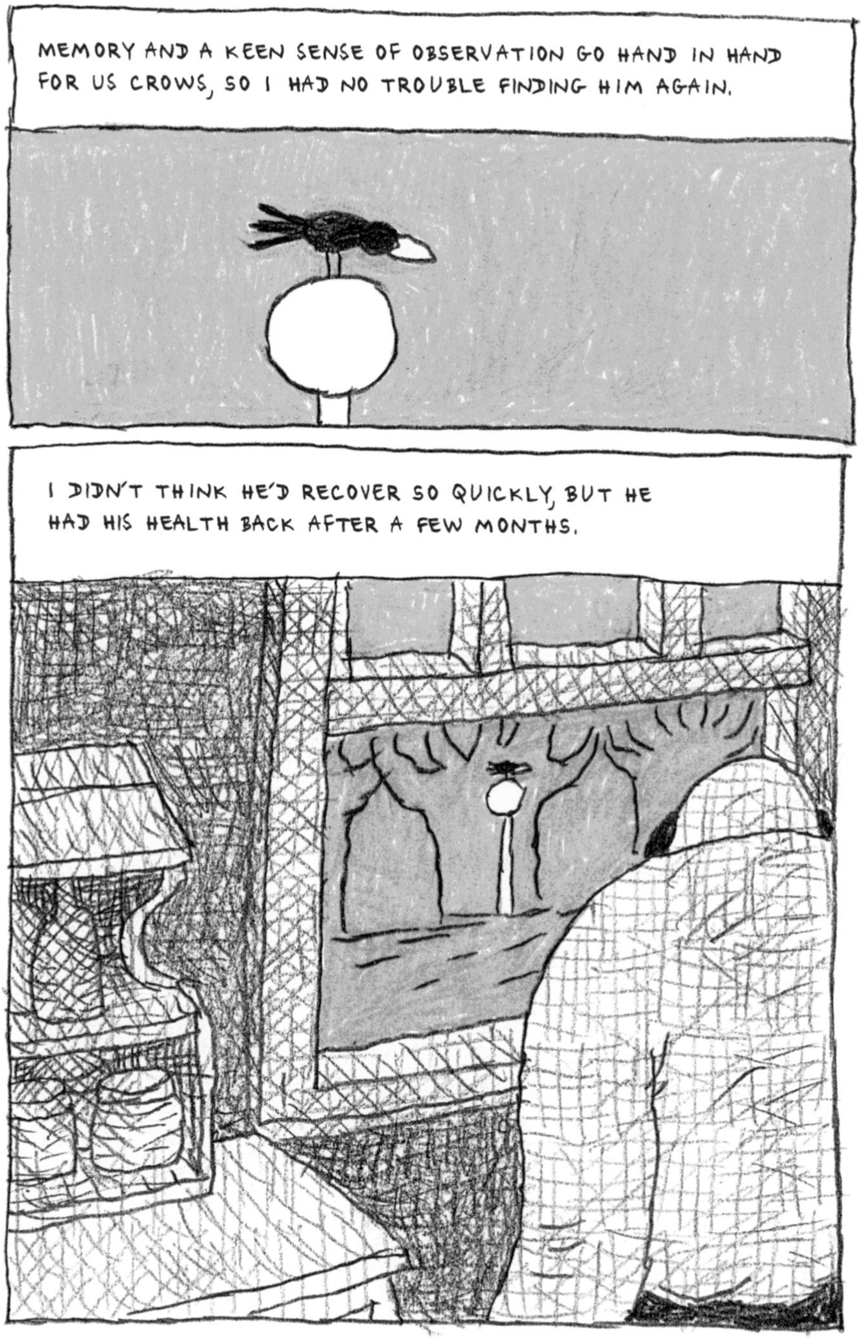
MEMORY AND A KEEN SENSE OF OBSERVATION GO HAND IN HAND FOR US CROWS, SO I HAD NO TROUBLE FINDING HIM AGAIN.
I DIDN'T THINK HE'D RECOVER SO QUICKLY, BUT HE HAD HIS HEALTH BACK AFTER A FEW MONTHS.

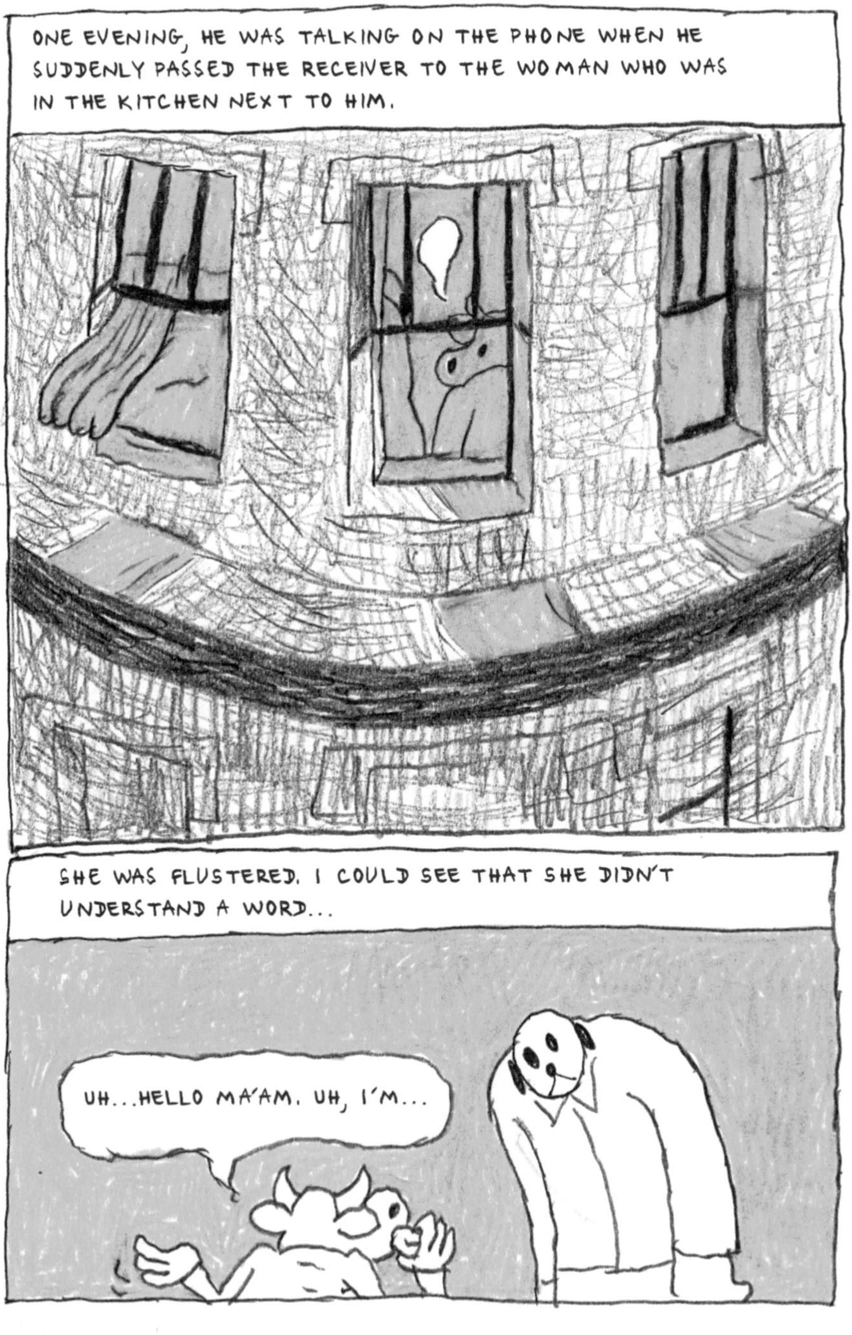
ONE EVENING, HE WAS TALKING ON THE PHONE WHEN HE SUDDENLY PASSED THE RECEIVER TO THE WOMAN WHO WAS IN THE KITCHEN NEXT TO HIM.
SHE WAS FLUSTERED. I COULD SEE THAT SHE DIDN'T UNDERSTAND A WORD...
UH...HELLO MA'AM. UH, I'M...

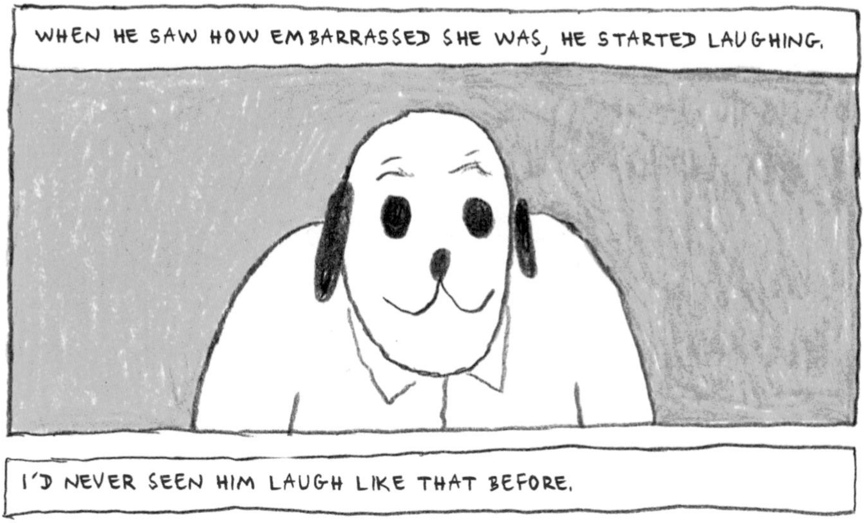
WHEN HE SAW HOW EMBARRASSED SHE WAS, HE STARTED LAUGHING.
I'D NEVER SEEN HIM LAUGH LIKE THAT BEFORE.

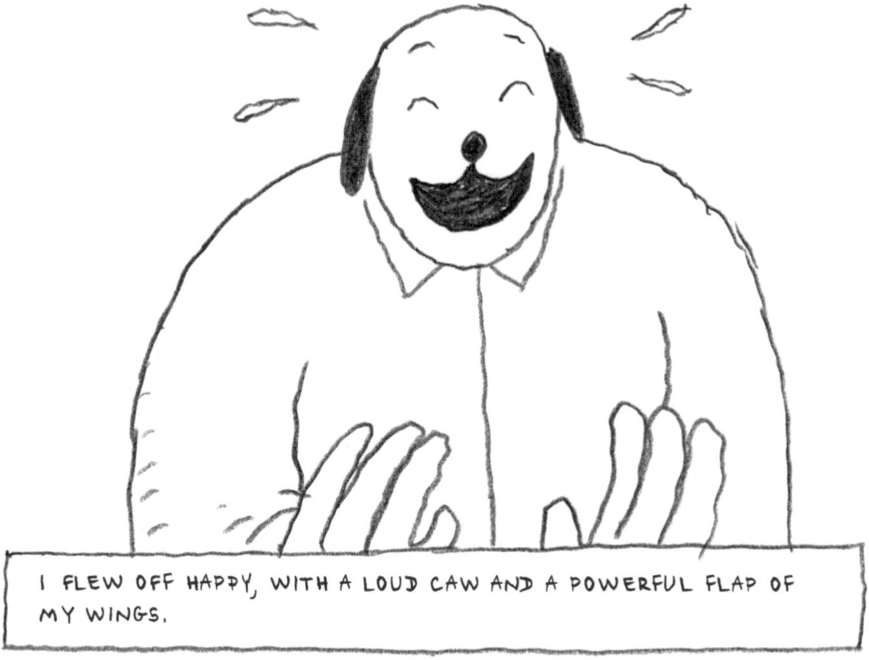
I FLEW OFF HAPPY, WITH A LOUD CAW AND A POWERFUL FLAP OF MY WINGS.

The cleaning lady

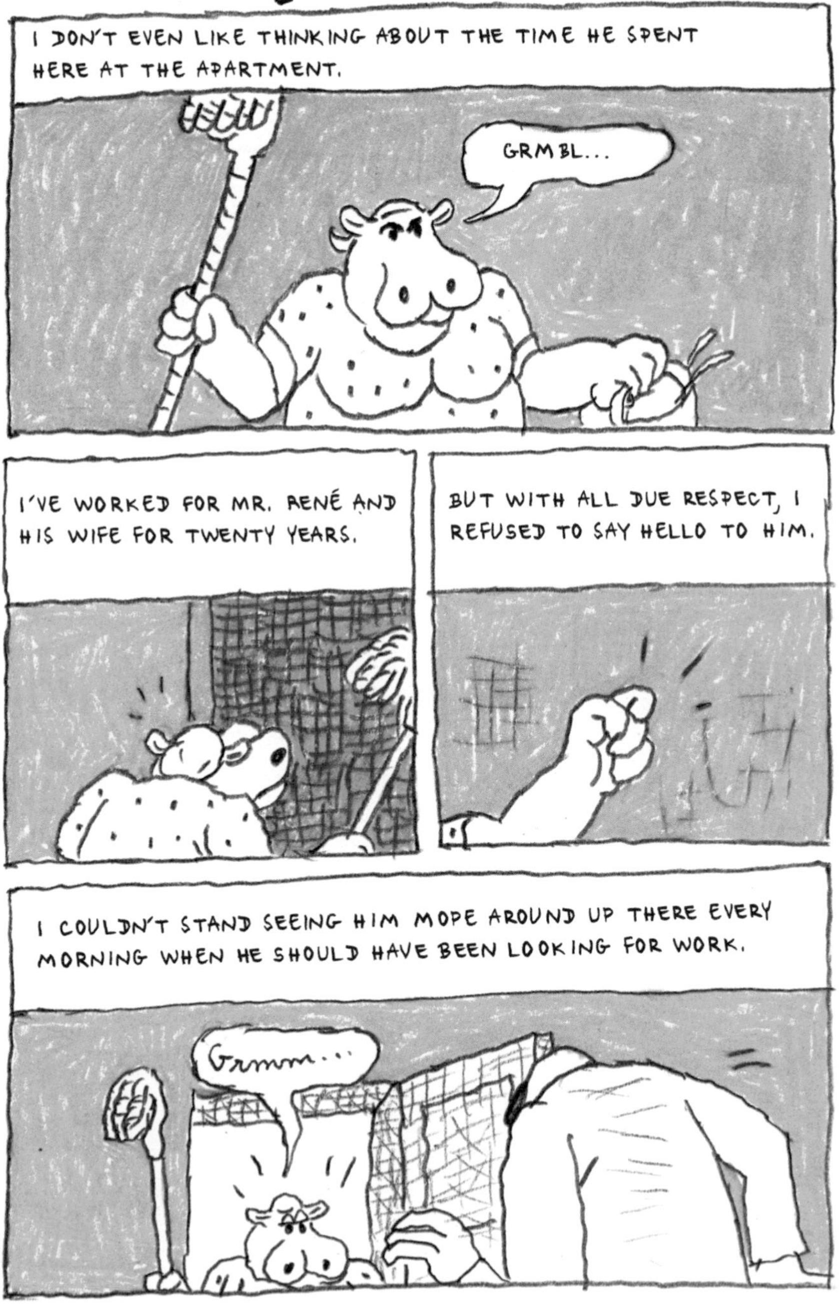
I DON'T EVEN LIKE THINKING ABOUT THE TIME HE SPENT HERE AT THE APARTMENT.
GRMBL...
I'VE WORKED FOR MR. RENÉ AND HIS WIFE FOR TWENTY YEARS.
BUT WITH ALL DUE RESPECT, I REFUSED TO SAY HELLO TO HIM.
I COULDN'T STAND SEEING HIM MOPE AROUND UP THERE EVERY MORNING WHEN HE SHOULD HAVE BEEN LOOKING FOR WORK.
Grmm...

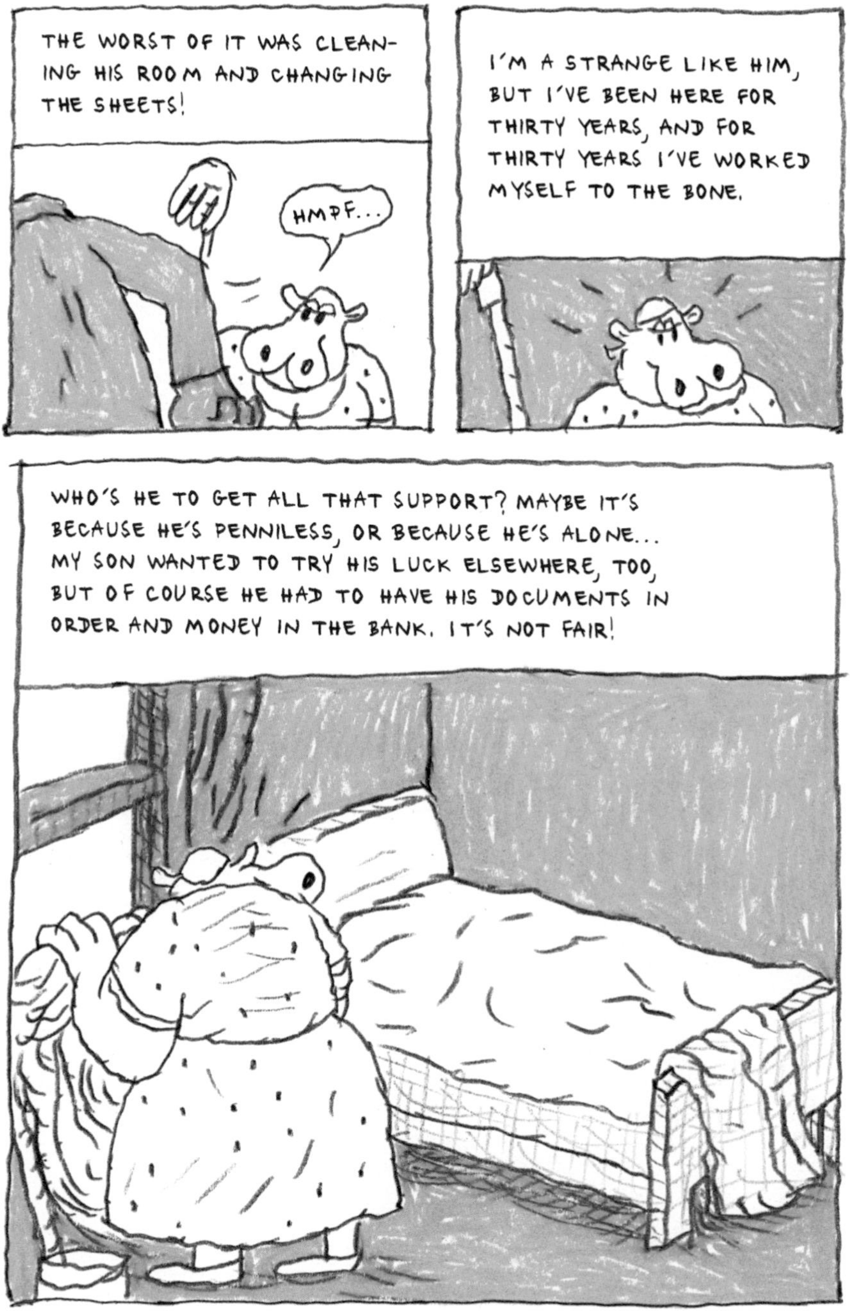
THE WORST OF IT WAS CLEANING HIS ROOM AND CHANGING THE SHEETS!
HMPF...
I'M A STRANGE LIKE HIM, BUT I'VE BEEN HERE FOR THIRTY YEARS, AND FOR THIRTY YEARS I'VE WORKED MYSELF TO THE BONE.
WHO'S HE TO GET ALL THAT SUPPORT? MAYBE IT'S BECAUSE HE'S PENNILESS, OR BECAUSE HE'S ALONE... MY SON WANTED TO TRY HIS LUCK ELSEWHERE, TOO, BUT OF COURSE HE HAD TO HAVE HIS DOCUMENTS IN ORDER AND MONEY IN THE BANK. IT'S NOT FAIR!

BUT HE DID MOVE OUT EVENTUALLY, AFTER THREE YEARS. HE BROUGHT HIS WIFE AND DAUGHTER INTO THE COUNTRY WITH THE HELP OF SMUGGLERS. AND WHEN HE FINALLY GOT AROUND TO LOOKING FOR LEGAL WORK, HE FOUND AN EMPLOYER WHO WAS WILLING TO HIRE HIM. IT WAS ABOUT TIME, BECAUSE I'D HAD IT!

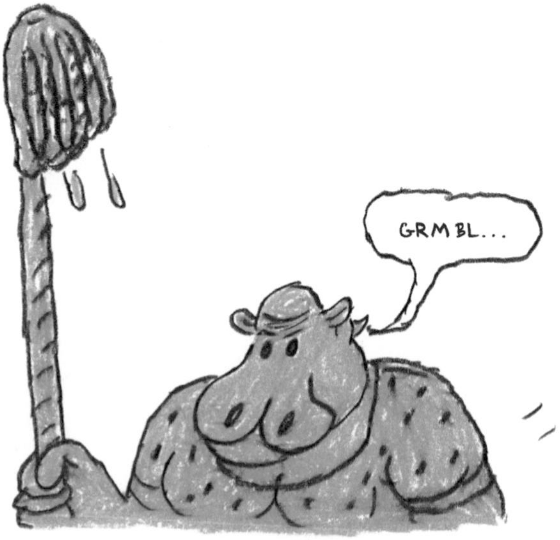
GRMBL...

His wife

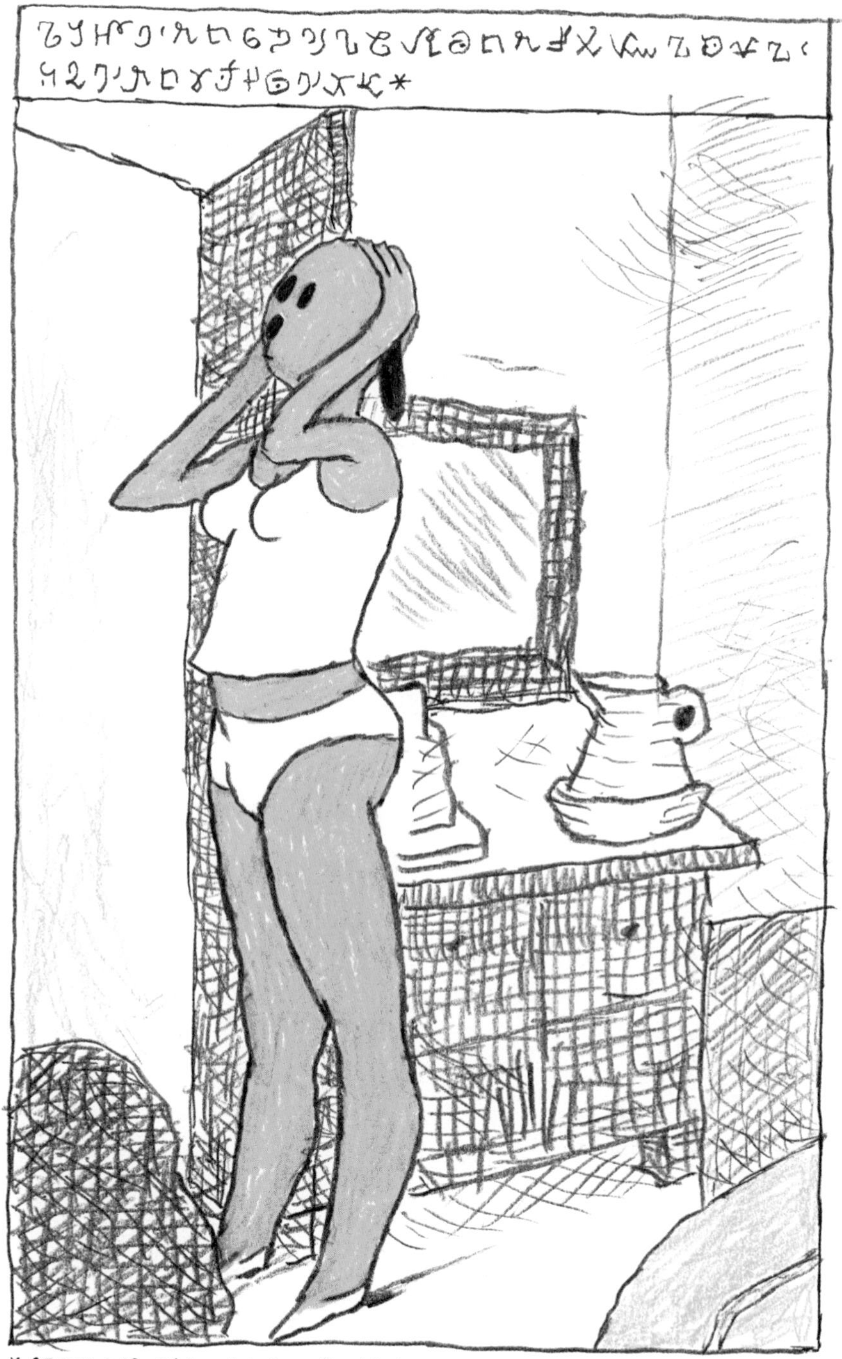

* SETTLING BACK INTO LIFE AS A COUPLE WASN'T EASY. OUR DAUGHTER WAS JUST A YEAR OLD WHEN HE LEFT, AND SHE WAS FIVE WHEN WE WERE REUNITED!

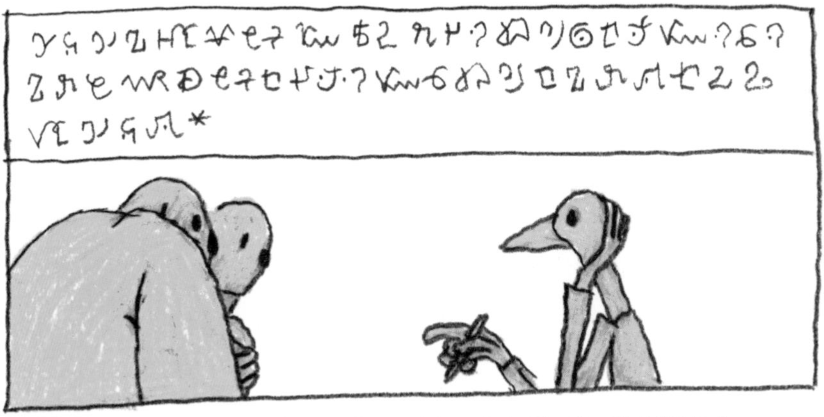

* SINCE THEN, THE ONLY THING WE'VE WANTED IS TO BUILD A BETTER FUTURE HERE FOR OUR DAUGHTER. THE NETWORK HAS BEEN HELPING US TAKE ALL THE NECESSARY STEPS TO GET REGULARIZED.

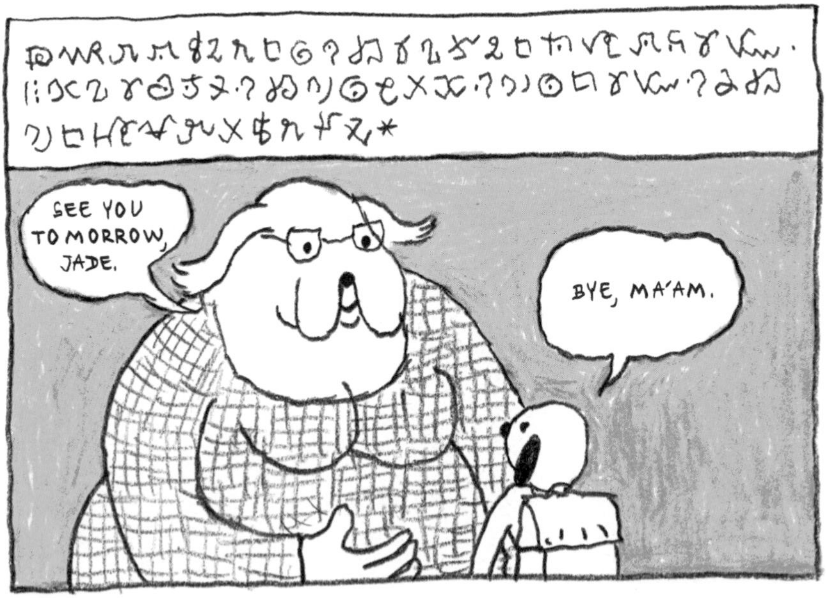
SEE YOU TOMORROW, JADE.
BYE, MA'AM.

* OUR DAUGHTER STARTED SCHOOL HERE FIVE YEARS AGO, AND SHE INTEGRATED EASILY. THE TEACHERS ARE PLEASED WITH HOW SHE'S DOING, AND SHE SPEAKS THE LANGUAGE FLUENTLY.

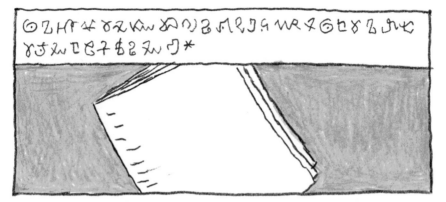

* BUT NOW OUR RESIDENCY APPLICATION HAS BEEN TURNED DOWN AND WE'VE BEEN ASKED TO LEAVE THE COUNTRY.

JULY
9
AUGUST
30
SEPTEMBER
2
OCTOBER
11

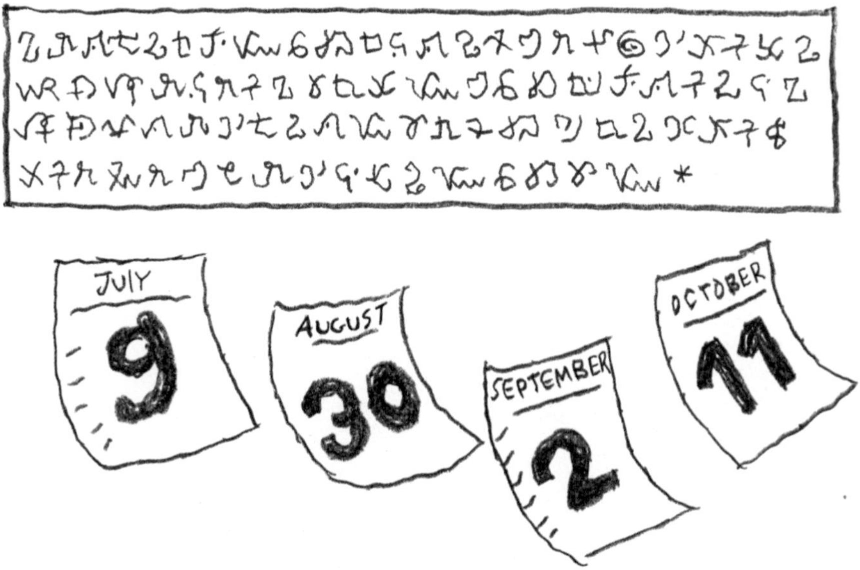

* WE APPEALED THE DECISION AND OUR FILE IS BEING REVIEWED. IT CAN TAKE AS LONG AS NINE MONTHS FOR A FILE TO GET PROCESSED... WE THOUGHT NOTHING COULD HAPPEN TO MY HUSBAND IF HE STAYED IN THE CITY.

"WE'RE FOOLING OURSELVES IF WE THINK WE CAN SOLVE
THE PROBLEM OF THE STRANGES THROUGH INTEGRATION ALONE.
THESE PEOPLE HAVE WAYS OF LIFE THAT ARE VERY DIFFERENT
FROM OUR OWN, AND THAT'S WHY THEY'RE DESTINED TO
RETURN TO THEIR COUNTRY OF ORIGIN."

* I SAW IT CLEARLY IN A DREAM. I CAN'T EXPLAIN IT,
BUT IT'S TRUE: I SEE EVERYTHING IN MY DREAMS.

* I SAW TWO MEN ARRIVE IN CIVILIAN CLOTHES.
THEY WERE WEARING TIES.

* ONE OF THEM WAS HOLDING MY PAPERS. THEY WERE
COPS—I SAW IT ALL—AND THEY HAD COME TO GET ME
AT THE RESTAURANT.

* AFTERWARD, I DON'T KNOW...I DREAMED THEY DROVE
ME RIGHT UP TO THE PLANE.

ᒡᔅᕐᒄᒡᐧᐲᕭᕐＲ*

* I SAW THE PLANE...

ꝃᏎ᠀᠍ꝗᎧᎷᏰᎷᏠᏰᎧᎧᎧ*

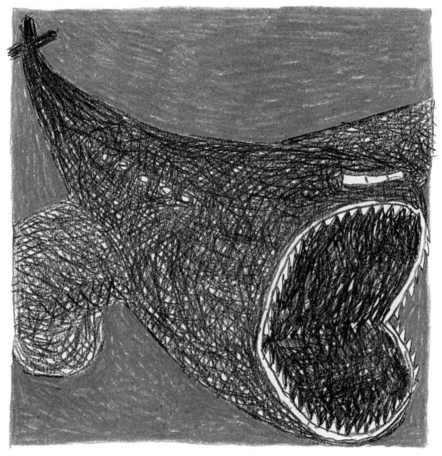

* AND I SAW THAT I WAS IN TROUBLE...

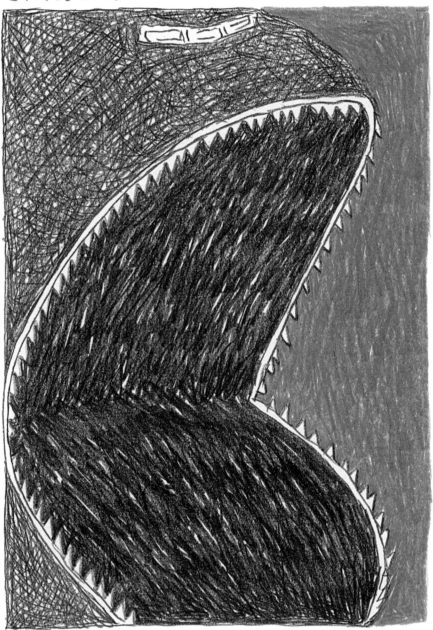

* ...REALLY DEEP TROUBLE.

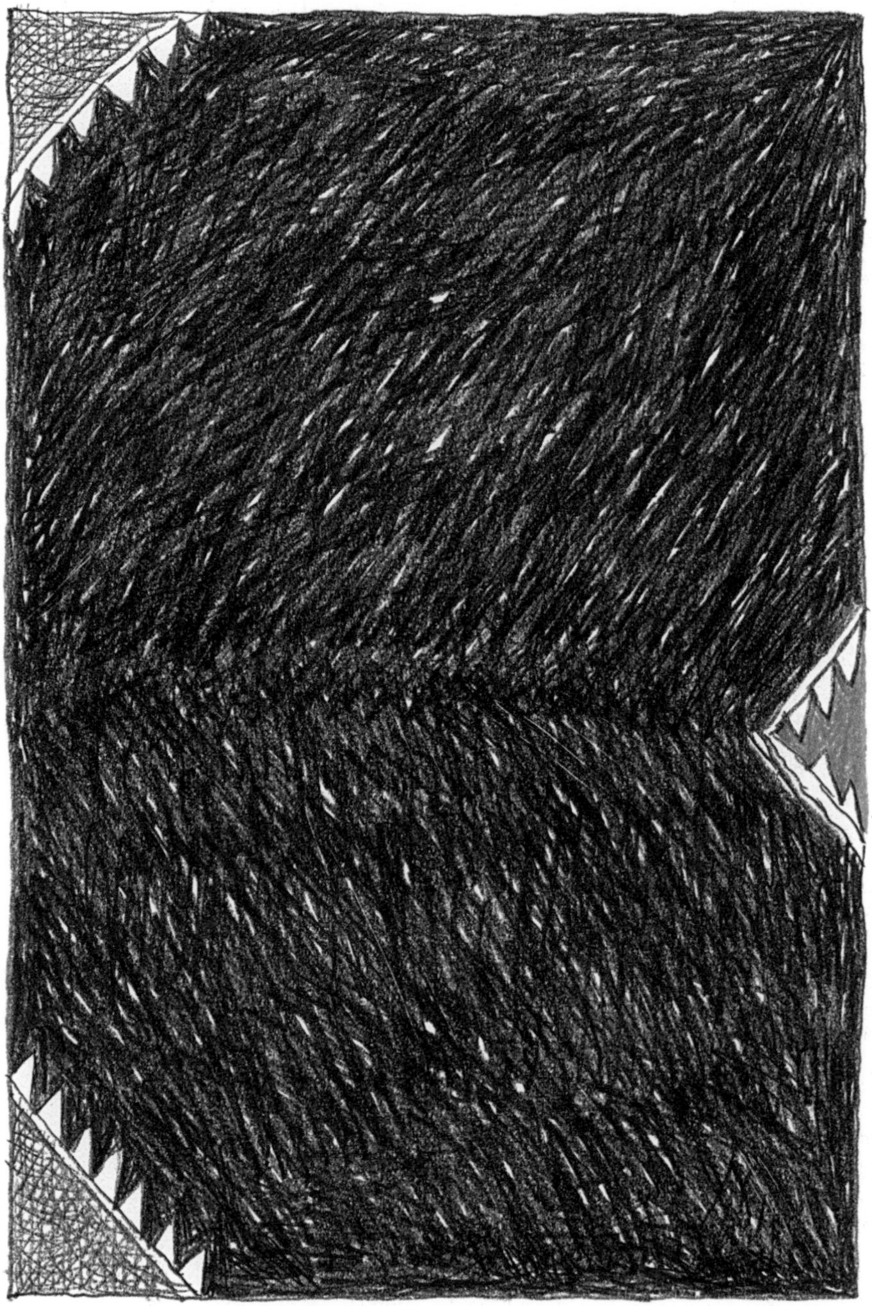

Epilogue

ON THURSDAY, APRIL 19, ELEVEN OFFICERS FROM THE AIR
AND BORDER POLICE TURNED UP AT THE STRANGE PALACE
RESTAURANT AND ASKED TO SEE THE COOK. HE WAS TAKEN
TO A DETENTION CENTER PENDING DEPORTATION.

NOTHING COULD CHANGE THE PREFECT'S MIND—NOT THE
DAILY DEMONSTRATIONS AT CITY HALL, SUPPORTED BY THE
MAYOR, NOT THE RALLY IN FRONT OF THE PREFECTURE, AND
NOT EVEN THE PROOF OF A FORMAL JOB OFFER.

THIRTY DAYS LATER, THE AUTHORITIES PUT HIM ON A
PLANE TO THE COUNTRY HE HAD LEFT NINE YEARS EARLIER.
HE FOUND HIMSELF ONCE AGAIN SEPARATED FROM HIS
WIFE AND DAUGHTER, WHO WERE STILL IN HIDING SOME-
WHERE IN THE CITY.

IN 2011, WHEN I WAS WORKING ON MY PREVIOUS GRAPHIC
NOVEL ABOUT THE SCAPEGOATING OF PEOPLE FROM IMMIGRANT
BACKGROUNDS, THE POLITICAL CONTEXT SHIFTED THE FOCUS OF
THE "IMMIGRATION PROBLEM" TO UNDOCUMENTED IMMIGRANTS,
AND THEN TO THE ROMA.

WITH THE HELP OF BETTY, A FRIEND WHO ACCOMPANIES
IMMIGRANTS AND IS ACTIVE IN THE ADVOCACY NETWORK
RÉSEAU D'ÉDUCATION SANS FRONTIÈRES, I BEGAN GATHERING
THE ACCOUNTS OF UNDOCUMENTED IMMIGRANTS AND THEIR
FAMILIES, AS WELL AS POLICE OFFICERS AND OTHER PEOPLE
CLOSE TO THE ISSUE. I THEN SELECTED, SCRAMBLED, COMBINED,
AND WOVE TOGETHER PIECES OF THEIR STORIES TO CREATE
THIS FICTIONAL ACCOUNT.

Thanks to

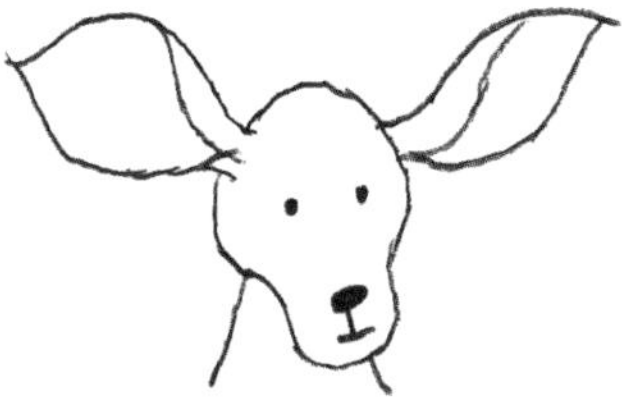

Manty

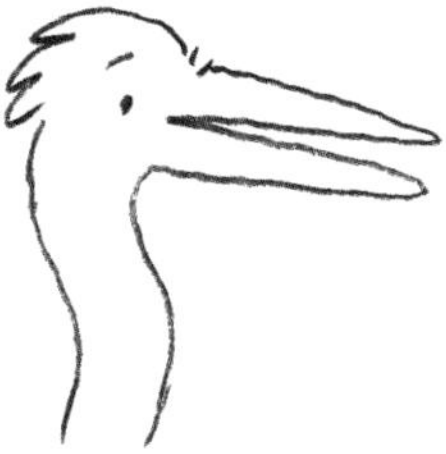

Mrs. T.

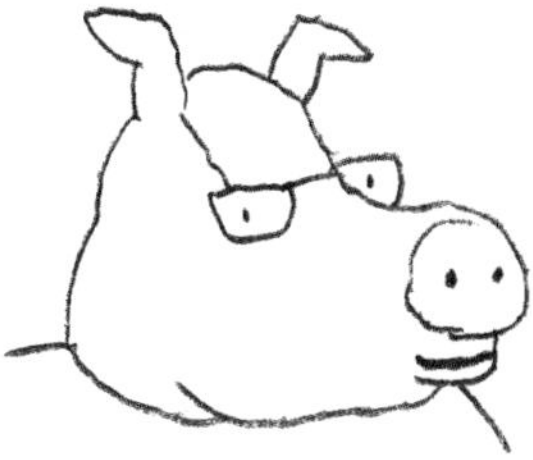

Mrs. M.

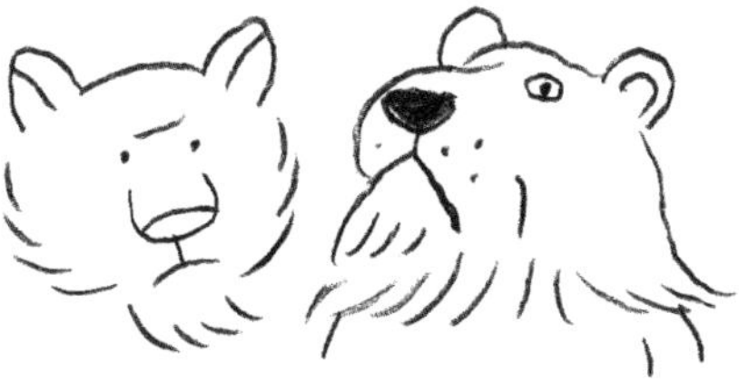

Mrs. and Mr. K.

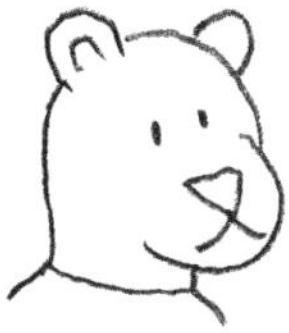

Mervé

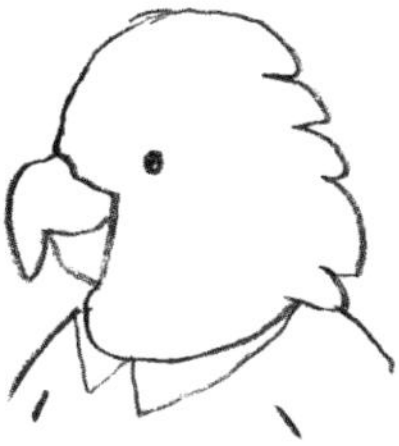

Mrs. L.

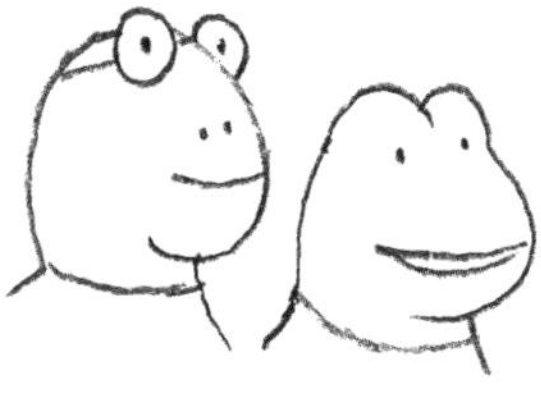

Mr. and Mrs. T.

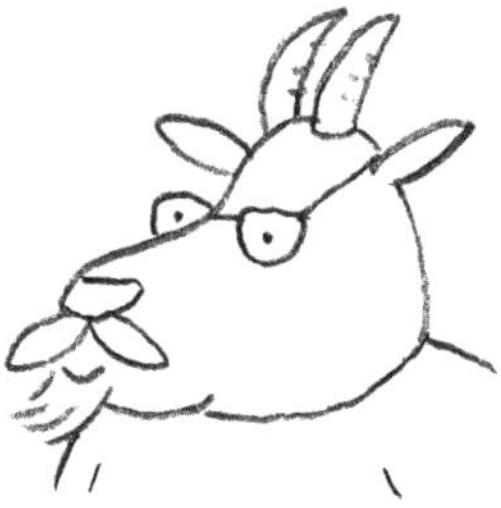

Mr. N

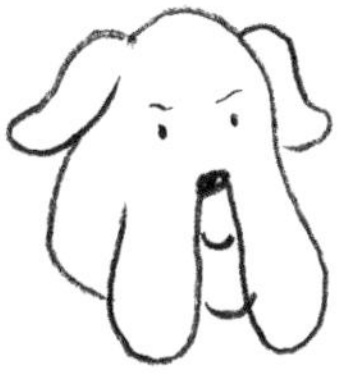

Jean Marie

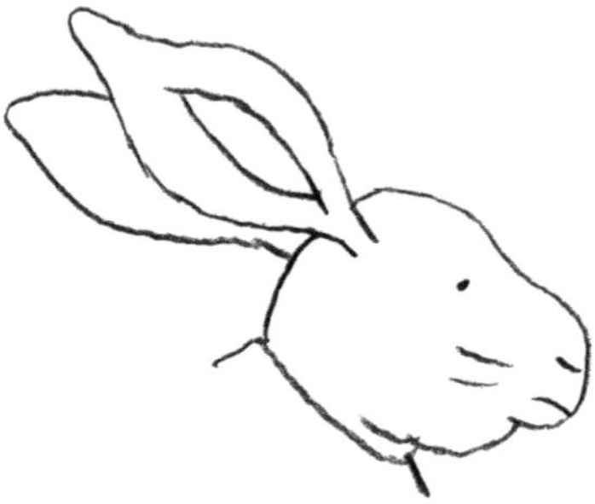

Nadège

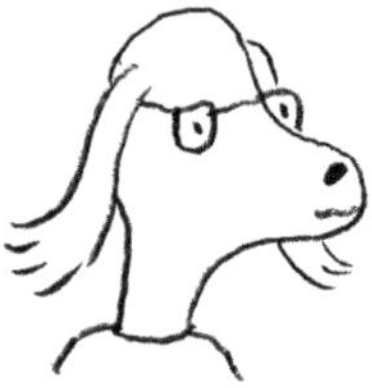

Martine

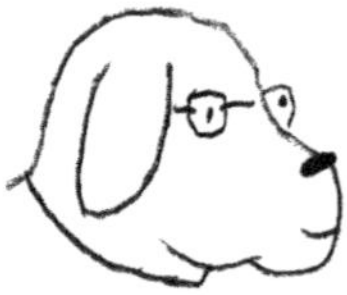

Mamadi

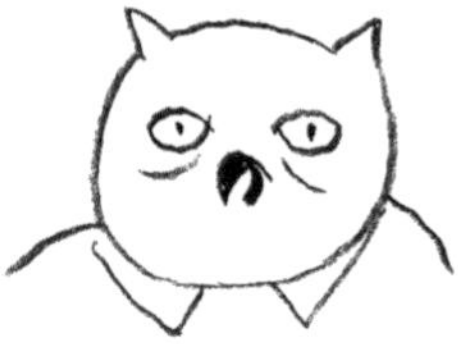

Éric

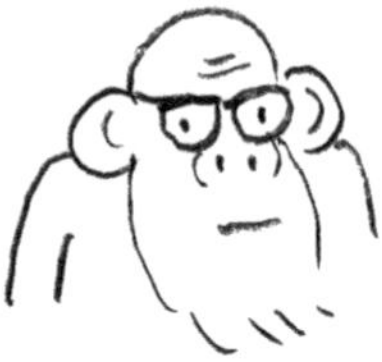

Christian

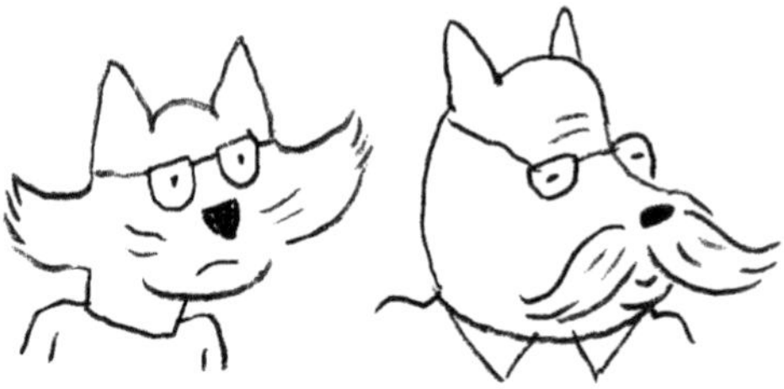

Catherine and René

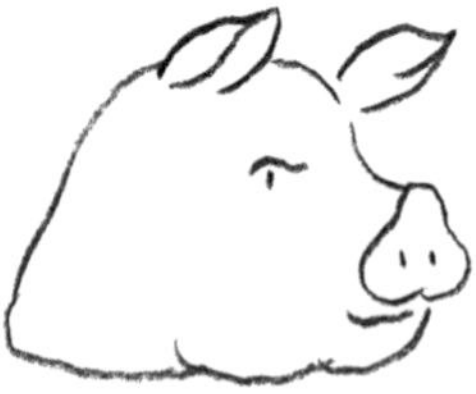

The officer

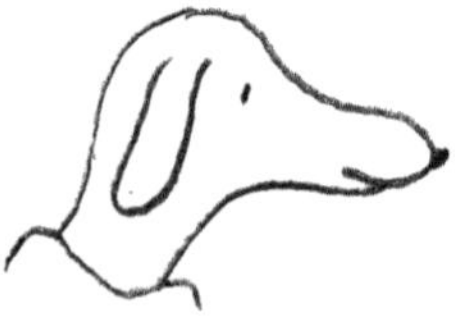

Isabelle

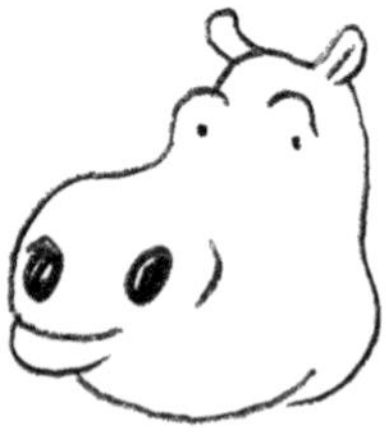

Fabrice

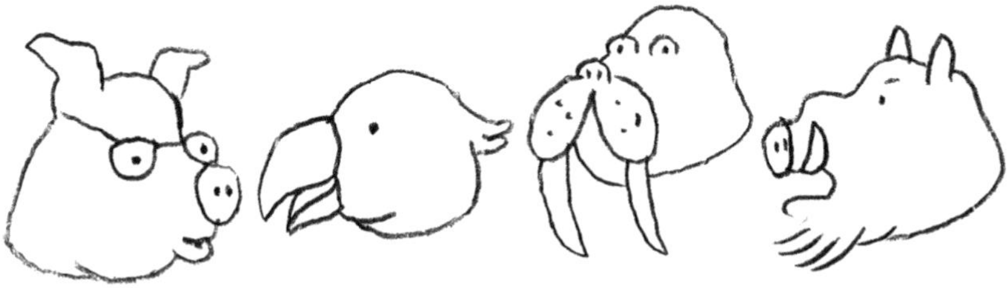

The RESF network in Voiron.

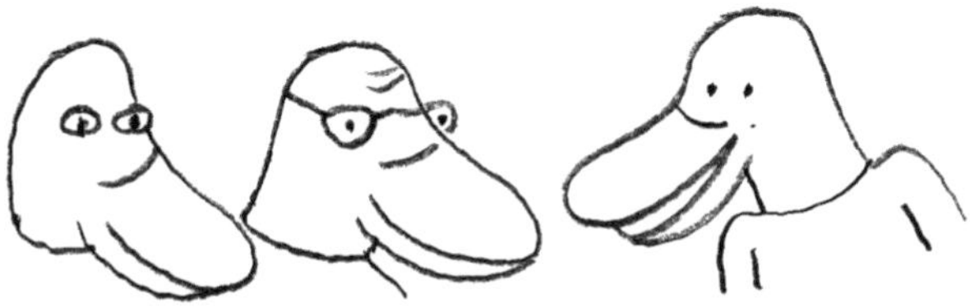

Marcelle, Théo, and Pierre, for their feedback.

And especially:

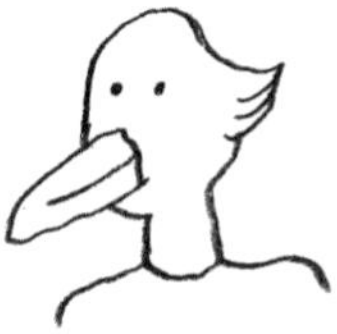

Betty
for her unfailing support.

And, as always, Isa for her eternal patience

Quotations:

Nicolas Sarkozy: pp. 21, 33-34 (radio), 43, 65, and 119.

And:

Manuel Valls: p. 137.

"TOLERANCE? WHAT DOES TOLERANCE EVEN MEAN? I'M A VERY TOLERANT PERSON, JUST LIKE YOU. DOES THAT MEAN YOU'RE GOING TO LET TWELVE ILLEGAL MIGRANTS MOVE INTO YOUR LIVING ROOM? AND WHAT ABOUT WHEN THEY START TAKING DOWN THE WALLPAPER? OR WHEN SOME OF THEM EVEN STEAL YOUR WALLET OR HARASS YOUR WIFE?"
—MARINE LE PEN

A Word from Amnesty International

Where does this story take place? What are we to make of the unusual character whose journey we follow? And what of the others who cross his path?

The world we encounter is vague yet familiar. Using real-life accounts, *The Strange*, with its chronological, precise, and well-documented story, draws us into a complicated and unfriendly landscape—one that begs examination.

And that is no doubt its strength: by avoiding specificity, *The Strange* sheds light on issues of xenophobia, immigration, and discrimination all across the globe. Traces and echoes of events and realities that were seen, read, or experienced remain. But instead of trying to connect the story through the specific instances that inspired it, we need to let ourselves be carried by the power and simplicity of the story—one that focuses directly on the effects of exile.

The condition of exile may vary in form and circumstance, but for those who experience it, it always involves a confrontation with otherness and difference. And for countless refugees and migrants throughout the world (many of whom have left their countries to escape threats or violence), exile often involves danger and violations of their rights—including the right to life.

The succession of characters ensures that no single point of view prevails. Instead, we gain insight into the many ways people perceive the circumstances of this uprooted, exiled refugee, whose name and background we'll never know.

Along the way, we come to realize that we could all be one of these characters. The plurality of voices forces us to recognize that this isn't just somebody else's story—that of the strange—but our story as well.

The driving force throughout is a deep humanity. The book is a reminder that we all have the capacity to respond when others are deprived of their rights and dignity. Bernard, Christine, and Susie are not superhuman and their actions are not exceptional. They are ordinary men and women who, simply and compassionately, decide that failing to act or to resist would mean abandoning the basic humanitarian principle that we are all entitled to the respect of our human rights. With great sensitivity, the book invites us to consider that each and every one of us has a role to play to ensure that our world does not succumb to indifference. This vision is shared by all those involved in Amnesty International.

Amnesty International
November 2015

Originally a children's book illustrator, in 2009, Jérôme Ruillier published his first graphic novel, *Le Coeur-enclume*, which is a deeply personal account of the first six days following the birth of a child with disabilities. His second comic, *Les Mohamed*, is based on interviews with immigrants from North Africa conducted by writer Yamina Benguigui. *Les Mohamed* explores the challenges that many immigrants face as they attempt to integrate into a new society. Exploring similar themes, *The Strange* is Ruillier's first graphic novel to be translated in English. Ruillier was born in 1966 in Madagascar and has spent much of his adult life living in France.